Marcus Tullius Cicero, William Melmoth

The Letters of Marcus Tullius Cicero to Several of his Friends

Volume III

Marcus Tullius Cicero, William Melmoth

The Letters of Marcus Tullius Cicero to Several of his Friends
Volume III

ISBN/EAN: 9783337017460

Printed in Europe, USA, Canada, Australia, Japan

Cover: Foto ©Thomas Meinert / pixelio.de

More available books at **www.hansebooks.com**

THE LETTERS

OF

Marcus Tullius Cicero

TO

Several of his FRIENDS:

With REMARKS

By WILLIAM MELMOTH, Esq;

——————— *Quo fit ut omnis*
Votiva pateat veluti descripta tabella
Vita senis.   Hor.

THE THIRD EDITION.

IN THREE VOLUMES.

VOL. III.

Ex Mus. Reg. Gall.

LONDON:

Printed for J. DODSLEY, in Pall-mall. 1778.

[1]

LETTERS

OF

Marcus Tullius Cicero

TO

Several of his FRIENDS.

BOOK XI.

LETTER I.

TO TIRO.

YOUR letter encourages me to hope that A.U.708. you find yourself better: I am sure at leaft, I moft sincerely wish that you may. I intreat you therefore to confecrate all your cares to that end; and by no means indulge fo miftaken a fufpicion as that I am difpleafed you are not with me. With me you are, in the beft fenfe of that expreffion, if you are taking care of your health: which I had much rather you fhould attend, than on myfelf. For

A.U. 708. tho' I always both fee and hear you with plea-
fure; that pleafure will be greatly increafed,
when I fhall have the fatisfaction at the fame time
to be affured that you are perfectly well.

My work is at prefent fufpended [1], as I can-
not make ufe of my own hand: however I em-
ploy myfelf a good deal in reading. If your
tranfcribers fhould be puzzled with my manu-
fcript, I beg you would give them your affift-
ance: as indeed there is an interlineation relat-
ing to a circumftance in Cato's behaviour when
he was only four years of age [2], that I could

---

[1] The work to which Cicero alludes, was probably a pa-
negyric upon Cato; which he wrote and publifhed about
this time.

[2] Plutarch mentions feveral inftances in the life of Cato,
wherein that confummate patriot had given very early indi-
cations of his refolute and inflexible fpirit. But the moft
remarkable, and probably the fame which Cicero had cele-
brated in the paffage he is here fpeaking of, was one that
happened when Cato was in the houfe of his uncle Livius
Drufus, who had taken upon himfelf the care of his educa-
tion. At that time the feveral ftates of Italy in alliance with
the republic, were ftrenuoufly foliciting the privileges of Ro-
man citizens: and Pompedius Silo, a perfon of great note,
who came to Rome in order to profecute this affair, was the
gueft of Drufus. As Pompedius was one day amufing himfelf
with the children of the family, " Well, young gentlemen,
faid he, addreffing himfelf particularly to the little Cato
and his brother, " I hope you will ufe your intereft with
" your uncle, to give his vote in our favour." The latter
very readily anfwered in the affirmative; while Cato figni-
fied his refufal by fixing his eyes fternly upon Pompedius,
without faying a fingle word in reply. Pompedius fnatch-
ing him up in his arms, ran with him to the window, and
in a pretended rage threatened to throw him out, if
he did not immediately yield to his requeft. But in vain:

fcarce

scarce decypher myself. You will continue your
care likewise, that the dining-room be in proper
order for the reception of our guests: in which
number, I dare say, I may reckon Tertia, pro-
vided Publius be not invited.

That strange fellow Demetrius was always,
I know, the very reverse of his name-sake of
Phaleris [3]: but I find he is now grown more in-
sufferable than ever, and is degenerated into an
arrant Bilienus [4]. I resign the management of
him therefore intirely into your hands; and you
will pay your court to him accordingly. But
however—d'ye see—and as to that—(to present
you with a few of his own elegant expletives) if
you should have any conversation with him, let
me know; that it may furnish me with the
subject of a letter, and at the same time af-
ford me the pleasure of reading so much longer

nature had not formed the *atrocem animum Catonis*, of a tex-
ture to be menaced out of its purposes. Accordingly Pom-
pedius was so struck with that early symptom of an undaunt-
ed spirit, that he could not forbear saying to some of his
friends who were present, " How happy will it be for
" Italy if this boy should live! for my part, continued he,
" I am well perfuaded if he were now a man, we should
" not be able to procure a single suffrage throughout all
" Rome." *Plut. in vit. Caton. Uticen.*
   [3] Demetrius, sur-named Phalerius, from Phaleris a sea-
port town in Greece, was a celebrated orator, who flourish-
ed about three centuries before the birth of Christ.
   [4] Who this person and Demetrius were, is utterly un-
known: but it is probable that the ridiculous part of their
characters, to which Cicero here alludes, was that of being
very dull and inelegant orators.

B 2

A.U.708. an one from yourfelf.   In the mean while take care of your health, my dear Tiro, I conjure you: and be well perfuaded, that you cannot render me a more pleafing fervice.   Farewel.

LETTER II.

To Dolabella [1].

OH! that the filence you fo kindly regret, had been occafioned by my own death, rather than by the fevere lofs [2] I have fuffered: a lofs I fhould be better able to fupport, if I had

[1] He was at this time with Cæfar in Spain.

[2] The death of his daughter Tullia.   It appears by a former letter, that fhe had lately lain-in at Rome : from whence fhe was probably removed for the benefit of the air, to her father's Tufculan villa, where fhe feems to have died.   This letter furnifhes a prefumptive argument againft the opinion of thofe who imagine, that Dolabella and Tullia were never actually divorced.   For in the firft place, notwithftanding it appears that there was fome diftance of time between the accident of her death and the prefent epiftle ; yet it feems to have been the firft letter which Cicero had written to Dolabella upon the occafion.   Now it is altogether improbable, if the marriage had fubfifted, that Cicero fhould not have given him immediate notice of an event in which, if not from affection, at leaft from intereft, he would have been greatly concerned.   In the next place, it is equally improbable, fuppofing there had been no divorce, that Cicero fhould fpeak of this misfortune only in general and diftant terms, as he does throughout this whole letter, without fo much as mentioning the name of Tullia, or intimating even the remoteft hint of any connection between her and Dolabella.   But the following letter will fupply a farther and more pofitive argument againft the opinion above mentioned. See rem. 4. on the next letter. *Ad At.* xii. 45, 46.

you

you with me.   For your judicious counfels, and
fingular affection towards me, would greatly con-
tribute to alleviate its weight.   This good office
indeed I may yet perhaps receive : for, as I
imagine we fhall foon fee you here, you will
find me ftill fo deeply affected, as to have an op-
portunity of affording me great affiftance.   Not
that this affliction has fo broken my fpirit as to
render me unmindful that I am a man, or ap-
prehenfive that I muft totally fink under its pref-
fure.   But all that chearfulnefs and vivacity of
temper, which you once fo particularly admired,
has now, alas! entirely forfaken me.   My forti-
tude and refolution neverthelefs, (if thefe virtues
were ever mine) I ftill retain : and retain them
too in the fame vigour as when you left me.

As to thofe battles which, you tell me, you
have fuftained upon my account; I am far lefs
folicitous that you fhould confute my detractors [3],
than that the world fhould know (as it unquef-
tionably does) that I enjoy a place in your af-
fection : and may you ftill continue to render

[3] The perfon to whom Cicero alludes, was in all pro-
bability his own nephew ; who was at this time in the ar-
my with Cæfar.   This young man had taken great liberties
with his uncle's character, afperfing it upon all occafions,
and in all companies ; in particular, (and what gave Cicero
the greateft uneafinefs) he attempted to infufe a fufpicion
among the principal officers of the army, that Cicero was a
man of dangerous defigns, and one againft whom Cæfar ought
to be particularly upon his guard.   *Ad At.* xii. 38. xiii. 37.

                     that

 that truth conspicuous. To this request I will add another, and intreat you to excuse me for not sending you a longer letter. I shorten it, not only as imagining we shall soon meet, but because my mind is at present by no means sufficiently composed for writing. Farewel.

LETTER III.

SERVIUS SULPICIUS to CICERO.

I Received the news of your daughter's death, with all the concern it so justly deserves: and indeed I cannot but consider it as a misfortune in which I bear an equal share with yourself. If I had been near you when this fatal accident happened, I should not only have mingled my tears with yours, but assisted you with all the consolation in my power. I am sensible at the same time, that offices of this kind afford at best but a wretched relief: for as none are qualified to perform them, but those who stand near to us by the ties either of blood or affection, such persons are generally too much afflicted themselves, to be capable of administering comfort to others. Nevertheless, I thought proper to suggest a few reflections, which occurred to me upon this occasion: not as imagining they would be new to you, but believing that in your present

dis-

discompofure of mind, they might poffibly have A.U.708.
efcaped your attention.   Tell me then, my
friend, wherefore do you indulge this excefs of
forrow ? Reflect, I intreat you, in what manner
fortune has dealt with every one of us : that fhe
has deprived us of what ought to be no lefs dear
than our children, and overwhelmed in one gene-
ral ruin our honours, our liberties, and our
country.   And after thefe loffes, is it poffible
that any other fhould increafe our tears ? Is it
poffible that a mind long exercifed in calamities
fo truly fevere, fhould not become totally callous,
and indifferent to every event ? But you will tell
me, perhaps, that your grief arifes not fo much
on your own account, as on that of Tullia. Yet
furely you muft often, as well as myfelf, have
had occafion in thefe wretched times to reflect,
that their condition by no means deferves to be.
regretted, whom death has gently removed from
this unhappy fcene.   What is there, let me afk,
in the prefent circumftances of our country, that
could have rendered life greatly defirable to your
daughter ? What pleafing hopes, what agreeable
views, what rational fatisfaction could fhe poffibly
have propofed to herfelf from a more extended
period ? Was it in the profpect of conjugal hap-
pinefs in the fociety of fome diftinguifhed youth [*] ?

* This paffage feems ftrongly to intimate, that the marriage
between Dolabella and Tullia was actually diffolved before

 as if, indeed, you could have found a son-in-law amongst our present set of young men, worthy of being entrusted with the care of your daughter! Or was it in the expectation of being the joyful mother of a flourishing race, who might possess their patrimony with independence, who might gradually rise thro' the several dignities of the state, and exert the liberty to which they were born in the service and defence of their friends and country? But is there one amongst all these desirable privileges, of which we were not deprived before she was in a capacity of transmitting them to her descendants? Yet after all, you may still alledge, perhaps, that the loss of our children is a severe affliction: and unquestionably it would be so, if it were not a much greater to see them live to endure those indignities which their parents suffer.

her death. It must be acknowledged however, that a very learned and accurate critic is of opinion, that the affirmative side of this question can no more be proved from these words of Sulpicius, than it can be inferred from those which he immediately adds, *an ut ea liberos ex sese pareret*, that Tullia died without issue; which it is well known she did not. But there seems to be this difference between the two instances: that with respect to the latter, Sulpicius might very properly put the question he there does, notwithstanding Tullia's having left a son: for altho' she had *one*, she might reasonably indulge the expectation of having more. Whereas with regard to the former; would it not have been highly injurious to her character, if Sulpicius had argued from a supposition which implied that Tullia entertained thoughts of another husband, whilst her marriage with Dolabella was still subsisting? *Vid. epist. Tunstal. ad vir. erud. Con. Middleton, p.* 186.

I lately

I lately fell into a reflection, which as it af- A.U. 708.
forded great relief to the difquietude of my own
heart, it may poffibly contribute likewife to af-
fuage the anguifh of yours.   In my return out of
Afia, as I was failing from Ægina towards Me-
gara [5], I amufed myfelf with contemplating the
circumjacent countries.   Behind me lay Ægina,
before me Megara; on my right I faw Piræeus [6],
and on my left, Corinth [7].   Thefe cities, once fo
flourifhing and magnificent, now prefented no-
thing to my view but a fad fpectacle of defolation.
" Alas, (I faid to myfelf) fhall fuch a fhort-
" lived creature as man complain, when one of
" his fpecies falls either by the hand of vio-
" lence, or by the common courfe of nature;
" whilft in this narrow compafs fo many great
" and glorious cities, formed for a much longer
" duration, thus lie extended in ruins? Remem-
" ber then, oh my heart! the general lot to
" which man is born: and let that thought fup-
" prefs thy unreafonable murmurs."   Believe
me, I found my mind greatly refrefhed and com-
forted by thefe reflections.   Let me advife you in
the fame manner to reprefent to yourfelf, what

[5] Ægina, now called Engia, is an ifland fituated in the
gulf that runs between the Peloponnefus and Attica, to
which it gives its name.   Megara was a city near the ifth-
mus of Corinth.

[6] A celebrated fea-port at a fmall diftance from Athens,
now called Port-Lion.

[7] A city in the Peloponnefus.

numbers

A.U. 708. numbers of our illuftrious countrymen have lately been cut off at once [a], how much the ftrength of the Roman republic is impaired, and what dreadful devaftation has gone forth throughout all its provinces! And can you, with the impreffion of thefe greater calamities upon your mind, be fo immoderately afflicted for the lofs of a fingle individual, a poor, little, tender woman? who, if fhe had not died at this time, muft in a few fleeting years more, have inevitably undergone that common fate to which fhe was born [s].

Reafonable however as thefe reflections are, I would call you from them awhile, in order to

---

[a] In the civil wars.

[s] One of the fineft and moft elegant of all writers, either antient or modern, has given us fome reflections which arofe in his mind in walking amongft the repofitories of the dead; which, as they are not altogether foreign to the fubject of this letter, the reader perhaps will indulge me in the pleafure of producing, as a fort of corollaries to the fentiments of Sulpicius. "When I look upon the tombs of the great, (fays the incomparable Addifon) "every emotion of envy "dies within me; when I read the epitaphs of the beautiful, "every inordinate defire goes out; when I meet with the "grief of parents upon a tomb-ftone, my heart melts with "compaffion; when I fee the tomb of the parents them- "felves, I confider the vanity of grieving for thofe whom "we muft quickly follow: when I fee kings lying by thofe "who depofed them; when I confider rival wits, placed "fide by fide, or the holy men that divided the world with "their contefts and difputes, I reflect with forrow and "aftonifhment on the little competitions, factions and de- "bates of mankind. When I read the feveral dates of the "tombs, of fome that died yefterday, and fome fix hundred "years ago, I confider that great day when we fhall all of "us be contemporaries, and make our appearance toge- "ther." *Spect. Vol.* 1. *Numb.* 26.

lead

lead your thoughts to others more peculiarly A.U. 708.
fuitable to your circumftances and character.
Remember then, that your daughter lived as long
as life was worth poffeffing, that is, till liberty
was no more: that fhe lived to fee you in the
illuftrious offices of prætor, conful, and augur;
to be married to fome of the nobleft youths in
Rome ; to be bleffed with almoft every valuable
enjoyment; and at length to expire with the re-
public itfelf.   Tell me now, what is there in this
view of her fate, that could give either her or
yourfelf juft reafon to complain ? In fine, do not
forget that you are Cicero ; the wife, the philofo-
phical Cicero, who were wont to give advice to
others : nor refemble thofe unfkilful empirics,
who at the fame time that they pretend to be fur-
nifhed with remedies for other men's diforders,
are altogether incapable of finding a cure for
their own.   On the contrary, apply to your pri-
vate ufe, thofe judicious precepts you have ad-
miniftered to the public. Time neceffarily weak-
ens the ftrongeft impreffions of forrow : but it
would be a reproach to your character not to an-
ticipate this its certain effect, by the force of your
own good fenfe and judgment. If the dead retain
any confcioufnefs of what is here tranfacted, your

9 To Pifo, Craffipes, and Dolabella : of each of whom
an account has been occafionally given in the preceding
obfervations.

daughter's

 daughter's affection, I am sure, was such both to you and to all her relations, that she can by no means desire you should abandon yourself to this. excess of grief. Restrain it then, I conjure you, for her sake, and for the sake of the rest of your family and friends, who lament to see you thus afflicted. Restrain it too, I beseech you, for the sake of your country; that whenever the opportunity shall serve, it may reap the benefit of your counsels and assistance. In short, since such is our fortune that we must necessarily submit to the present system of public affairs, suffer it not to be suspected, that it is not so much the death of your daughter, as the fate of the republic, and the success of our victors, that you deplore.

But it would be ill-manners to dwell any longer upon this subject, as I should seem to question the efficacy of your own good sense. I will only add therefore, that as we have often seen you bear prosperity in the noblest manner, and with the highest applause; shew us likewise that you are not too sensible of adversity, but know how to support it with the same advantage to your character. In a word, let it not be said, that fortitude is the single virtue to which my friend is a stranger [10].

[10] Sulpicius has drawn together in this admired letter, whatever human philosophy has of force to compose the perturbations of a mind under the disquietude of severe af-

As

As for what concerns myfelf; I will fend you A.U.708.
an account of the ftate of this province, and
of what is tranfacting in this part of the world, as
foon as I fhall hear that you are fufficiently com-
pofed to receive the information.   Farewel.

L E T T E R IV.

To Servius Sulpicius.

I Join with you, my dear Sulpicius, in wifh-
ing that you had been in Rome when this
moft fevere calamity befell me. I am fenfible
of the advantage I fhould have received from
your prefence, and I had almoft faid your
equal participation of my grief, by having found
myfelf fomewhat more compofed after I had
read your letter. It furnifhed me indeed with ar-
guments extremely proper to footh the anguifh
of affliction; and evidently flowed from a heart
that fympathized with the forrows it endeavour-
ed to affuage. But altho' I could not enjoy the
benefit of your own good offices in perfon, I had
the advantage however of your fon's: who gave

flictions. But it is evident, that all arguments of the fort
here produced, tend rather to filence the clamours of forrow,
than to foften and fubdue its anguifh. It is a much more
exalted philofophy indeed, that muft fupply the effectual
remedies for this purpofe: to which, no other but that of
chriftianity alone, will be found on the trial to be in any
rational degree fufficient.

me

A.U.708. me a proof by every tender affiftance that could be contributed upon fo melancholy an occafion; how much he imagined that he was acting agreeably to your fentiments, when he thus difcovered the affection of his own. More pleafing inftances of his friendfhip, I have frequently received; but never any that were more obliging. As to thofe for which I am indebted to yourfelf; it is not only the force of your reafonings, and the very confiderable fhare you take in my afflictions, that have contributed to compofe my mind; it is the deference likewife which I always pay to the authority of your fentiments. For knowing, as I perfectly do, the fuperior wifdom with which you are enlightened, I fhould be afhamed not to fupport my diftreffes in the manner you think I ought. I will acknowledge neverthelefs, that they fometimes almoft intirely overcome me: and I am fcarce able to refift the force of my grief when I reflect, that I am deftitute of thofe confolations which attended others, whofe examples I propofe to my imitation. Thus Quintus Maximus [1] loft a fon of confular rank, and diftinguifhed by many brave and illuftri-

---

[1] Quintus Fabius Maximus, fo well known for his brave and judicious conduct in oppofing the progrefs of Hannibal's arms in Italy, was five times advanced to the confular office: the laft of which was in the year of Rome 545. At the expiration of his fourth confulate, he was fucceeded in that office by his fon Marcus Fabius, who likewife diftin-

ous

ous actions; Lucius Paulus [2] was deprived of A.U.708.
two sons in the space of a single week; and your
relation Gallus [3], together with Marcus Cato [4],
had both of them the unhappiness to survive
their respective sons, who were endowed with

guished himself by his military atchievements. It does not
appear when, or by what accident Marcus died: but his il-
lustrious father was so much master of his grief upon that oc-
casion, as to pronounce a funeral eulogy in honour of his son,
before a general assembly of the people. *Liv.* xxiv. 43. *Plut.
in vit. Fab.*

[2] A very few days before Paulus Æmilius made his public
entry into Rome in the year 585, on occasion of his victory
over Perseus, he had the misfortune to lose one of his sons:
and this calamity was succeeded by another of the same
kind which befel him about as many days *after* his triumph.
Liv. xlv. 41.

Manutius conjectures, that the person here mentioned,
is Caius Sulpicius Gallus, who was consul in the year 586.

[4] The censor. His son was prætor in the year of Rome
638, and died whilst he was in the administration of that
office. I cannot forbear transcribing upon this occasion a
noble passage from Cicero's treatise concerning old age, as I
find it extremely well translated to my hand by a late inge-
nious writer (Mr. Hughes, if I mistake not) in the Spectator.
Our author represents Cato as breaking out into the follow-
ing rapture at the thoughts of his approaching dissolution:
" O happy day, (says this amiable moralist) when I shall
" escape from this crowd, this heap of pollution, and be ad-
" mitted to that divine assembly of exalted spirits! when
" I shall go—to my Cato, my son; than whom a better
" man was never born; and whose funeral rites I myself
" performed, whereas he ought rather to have attended
" mine. Yet has not his soul deserted me, but seeming to
" cast a look on me, is gone before to those habitations to
" which it was sensible I should follow him. And tho' I
" might appear to have borne my loss with courage; I was
" not unaffected with it: but I comforted myself in the as-
" surance that it would not be long before we should meet
" again, and be divorced no more." *Pigh. Annal.* ii.
99. *Plut. in vit. Caton. Cic. de Senect.* 23. *Spect. Vol.* 7.
Numb. 537.

the

A.U. 708. the higheft abilities and virtues. Yet thefe un-
fortunate parents lived in times when the honours
they derived from the republic, might in fome
meafure alleviate the weight of their domeftic
misfortunes. But as for myfelf, after having
been ftripped of thofe dignities you mention, and
which I had acquired by the moft laborious exer-
tion of my abilities, I had one only confolation
remaining: and of that I am now bereaved! I
could no longer divert the difquietude of my
thoughts, by employing myfelf in the caufes of
my friends, or the bufinefs of the ftate: for I
could no longer with any fatisfaction appear either
in the forum, or the fenate. In fhort, I juftly
confidered myfelf as cut off from the benefit of
all thofe alleviating occupations in which fortune
and induftry had qualified me to engage. But I
confidered too, that this was a deprivation which
I fuffered in common with yourfelf and fome
others: and whilft I was endeavouring to recon-
cile my mind to a patient indurance of thofe ills;
there was *one* to whofe tender offices I could
have recourfe, and in the fweetnefs of whofe con-
verfation I could difcharge all the cares and an-
xiety of my heart. But this laft fatal ftab to my
peace, has torn open thofe wounds which feem-
ed in fome meafure to have been tolerably heal-
ed. For I can now no longer lofe my private
forrows in the profperity of the commonwealth,

as

as I was wont to difpel the uneafinefs I fuffered A.U. 708.
upon the public account, in the happinefs I re-
ceived at home.   Accordingly I have equally
banifhed myfelf from my houfe [5], and from the
public; as finding no relief in either, from the ca-
lamities I lament in both.   It is this, therefore,
that heightens my defire of feeing you here;
as nothing can afford me a more effectual confo-
lation than the renewal of our friendly intercourfe:
a happinefs which I hope, and am informed in-
deed, that I fhall fhortly enjoy.   Among the
many reafons I have for impatiently wifhing your
arrival, one is, that we may previoufly concert
together our fcheme of conduct in the prefent con-
juncture; which, however, muft now be intirely
accommodated to another's will.   This perfon [a],
'tis true, is a man of great abilities and genero-
fity; and one, if I miftake not, who is by no
means my enemy; as I am fure he is extremely
your friend.   Neverthelefs it requires much
confideration, I do not fay in what manner we
fhall act with refpect to public affairs, but by
what methods we may beft obtain his permiffion
to retire from them.   Farewel.

---

[5] Cicero, upon the death of his daughter, retired from his
own houfe, to one belonging to Atticus near Rome: from
which, perhaps, this letter was written.
[a] Cæfar.

LETTER V.

TO LUCIUS LUCCEIUS [6].

A.U. 708. ALL the letters I have received from you
upon the subject of my late misfortune,
were extremely acceptable to me, as instances of
the highest affection and good sense. But the
great advantage I have derived from them, prin-
cipally results from that animating contempt
with which you look down upon human af-
fairs, and that exemplary fortitude which arms
you against all the various assaults of fortune.
I esteem it the most glorious privilege of
philosophy, to be thus superior to external acci-
dents, and to depend for happiness on ourselves
alone: a sentiment, which, altho' it was too
deeply planted in my heart to be totally eradi-
cated, has been somewhat weakened, I confess,
by the violence of those repeated storms to which
I have been lately exposed. But you have en-
deavoured, and with great success indeed, to re-
store it to all its usual strength and vigour. I can-
not therefore either too often, or too strongly
ly assure you, that nothing could give me an

---

[6] The same to whom the 20th letter of the first book is
written. See an account of him in rem. 1. on that epistle.

9

A.U. 705.

higher satisfaction than your letter.   But power-
ful as the various arguments of consolation are
which you have collected for my use, and ele-
gantly as you have enforced them ; I must ac-
knowledge, that nothing proved more effectual
than that firmness of mind which I remarked in
your letters, and which I should esteem as the
utmost reproach not to imitate. But if I imitate,
I must necessarily excel my guide and instructor
in this lesson of fortitude : for I am altogether
unsupported by the same hopes which I find you
entertain, that public affairs will improve. Those
illustrations indeed which you draw from the gla-
diatorial combats [7], together with the whole ten-
dency of your reasoning in general, all concur in
forbidding me to despair of the commonwealth.
It would be nothing extraordinary therefore if
you should be more composed than myself,
whilst you are in possession of these pleasing
hopes : the only wonder is, how you can possibly
entertain any.   For say, my friend, what is there
of our constitution that is not utterly subverted ?
Look round the republic and tell me, (you who

[7] Manutius supposes, with great probability, that Luccei-
us in the letter to which this is an answer, had endeavoured
to persuade Cicero not to despair of better times, by remind-
ing him of what sometimes happened at the gladiatorial
shews : where it was not unusual to see a combatant that
seemed almost intirely vanquished, unexpectedly recover
his ground, and gain the day from his antagonist.

C 2

 fo well underftand the nature of our government)
what part of it remains unbroken, or unim-
paired? Moft unqueftionably there is not one;
as I would prove in detail, if I imagined my
own difcernment was fuperior to yours, or were
capable (notwithftanding all your powerful ad-
monitions and precepts) to dwell upon fo melan-
choly a fubject without being extremely affected.
But I will bear my domeftic misfortunes in the
manner you affure me that I ought: and as to
thofe of the public, I fhall fupport them, per-
haps, with greater equanimity than even my
friend. For (to repeat it again) you are not, it
feems, without fome fort of hopes; whereas for
myfelf, I have abfolutely none: and fhall there-
fore, in purfuance of your advice, preferve my
fpirits even in the midft of defpair.   The pleaf-
ing recollection of thofe actions you recall to my
remembrance, and which indeed I performed
chiefly by your encouragement and recommenda-
tion, will greatly contribute to this end.   To fay
the truth, I have done every thing for the fervice
of my country that I ought, and more than could
have been expected from the courage and coun-
fels of any man.   You will pardon me, I hope,
for fpeaking in this advantageous manner of my
own conduct: but as you advife me to alleviate
my prefent uneafinefs by a retrofpect on my paft
actions:

actions ; I will confefs, that in thus commemo- A.U. 708.
rating them, I find great confolation.

I fhall punctually obferve your admonitions,
by calling off my mind as much as poffible from
every thing that may difturb its peace, and fixing
it on thofe fpeculations which are at once an
ornament to profperity, and the fupport of ad-
verfity. For this purpofe I fhall endeavour to
fpend as much of my time with you, as our
health and years will mutually permit : and if we
cannot meet fo often as I am fure we both wifh,
we fhall always at leaft feem prefent to each other
by a fympathy of hearts, and an union in the
fame philofophical contemplations.   Farewel.

L E T T E R   VI.

L u c c e i u s to C i c e r o.

I Shall rejoice to hear that you are well. As to
my own health, it is much as ufual ; or ra-
ther, I think, fomewhat worfe.

I have frequently called at your door ; and am
much furprized to find, that you have not been
in Rome fince Cæfar left it. What is it that
fo ftrongly draws you from hence ? If any of
your ufual engagements of the literary kind,
renders you thus enamoured of folitude, I am fo

C 3 far

 far from condemning your retirement, that I think of it with pleasure. There is no sort of life indeed that can be more agreeable, not only in times so disturbed as the present, but even in those of the most desirable calm and serenity: especially to a mind like yours, which may have occasion for repose from its public labours, and which is always capable of producing something that will afford both pleasure to others and honour to yourself. But if you have withdrawn from the world in order to give a free vent to those tears which you so immoderately indulged when you were here; I shall lament indeed your grief; but (if you will allow me to speak the truth) I never can excuse it. For tell me, my friend, is it possible that a man of your uncommon discernment should not perceive, what is obvious to all mankind? Is it possible you can be ignorant that your perpetual complaints can profit nothing, and only serve to increase those disquietudes which your good sense requires you to subdue? But if arguments cannot prevail, intreaties perhaps may. Let me conjure you then by all the regard you bear me, to dispel this gloom that hangs upon your heart; to return to that society and to those occupations which were either common to us both, or peculiar to yourself. But though I would fain dissuade

you

you from continuing your prefent way of life, A.U. 708.
yet I would by no means fuffer my zeal to be
troublefome.   In the difficulty therefore of fteer-
ing between thefe two inclinations, I will only
add my requeft, that you would either comply
with my advice, or excufe me for offering it.
Farewel.

LETTER VII.

To Lucius Lucceius.

EVERY part of your laft letter glowed with
that warmth of friendfhip, which, tho' it
was by no means new to me, I could not but ob-
ferve with peculiar fatisfaction ; I would fay
pleafure, if that were not a word to which I have
now for ever bidden adieu. Not merely, however,
for the caufe you fufpect, and for which, under
the gentleft and moft affectionate terms, you in
fact very feverely reproach me ; but becaufe all
that ought in reafon to affuage the anguifh of fo
deep a wound, is abfolutely no more. For whi-
ther fhall I fly for confolation ? Is it to the bofom
of my friends ? But tell me (for we have gene-
rally fhared the fame common amities together)
how few of that number are remaining ? how few
that have not perifhed by the fword, or that
are not become ftrangely infenfible ? You will
C 4 . fay,

A.U.708. say, perhaps, that I might seek my relief in your society : and there indeed I would willingly seek it. The same habitudes and studies, a long intercourse of friendship—in short, is there any sort of bond, any single circumstance of connection wanting to unite us together? Why then are we such strangers to one another? For my own part, I know not: but this I know, that we have hitherto seldom met, I do not say in Rome, where the Forum usually brings every body together[8], but when we were near neighbours at Tusculum and Puteolæ.

I know not by what ill fate it has happened, that at an age, when I might expect to flourish in the greatest credit and dignity, I should find myself in so wretched a situation as to be ashamed that I am still in being. Despoiled indeed of every honour and every comfort that adorned my public life, or smoothed my private; what is it that can now afford me any refuge? My books, I imagine you will tell me: and to these indeed I very assiduously apply. For to what else can I possibly have recourse? Yet even these seem to exclude me from that peaceful port

[8] The forum was a place of general resort for the whole city. It was here that the lawyers pleaded their causes, that the poets recited their works, and that funeral orations were spoken in honour of the dead. It was here, in short, every thing was going forward, that could engage the active, or amuse the idle. *Vid. Hor. lib.* 1. *sat.* 4. 74. *sat.* 6. 42.

which

which I fain would reach, and reproach me, as it were, for prolonging that life which only increases my sorrows with my years. Can you wonder then that I absent myself from Rome, where there is nothing under my own roof to afford me any satisfaction, and where I abhor both public men and public measures, both the forum and the senate ? For this reason it is that I wear away my days in a total application to literary pursuits: not indeed as entertaining so vain a hope, that I may find in them a complete cure for my misfortunes, but in order to obtain at least some little respite from their bitter remembrance.

If those dangers with which we were daily menaced, had not formerly prevented both you and myself from reflecting with that coolness we ought, we should never have been thus separated. Had that proved to have been the case, we should both of us have spared ourselves much uneasiness: as I should not have indulged so many groundless fears for your health, nor you for the consequences of my grief. Let us repair then this unlucky mistake as well as we may : and as nothing can be more suitable to both of us, than the company of each other, I purpose to be with you in a few days. Farewel.

LETTER VIII.

To Marcus Marcellus.

A.U. 703. NOtwithstanding that I have nothing new to communicate to you, and am in expectation of a letter from you very shortly, or rather indeed of seeing you in person; yet I would not suffer Theophilus to go away, without sending you a line or two by his hands. Let me intreat you then to return amongst us[9], as soon as possible: and be assured you are impatiently expected, not only by myself and the rest of your friends, but by all Rome in general. I am sometimes however inclined to fear, that you will not be extremely forward to hasten your journey: and indeed if you were possessed of no other sense but that of seeing, I could easily excuse you if there are some persons whom you would chuse to avoid. But as the difference is very inconsiderable between hearing and being a spectator of what one disapproves; and as I am persuaded it is of great consequence, both in respect to your private affairs, as well as upon every other consideration, that you should expedite your return; I thought it incumbent upon me to tell you so. And now

[9] See let. 19. vol. ii. p. 343.

having

having acquainted you with my fentiments, the A.U.708.
reft muft be left to your own determination: but
I fhould be glad to know, however, when we
may expect you.   Farewel.

L E T T E R   IX.
To Tiro.

BElieve me, my dear Tiro, I am greatly
anxious for your health : however if you
perfevere in the fame cautious regimen which you
have hitherto obferved, you will foon, I truft,
be well.   As to my library; I beg you would
put the books in order, and take a catalogue of
them, when your phyfician fhall give you his con-
fent: for it is by his directions you muft now be
governed.   With refpect to the gardener; I leave
you to adjuft matters as you fhall judge proper.

I think you might come to Rome on the firft
of next month, in order to fee the gladiatorial
combats, and return the following day : but let
this be entirely as is moft agreeable to your own
inclinations.   In the mean time, if you have any
affection for me, take care of your health.   Fare-
wel.

L·E T-

LETTER X.

SERVIUS SULPICIUS to CICERO.

A.U. 708. THE news I am going to acquaint you with, will, I am sure, prove extremely unwelcome: yet as you cannot but in some measure be prepared for it, by being sensible that every man's life is subject to casualties, as well as to the general laws of nature, I thought proper to send you a circumstantial account of the unhappy accident that has lately happened.

I arrived at Piræeus, from Epidaurus [1], on the 23d instant: where I continued all that day merely to enjoy the company of my collegue [2] Marcellus. The next day I took my leave of him, with an intention of going from Athens into Bœotia [3], in order to finish the remainder of my circuit [4]: and I left him in the resolution, as he told me, of sailing to Italy by the way of Malea [5].

[1] A city in the Peloponnesus, now called *Pigrada*, situated upon the bay of *Engia*.

[2] It has already been noted, that Marcellus and Sulpicius were collegues in the consular office, A. U. 702.

[3] A district of Greece, under the jurisdiction of Sulpicius governor of that province.

[4] The Roman governors were obliged to visit the principal cities of their province, in order to administer justice, and settle other affairs relating to their function.

[5] A promontory in the south-east point of the Peloponnesus, now called cape *Malis*.

The

The day following, as I was preparing to set out from Athens, his friend Posthumius came to me about four in the morning, and informed me Marcellus had been stabbed the night before by Magius Cilo, whilst they were sitting together after supper [6]; that he had received two wounds from a dagger, one of which was in his breast, and the other under his ear; but that neither of them, he hoped, was mortal. He added, that Magius after having committed this barbarous action, immediately killed himself; and that Marcellus had dispatched him in order to give me this account, and likewise to desire that I would direct my physicians [7] to attend him. This I instantly did: and followed them myself as soon as it was light. But when I had almost reached Piræeus, I met a servant of Acidanus with a note to acquaint me, that our friend expired a little before day-break. Thus did the noble Marcellus unworthily fall by the hand of a villainous assassin: and he whose life his very ene-

A.U. 708.

[6] The reason which induced Cilo to murder his friend, is not certainly known. It was suspected by some at Rome, that it was at the secret instigation of Cæsar: but the circumstance of Cilo immediately afterwards killing himself, renders that suspicion altogether improbable, and seems to determine the motive to some personal, and perhaps sudden resentment. *Vid. ad Att.* xiii. 10.

[7] The antient physicians practised surgery as well as medicine.

mies

 mies had fpared in reverence to his illuftrious virtues, met with an executioner at laft in his own friend! However, I proceeded to his pavilion : where I found only two of his freedmen and a few flaves; the reft, I was told, having fled in apprehenfion of the confequences in which they might be involved by this murder of their mafter [8]. I was obliged to place the body of Marcellus in the fame fedan that brought me, and to make my chair-men carry it into Athens : where I paid him all the funeral honours that city could fupply : which indeed were not inconfiderable. But I could not prevail with the Athenians to fuffer him to be buried within their walls : a privilege, they affured me, which their religious ordinances would by no means admit. They granted me, however, what was the next honour, and which they had never permitted to any ftranger before : they allowed me to depofite his afhes in any of the Gymnafia I fhould think proper. Accordingly I fixed upon a fpot belonging to the Academy [9]; one of the nobleft colleges in the

---

[8] Manutius remarks, that by the Roman law, where a man was murdered in his own houfe, his flaves were punifhable with death. *Vid. Tacit. Annal.* xiv. 42.

[9] " This celebrated place took its name from one Academus, an antient hero, who poffeffed it in the time of the " Tyndaridæ. But famous as it was, it was purchafed afterwards for about 100l. and dedicated to the public for the " convenience of walks and exercifes for the citizens of

whole

whole world.   In this place I caufed a funeral A.U.708.
pile to be erected: and afterwards perfuaded the
Athenians to raife a marble monument to his me-
mory, at the public expence.   Thus have I paid
to my relation and collegue, both during his life
and after his death, every friendly office he had a
right to expect from me.   Farewel.

Athens, May 31.

L E T T E R XI.

To Tiro.

I Impatiently expect a letter from you upon
affairs of many and various kinds: but it is
with much greater impatience however that I ex-
pect yourfelf.   In the mean time, endeavour to
gain Demetrius over to my intereft, and to ob-
tain whatever other advantage you fhall be able.
I know your care is not wanting to recover the
money which is owing to me from Aufidius: but
I beg you would be as expeditious in that matter
as poffible.   If it is upon that account you delay
your return ; I admit it to be a good reafon : if
not ; fly hither, I charge you, with the utmoft

" ·Athens, and was gradually improved by the rich, who
" had received benefit or pleafure from it, with plantations
" of groves, ftately porticos, and commodious apartments,
" for the profeffors of the academic fchool." *Middleton's*
life of Cic. iii. 325.

fpeed.

 speed.   To repeat it once more: I expect a let-
ter from you with great impatience.   Farewel.

LETTER XII.

VATINIUS[1] TO CICERO.

IF you have not renounced your usual custom of defending the cause of your friends, an old client of yours desires to engage you as his advocate: and as you formerly protected him in his humiliation[2], I dare say, you will not now abandon him in his glory. Whose aid indeed can I so properly invoke upon the occasion of my victories, as that generous friend's, who first taught me how to *vanquish*[3]? Can I doubt, that he who had the courage to withstand a combination of

---

[1] I have already had occasion to give an account of the character of Vatinius, in rem. 5. p. 160. vol. 1. He was at this time, by the appointment of Cæsar, governor of Illyricum: which comprehended part of Austria, Hungary, Sclavonia, Bosnia and Dalmatia. He was sent thither with a considerable army, to reduce the people of that province to obedience; and having obtained some success, he wrote the present letter to Cicero, in order to engage him to support his pretensions to the honour of a public thanksgiving. *Pigh. Annal.* ii. 454.

[2] When Cicero, much to his dishonour, defended Vatinius against the impeachment of Licinius Calvus. See vol. i. p. 189.

[3] Alluding to his having, by the assistance of Cicero's eloquence, vanquished his adversaries in the prosecution mentioned in the preceding note.

the

the moft powerful men in Rome, who had con- A.U. 708.
fpired my ruin; will not be able to beat down
the envious and malignant efforts of a little con-
temptible party, that may endeavour to oppofe
my honours ? If I ftill then retain the fhare I once
enjoyed of your friendfhip, take me, I intreat
you, wholly under your protection, as one whofe
dignities it is incumbent upon you both to fupport
and advance. You are fenfible that I have many
enemies, whofe malevolence I have in no fort de-
ferved: but what avails innocence againft fo un-
accountable a fate ? If thefe therefore fhould any
of them attempt to obftruct the honours I am
folliciting; I conjure you to exert your generous
offices, as ufual, in defence of your abfent friend.
In the mean time, you will find at the bottom of
this letter a copy of the difpatches I fend by this
exprefs to the fenate, concerning the fuccefs of
my arms.

Being informed that the flave whom you em-
ploy as your reader, had eloped from you into
the country of the Vardæi [4], I have caufed dili-
gent fearch to be made after him; altho' I did
not receive your commands, for that purpofe.
I doubt not of recovering him, unlefs he fhould
take refuge in Dalmatia [5] : and even in that cafe,

[4] A people contiguous to Dalmatia.
[5] Dalmatia made part of the province of Illyricum : but
it was not at this time entirely fubdued to the Roman go-
vernment.

Vol. III.   D   I do

A.U.708. I do not entirely defpair. Farewel, and con-
tinue to love me.

From the camp at Narona [6], July the 11th.

LETTER XIII.

To Tiro.

YOU are not miftaken in fuppofing me de-
firous of your company : but indeed I am
extremely apprehenfive of your venturing upon
fo long a journey. The abftinence you have
been obliged to obferve, the evacuations you have
undergone, together with the violence of your
diftemper itfelf, have too much impaired your
ftrength for fo great a fatigue : and any negli-
gence after diforders fo fevere as yours, is gene-
rally attended with confequences of the moft
dangerous kind. You cannot reach Cuma in lefs
than two days : and it will coft you five more to
complete your expedition. But I purpofe to be
with you at Formiæ towards the end of this
month : and I hope, my dear Tiro, it will not
be your fault if I fhould not have the fatisfaction
of finding you perfectly recovered.

My ftudies languifh for want of your affift-
ance : however, the letter you fent by Acaftus

* In Liburnia, now called Croatia, and which formed
part of Vatinius's government.

has

has somewhat enlivened them. Pompeius is now
here, and presses me much to read some of my
compositions : but I jocosely, tho' at the same
time truly assure him, that all my muses are si-
lent in your absence.   I hope therefore you will
prepare to attend them with your usual good of-
fices.   You may depend upon mine in the article
and at the time I promised : for as I taught you
the etymology of the word *fides*, be assured I shall
act up to its full import.   Take care, I charge
you, to re-establish your health : mine is perfectly
well.   Adieu.

L E T T E R XIV.

To Varro.

TO importune the execution of a promise is
a sort of ill-manners, of which the popu-
lace themselves, unless they are particularly in-
stigated for that purpose, are seldom guilty [7].   I
cannot, however, forbear, I will not say to de-
mand, but to remind you of a favour, which you
long since gave me reason to expect.   To this end,

---

[7] This alludes to the promises of public shews which
were frequently made to the people, by the magistrates and
others, who affected popularity : some particular instances
of which have been occasionally produced in the course of
the preceding remarks.

D 2

I have

A.U. 70?. I have sent you four admonitors[1]: but admonitors, perhaps, whom you will not look upon as extremely modeft. They are certain philofophers, whom I have chofen from among the difciples of the later Academy[2]: and confidence, you know, is the characteriftic of this fect[3]. I am apprehenfive therefore that you may confider them as fo many importunate duns, when my meaning only is, that they fhould prefent themfelves before you as modeft petitioners. But to drop my metaphor; I have long denied myfelf the fatisfaction of addreffing to you fome of my works, in expectation of receiving a compliment of the fame kind from yourfelf. I waited therefore in order to make you a return as nearly as poffible of the fame nature. But as I am willing to impute your delaying this favour, to the defire of rendering it fo much the more perfect; I could no longer refrain from telling the world,

[1] Thefe were dialogues entitled *Academica :* which appear from hence to have originally confifted of four books, tho' there is only part of one now remaining.

[2] The followers of the Academic philofophy were divided into two fects ; called the *old* and the *new.* The founder of the former was Plato ; of the latter Arcefilas. The principal difpute between them feems to have related to the degree of evidence upon which human knowledge is founded ; the earlier Academics maintaining that fome propofitions were certain ; the latter, that none were more than probable. *Vid. Academ.* 1. *paffim.*

[3] Alluding to their practice of queftioning all opinions, and affenting to none.

in the beſt manner I was able, that we are united A.U. 708.
both in our affections and in our ſtudies. With
this view, I have drawn up a dialogue which I
ſuppoſe to have paſſed between you and myſelf
in conjunction with Atticus : and have laid the
ſcene in your Cuman villa. The part I have aſ-
ſigned to you, is to defend, (what if I miſtake not
you approve) the ſentiments of Antiochus [2] : as
I have choſen myſelf to maintain the principles
of Philo [3]. You will wonder to find, perhaps,
in the peruſal of this piece, that I have repreſent-
ed a converſation, which in truth we never had :
but you muſt remember the privilege which dia-
logue writers have always aſſumed.

And now, my dear Varro, let me hope that we
ſhall hereafter enjoy together many of theſe phi-
loſophical converſations. If we have too long
neglected them ; the public occupations in which
we were engaged muſt be our apology : but the
time is now arrived when we have no ſuch ex-

---

[2] A philoſopher at Athens, whoſe lectures Varro had for-
merly attended. He maintained the doctrines of the *old*
Academy. *Cic. Academ.* 1. 3.

[3] A Greek philoſopher, who profeſſed the ſceptical prin-
ciples of the *new* Academy. Antiochus, mentioned in the
preceding note, had been bred up under him, tho' he after-
wards became a convert to the oppoſite ſect. Cicero took
the ſceptical part of this dialogue, not as being agreeable to
his own ſentiments, but in order to pay Varro the greater
compliment of maintaining the more rational opinion. *Aca-
dem. ubi ſup. ad At.* xiii. 19.

                        cuſe

 cuſe to plead. May we then exerciſe theſe ſpeculations together, under a fixed and peaceable government at leaſt, if not under one of the moſt eligible kind ! Tho' indeed if that were to prove the caſe, far other employments would engage our honourable labours. But as affairs are at preſent ſituated, what is there elſe that can render life deſirable ? For my own part, it is with difficulty I endure it, even with all the advantages of their powerful aſſiſtance : but without them, it would be utterly inſupportable. But we ſhall talk farther and frequently upon this ſubject, when we meet : in the mean time I give you joy of the new habitation you have purchaſed, and highly approve of your removal. Farewel.

LETTER XV.

To Tiro.

WHY ſhould you not direct your letters to me with the familiar ſuperſcription which one friend generally uſes to another ? However, if you are unwilling to hazard the envy which this ·privilege may draw upon you, be it as you think proper : tho' for my own part, it is a maxim which I have generally purſued with re-

ſpect

ſpect to myſelf, to treat envy with the utmoſt A.U.708.
diſregard.

I rejoice that you found ſo much benefit by
your ſudorific : and ſhould the air of Tuſculum
be attended with the ſame happy effect, how infi-
nitely will it increaſe my fondneſs for that favou-
rite ſcene ! If you love me then, (and if you
do not, you are undoubtedly the moſt ſucceſsful
of all diſſemblers) conſecrate your whole time to
the care of your health : which hitherto indeed
your aſſiduous attendance upon myſelf, has but
too much prevented.   You well know the rules
which it is neceſſary you ſhould obſerve for this
purpoſe; and I need not tell you that your diet
ſhould be light, and your exerciſes moderate ;
that you ſhould keep your body open, and your
mind amuſed.   Be it your care, in ſhort, to re-
turn to me perfectly recovered : and I ſhall ever
afterwards not only love you, but Tuſculum ſo
much the more ardently.

I wiſh you could prevail with your neighbour
to take my garden : as it will be the moſt effec-
tual means of vexing that raſcal Helico.   This
fellow, altho' he paid a thouſand feſterces [5]
for the rent of a piece of cold barren ground,
that had not ſo much as a wall or a ſhed upon it,

[5] About 8 l. of our money.

or

 or was fupplied with a fingle drop of water, has yet the affurance to laugh at the price I require for mine; notwithftanding all the money I have laid out upon improvements. But let it be your bufinefs to fpirit the man into our terms: as it fhall be mine to make the fame artful attack upon Otho.

Let me know what you have done with refpect to the fountain: tho' poffibly this wet feafon may now have overfupplied it with water. If the weather fhould prove fair, I will fend the dial, together with the books you defire. But how happened it that you took none with you? Was it that you were employed in fome poetical compofition upon the model of your admired Sophocles? If fo, I hope you will foon oblige the world with your performance.

Ligurius, Cæfar's great favourite, is dead. He was a very worthy man, and much my friend. Let me know when I may expect you: in the mean time be careful of your health. Farewel.

L E T T E R XVI.

To Quintus Valerius Orca[9].

I Have the ftrongeft attachment to the citizens A.U. 708. of Volaterræ[1], as a body of men, who having received great obligations from me, have abundantly returned them.   Their good offices indeed have never been wanting in any feafon of my life, whether of adverfity or profperity. But were I entirely void of all perfonal connections with this community, I fhould neverthelefs, merely from my great affection towards yourfelf, and in return to that which I am fenfible you equally bear for me, moft earneftly recommend them to your protection: efpecially as they have in fome fort a more than common claim to your juftice. For in the firft place, the gods themfelves feem to have interpofed in their behalf, when they fo wonderfully efcaped from the perfecutions of

---

[9] He was prætor in the year of Rome 697, and at the expiration of his office obtained the government of Africa. Upon the breaking out of the civil war he took poffeffion of Sardinia in the name of Cæfar: by whom he was at this time appointed one of the commiffioners for dividing thofe eftates, with which he propofed upon his return from Spain to reward the valour and fidelity of his foldiers. *Pigh. Annal.* ii. 384.

[1] A city in Tufcany.

Sylla:

 la [2] : and in the next, the whole body of the Roman people expreſſed the warmeſt concern for their intereſt, when I ſtood forth as their advocate in my conſulſhip. For when the tribunes were endeavouring to carry a moſt iniquitous law for the diſtribution of the lands belonging to this city; I found it extremely eaſy to perſuade the republic to favour the rights of a community, which fortune had ſo remarkably protected. And as Cæſar in the Agrarian law which he procured during his firſt conſulate [3], ſhewed his approbation of the ſervices I had thus performed for them, by expreſly exempting their lands from all future impoſitions; I cannot ſuppoſe that he who is perpetually diſplaying new inſtances of his generoſity, ſhould intend to reſume thoſe which his former bounty has beſtowed. As you have followed then his party and his power, with ſo much honour to yourſelf: it ſhould ſeem agreeable to your uſual prudence, to follow him likewiſe in this inſtance of his generoſity; or certainly at leaſt to leave this matter intirely to his own deciſion. One thing I am ſure you can

[2] They held out a ſiege of two years againſt the troops of Sylla: who in vain endeavoured to compel them to ſubmit to his edict for the confiſcation of their lands. *Quartier.*

[3] The law alluded to, ſeems to have been a branch of that propoſed by Rullus: an account of which has been given in theſe remarks. See rem. 13. p. 165. vol. I.

by

by no means doubt; and that is, whether you
fhould wifh to fix fo worthy and fo illu-
ftrious a corporation in your intereft, who are di-
ftinguifhed for their inviolable adherence to their
friends. Thus far I have endeavoured to perfuade
you to take thefe people under your protection, for
your own fake : but that you may not imagine I
have no other plea to urge in their favour, I will
now requeft it alfo for mine. You cannot, in
truth, confer upon me a more acceptable fervice,
than by proving yourfelf the friend and guardian
of their interefts. I recommend therefore to your
juftice and humanity the poffeffions of a city
which have been hitherto preferved by the pecu-
liar providence of the gods, as well as by the
particular favour of the moft diftinguifhed perfo-
nages in the whole Roman commonwealth. If
it were in my power as effectually to ferve thofe
who place themfelves under my patronage, as it
once was; there is no good office I would not ex-
ert, there is no oppofition I would not encoun-
ter, in order to affift the Volaterranians. But I
flatter myfelf I have ftill the fame intereft with
you, that I formerly enjoyed with the world in
general. Let me intreat you then by all the
powerful ties of our friendfhip, to give thefe
citizens reafon to look upon it as a providential
circumftance,

 circumſtance, that the perſon who is appointed to execute this commiſſion, happens to be one with whom their conſtant patron has the greateſt influence.   Farewel.

LETTER XVII.

TO LEPTA.

I Am glad that Macula has acted agreeably to the good offices I have a right to expect from him, by offering me the uſe of his houſe. I always thought the man's Falernian [6] was well enough for road-wine; and only doubted whether he had ſufficient room to receive my retinue: beſides, there is ſomething in the ſituation of his villa that does not diſpleaſe me.   However I do not give up my deſign upon Petrinum [7].   But it has too many charms to be uſed only as an occaſional lodging: its beauties deſerve a much longer ſtay.

Balbus is confined with a very ſevere fit of the gout, and does not admit any viſitors; ſo that I have not been able to ſee him ſince you left Rome.   However I have talked with Oppius concerning your requeſt to be appointed one of

---

[6] This was a favourite wine among the Romans, which took its name from Falernus, a little hill in Campania where the grape was produced.
[7] A town in Campania, where Lepta had a villa.

the

the managers of Cæfar's games [8].   But in my A.U.708.
opinion it would be moſt adviſeable not to under-
take this trouble; as you will by no means find
it ſubſervient to the point you have in view. For
Cæfar is ſurrounded with ſuch a multitude of
pretenders to his friendſhip, that he is more
likely to leſſen, than increaſe, the number; eſpe-
cially where a man has no higher ſervice to
recommend him, than what ariſes from little
offices of this kind: a circumſtance too, which
Cæſar poſſibly may never be acquainted with.
But if he ſhould, he would look upon himſelf
rather as having conferred, than received, a fa-
vour.   Nevertheleſs I will try if this affair can be
managed in ſuch a manner, as to give you any
reaſonable hope that it will anſwer your purpoſe:
otherwiſe, I think, you ſhould be ſo far from de-
ſiring the employment, that you ought by all
means to avoid it.

I believe I ſhall ſtay ſome time at Aſtura [9]; as
I purpoſe to wait there the arrival of Cæſar [5].
Farewel.

[8] Theſe were games which Cæſar purpoſed to exhibit in
the ſeveral quarters of Rome upon his return from Spain, in
honour of his victory over the ſons of Pompey. *Suet. in vit.
Jul.*

[9] A town in the *Campagna di Roma*, ſituated near the ſea
coaſt between Civita Vecchia and Monte Circello: where
Cicero had a villa.   It was about two years after the date of
this letter, that Cicero was murdered near this villa by the
order of Antony.

[5] From Spain.

LETTER XVIII.

To Quintus Valerius Orca [1].

A.U. 703.

I Am not difpleafed to find, that the world is ap-
prifed of the friendfhip which fubfifts between
us. But it is not, you may well imagine, from
any vain oftentation of this kind, that I interrupt
you in the honourable difcharge of that trouble-
fome and important commiffion which Cæfar has
entrufted to your care. On the contrary, not-
withftanding that the fhare I enjoy in your affec-
tion is fo generally known, as to occafion many ap-
plications to me; yet I would not be tempted by
any popular motives to break in upon you in the
execution of your office. However I could not
refufe the follicitations of Curtius; as he is one
with whom I have been intimately connected
from his earlieft youth. I took a very confidera-
ble part in the misfortunes he fuffered from the
unjuft perfecution of Sylla: and when it feemed
agreeable to the general fenfe of the people, that
my friend, together with the reft of thofe who
in conjunction with himfelf had been deprived
both of their fortunes and their country, fhould

[1] See rem. 9. on let. 16. of this B.

be

be reftored at leaft to the latter ; I affifted him A.U.708.
for that purpofe to the utmoft of my power.
Upon his return he invefted all that remained to
him from this general wreck of his fubftance, in
the purchafe of an eftate at Volaterræ : of which
if he fhould be difpoffeffed, I know not how he
will fupport the fenatorial rank to which Cæfar
has lately advanced him.   It would be an extreme
hardfhip indeed if he fhould fink in wealth, as
he rifes in honours : and it feems altogether in-
confiftent that he fhould lofe his eftate in confe-
quence of Cæfar's general order for the diftribu-
tion of thefe lands in queftion ; at the fame time
that by his particular favour he has gained a feat
in the fenate.   But I will not alledge all that I
well might for the equity of my friend's caufe ;
left by enlarging on the juftice, I fhould feem
to derogate from the favour of your compliance
with my requeft.   I moft earneftly conjure you
then to confider this affair of Curtius as my own ;
to protect his intereft as you would mine in the
fame circumftances ; and to be affured that what-
ever fervices you fhall thus confer upon my
friend, I fhall efteem as a perfonal obligation
to myfelf.   Farewel.

LETTER XIX.

TO FABIUS GALLUS[z].

A.U. 708. INstances of your friendſhip are perpetually meeting me wherever I turn: and I have lately, in particular, had occaſion to experience them in regard to my affair with Tigellius[3]. I perceive by your letter, that it has occaſioned you much concern: and I am greatly obliged by this proof of your affection. But let me give you a ſhort hiſtory how the caſe ſtands. It was Cipius, I think, that formerly ſaid, " *I am not aſleep for* " *every man*[4] : neither am I, my dear Gallus, ſo meanly complaiſant as to be the humble ſervant of every minion. The truth of it is, I am the humble ſervant of none: and am ſo far from being under the neceſſity of ſubmitting to any ſervile compliances in order to preſerve my friendſhip

---

[z] This is the ſame perſon to whom the 11th letter of the firſt book is addreſſed.

[3] Tigellius was an extravagant debauchee, who by his pleaſantry, his ſkill in muſic, his agreeable voice, together with his other ſoft and faſhionable qualifications, had extremely ingratiated himſelf with Cæſar.

[4] Cipius was a complaiſant huſband, who upon ſome occaſions would affect to nod, whilſt his wife was awake and more agreeably employed. But a ſlave coming into the room when he was in one of theſe obliging ſlumbers, and attempting to carry off a flaggon that ſtood upon the table, " Sirrah, ſays he, *non omnibus dormio.*"

with

with Cæsar's favourites ; that there is not one of
them, except this Tigellius, who does not treat
me with greater marks of refpect than I ever re-
ceived even when I was thought to enjoy the
higheft popularity and power.   But I think my-
felf extremely fortunate in being upon ill terms
with a man who is more corrupted than his own
native air [5], and whofe character is notorious, I
fuppofe, to the whole world by the poignant
verfes of the fatyric Calvus [6].   But to let you fee
upon what flight grounds he has taken offence ;
I had promifed, you muft know, to plead the
caufe of his grandfather Phameas: which I under-
took, however, merely in friendfhip to the man
himfelf.   Accordingly Phameas called upon me
in order to tell me, that the judge had fixed a
day for his trial : which happened to be the very
fame on which I was obliged to attend as advo-
cate for Sextius.   I acquainted him therefore,
that I could not poffibly give him any affiftance
at the time he mentioned ; but that if any other

[5] Tigellius was a native of Sardinia : an ifland noted for
its noxious air.   See rem. 3. p. 246. vol. ii.

[6] Fate feems to have decreed that Tigellius fhould not want
a poet to deliver his character down to pofterity : for altho' the
verfes of Calvus are loft, thofe of Horace remain, in which
Tigellius is delineated with all thofe inimitable ftrokes of ri-
dicule which diftinguifh the mafterly hand of that polite fa-
tyrift.   *Vid. Hor. fatyr. lib . 1. fat. 2 & 3.*

A.U. 708. had been appointed, I moſt aſſuredly would not have failed.   Phameas neverthelefs, in the conſcious pride, no doubt, of having a grandſon that could pipe and ſing to ſome purpoſe, left me with an air that ſeemed to ſpeak indignation. And now having thus ſtated my cafe, and ſhewn you the injuſtice of this ſongſter's complaints, may I not properly ſay with the old proverb, " *So many Sardinians, ſo many rival rogues* [7]."

I beg you would ſend me your Cato [8], which I am extremely defirous of reading.   It is indeed ſome reflection upon us both, that I have not yet enjoyed that pleafure.   Farewel.

[7] The literal interpretation of this proverb is, *you have Sardinians to ſell, each a greater rogue than the other;* but a ſhorter turn has been adopted in the tranſlation, in order to bring it nearer to the concifeneſs of the proverbial ſtile. This proverb took its rife (as Manutius obſerves) from the great number of Sardinian ſlaves with which the markets of Italy were overſtocked, upon the reduction of that iſland by Titus Sempronius Gracchus, in the year of Rome 512.

[8] The character of Cato was at this time the faſhionable topic of declamation at Rome : and every man that pretended to genius and eloquence, furniſhed the public with an inventive or panegyric upon that illuſtrious Roman, as party or patriotifm directed his pen.   In this refpect, as well as in all others, Cato's reputation feems to have been attended with every advantage that any man who is ambitious of a good name can defire : for the next honour to being applauded by the worthy, is to be abufed by the worthleſs.

L E T T E R   XX.

To CLUVIUS[a].

IN the visit which, agreeably to our friend-
ship and that great respect with which you
always treat me, I received from you upon your
setting out for Gaul, we had some general dif-
course relating to those estates in that province
which are held of the city of Atella[b] : and I then
expressed how much I was concerned for the in-
terest of that corporation.   But in confidence of
the singular affection you bear me, and in per-
formance of a duty which it is incumbent upon
me to discharge, I thought proper to write to
you more fully upon this affair : as it is indeed
of the last importance to a community with which
I have the strongest connections.   I am very sen-
sible at the same time both of the occasion and
extent of your commission; and that Cæsar has
not entrusted you in the execution of it, with any
discretionary power.   I limit my request there-

[a] He was one of the commissioners nominated by Cæsar
for settling the division of the lands for the purposes men-
tioned in note 9 on let. 16 of this B.   The department af-
signed to him was Cisalpine Gaul.

[b] A city in Campania, situated between Naples and Ca-
pua : it is now called *Santo Arpino*.

E 2

fore

A.U. 708. fore by what I imagine is no lefs within the bounds of your authority, than I am perfuaded it is not beyond what you would be willing to do for my fake. In the firft place then, I intreat you to believe, what is truly the fact, that the whole revenues of this corporation arife from thefe lands in queftion : and that the heavy impofitions with which they are at prefent burthened, have laid them under the greateft difficulties. But altho' in this refpect they may feem to be in no worfe condition than many other cities in Italy; yet believe me, their cafe is unhappily diftinguifhed by feveral calamitous circumftances peculiar to themfelves. I forbear however to enumerate them; left in lamenting the miferies of my friends, I fhould be thought to glance at thofe perfons whom it is by no means my defign to offend. Indeed if I had not conceived ftrong hopes that I fhall be able to prevail with Cæfar in favour of this city, there would be no occafion for my prefent very earneft application to you. But as I am well perfuaded that Cæfar will have regard to the dignity of this illuftrious corporation; to the zeal which they bear for his intereft; and above all, to the equity of their caufe; I venture to intreat you to leave the decifion of this affair entirely to his own determination [c].

Cæfar was not yet returned out of Spain.

If

If I could produce no precedent of your having A.U. 708.
already complied with a requeſt of this nature;
it is a requeſt which I ſhould neverthelefs have
made: but I have ſo much the ſtronger hopes
that you will not refuſe me in the preſent in-
ſtance, as I am informed you have granted the
ſame favour to the citizens of Regium[c]. 'Tis true,
you have ſome ſort of connection with that city.
But in juſtice to your affection towards me, I can-
not but hope, that what you have yielded to your
own clients, you will not deny to mine: eſpeci-
ally as it is for theſe alone that I ſollicit you, not-
withſtanding ſo many others of my friends are in
the ſame ſituation.   I dare ſay I need not aſſure
you, that it is neither upon any ambitious mo-
tives that I apply to you in their behalf, nor
without having juſt reaſon to be their advocate.
The fact is, I have great obligations to them:
and there has been no ſeaſon of my life in which
they have not given me ſignal proofs of their af-
fection.   As you are ſenſible therefore that the
intereſt of this corporation with which I am ſo
ſtrongly connected, is greatly concerned in the
ſucceſs of my preſent requeſt; I conjure you by
all the powerful ties of our mutual friendſhip,
and by all the ſentiments of your humanity, to

---

[c] Now called Regio: a maritime city in Calabria.

E 3   comply

A.U.703. comply with thefe my interceffions in their behalf.
If after having obtained this favour I fhould fuc-
ceed likewife (as I have reafon to hope) in my
application to Cæfar; I fhall confider all the ad-
vantages of that fuccefs as owing entirely to
yourfelf. Nor fhall I be lefs obliged to you tho'
I fhould not fucceed: as you will have contri-
buted all in your power at leaft that I might.
In one word, you will by thefe means not only
perform a moft acceptable fervice to myfelf; but
for ever attach to the intereft both of you and
your family, a moft illuftrious and grateful city.
Farewel.

LETTER XXI.

To Fabius Gallus.

YOU need be in no pain about your letter.
So far from having deftroyed it, as you
imagine; it is perfectly fafe: and you may call
for it whenever you pleafe.

Your admonitions are extremely obliging, and
I hope you will always continue them with the
fame freedom. You are apprehenfive, I per-
ceive, that if I fhould render this Tigellius my
enemy, he may probably make me merrier
than I like, and teach me the *Sardinian*
laugh.

laugh[9].   In return to your proverb, let me pre-
sent you with another, and advise you to " *throw
aside the pencil*[1]."   For our *master*[2] will be here
much sooner than was expected : and I am afraid
he should send the man who ventures to paint
Cato in such favourable colours, to join the hero
of his panegyric in the shades below.

Nothing, my dear Gallus, can be expressed
with greater strength and elegance than that part
of your letter which begins, " *The rest are fallen,*
&c."   But I whisper this applause in your ear;

[9] It is said, there was a sea weed frequently found upon
the coasts of Sardinia, the poisonous quality whereof occa-
sioned a convulsive motion in the features which had the ap-
pearance of laughter ; and that hence the *Sardinian laugh* be-
came a proverb usually applied to those who concealed a
heavy heart under a gay countenance.   Gallus seems to
have cited this proverb as a caution to Cicero not to be too
free in his railleries upon Tigellius : and there is a peculiar
propriety in his application of it, as Tigellius was a Sar-
dinian.   I must acknowledge however, that I have departed
from the sentiments of the commentators, in supposing that
Tigellius is the person here alluded to : they all imagine,
on the contrary, that it is Cæsar.   But this letter seems
evidently to be upon the same subject as the 19th of this
book : and was probably an answer to one which Gallus had
written in return to that epistle.
[1] This proverb, Victorius supposes, had its rise from the
schools of the painters : where the young pupils, who in the
absence of their master were amusing themselves, perhaps,
in drawing their pencils over the piece on which he was at
work, called upon each other when they saw him returning
to lay them aside.   Cicero in the application of this proverb
alludes to the panegyric which Gallus had written upon Cato.
See rem. 8. on the 19th letter of this book.
[2] Cæsar : who was at this time upon his return from
Spain.

A.U. 708. and defire it may be a fecret, even to your freedman Apella. No body indeed writes in this manner except ourfelves. How far it is to be defended or not, I may confider, perhaps, another time: but this at leaft is indifputable, that it is a ftyle entirely our own. Perfevere then in thefe compofitions, as the beft and fureft method of forming your eloquence. As for myfelf, I now employ fome part even of my nights, in exercifes of the fame kind. Farewel.

LETTER XXII.

To Marcus Rutilius[e].

IN the confcioufnefs of that affection I bear you, and from the proofs I have experienced of yours, I do not fcruple to afk a favour which a principle of gratitude obliges me to requeft. To what degree I value Publius Sextius[f], is a circumftance with which my own heart is beft acquainted: but how greatly I ought to do fo, both you and all the world are perfectly well apprifed. As he has been informed by fome of his friends, that you are upon all occafions ex-

---

[e] He was employed in a commiffion of the fame kind with that of Orca and Cluvius, to whom the 16th and 20th letters of this book are addreffed.

[f] See rem. 9. p. 163. vol. 1.

tremely

tremely well difpofed to oblige me, he has defired A.U. 708.
I would write to you in the ftrongeft terms in
behalf of Caius Albinius, a perfon of fenatorian
rank. Publius Sextius married his daughter:
and he has a fon by her, who is a youth of great
merit. I mention thefe circumftances, to let you
fee, that Sextius has no lefs reafon to be con-
cerned for the intereft of Albinius, than I have
for that of Sextius. But to come to the point.

Marcus Laberius purchafed under an edict of
Cæfar the confifcated eftate of Plotius, which he
afterwards affigned over to Albinius in fatisfaction
of a debt. If I were to fay, that it is not for the
credit of the government to include this eftate
among thofe lands which are directed to be di-
vided; I might feem to talk rather in the ftile of
a man who is dictating, than of one who is mak-
ing a requeft. But as Cæfar thought it neceffary
to ratify the fales and mortgages that had been
made of thofe eftates which were confifcated dur-
ing Sylla's adminiftration, in order to render his
own purchafers of the fame kind fo much the
more fecure; if thefe forfeited lands, which were
put up to auction by his particular order, fhould
be included in the general divifion he is now
making, will it not difcourage all future bidders?
I only hint this, however, for your own judici-
ous confideration. In the mean time, I moft

earneftly

A.U.708. earneftly intreat you not to difpoffefs Albinius of
the farms which Laberius has thus conveyed to
him: and be affured, as nothing can be more
equitable than this requeft, fo I make it in all the
warmth and fincerity of my heart. It will afford
me, indeed, not only much fatisfaction, but in
fome fort likewife great honour, if Sextius, to
whofe friendfhip I am fo deeply indebted, fhould
have an opportunity thro' my means of ferving a
man to whom he is thus nearly related. Again
and again therefore I intreat your compliance:
and as there is no inftance wherein you can more
effectually oblige me, fo you may depend upon
finding me infinitely fenfible of the obligation.
Farewel.

LETTER XXIII.

TO VATINIUS.

I Am by no means furprifed to find, that you
are fenfible of my fervices [1]. On the contrary,
I perfectly well knew, and have upon all occa-
fions declared, that no man ever poffeffed fo

---

[1] The fervices here alluded to, are probably thofe which
Vatinius follicited in the 12th letter of this book. Cicero's
anfwer to that letter is loft, as well as Vatinius's reply: but
the prefent epiftle feems to have been written in return to
the latter.

grateful

grateful a heart.   You have indeed not only ac- A.U.708.
knowledged, but abundantly returned my good
offices : be affured, therefore, you will always
experience in me the fame friendly zeal in every
other article of your concerns.   Accordingly,
after having received your laft letter, wherein
you recommend that excellent woman your wife
to my protection [4]; I immediately defired our
friend Sura to acquaint her, that if in any in-
ftance fhe had occafion for my fervices, I hoped
fhe would let me know; and that fhe might de-
pend upon my executing her requefts with the
utmoft warmth and fidelity.   This promife I
fhall very punctually fulfil : and if it fhould prove
neceffary, I will wait upon her myfelf.   In the
mean time I beg you would inform her by your
own hand, that I fhall not look upon any office
as difficult, or below my character, wherein my
affiftance can avail her : as indeed there is no
employment in which I could be engaged upon
your account, that I fhould not think both eafy
and honourable [5].

[4] If Vatinius was not a more tender hufband, than he ap-
pears to have been a fon, this lady might have had occafion
for Cicero's protection in fome inftances which fhe would
not, perhaps, have been very willing to own : for among
other enormities that are laid to the charge of Vatinius, it
is faid that he had the cruelty as well as the impiety to lay
violent hands on his mother.   *Orat. in Vatin.* 7.
[5] Who would imagine that this is the fame perfon of whom

I in-

 I intreat you to fettle the affair with Dionyfius: and any affurance that you fhall think proper to give him in my name, I will religioufly perform. But if he fhould continue obftinate, you muft e'en feize him as a prifoner of war to grace your triumphal entry.

May a thoufand curfes fall upon thefe Dalmatians for giving you fo much trouble. However, I join with you in being well perfuaded, that you will foon reduce them to obedience: and as they have always been efteemed a warlike people, their fubmiffion will greatly contribute to the glory of your arms.   Farewel.

Cicero has elfewhere faid, that " No one could look upon " him without a figh, or fpeak of him without execration : " that he was the dread of his neighbours, the difgrace of " his kindred, and the utter abhorrence of the public in " general ?" Indeed when Cicero gave this character of Vatinius, he was acting as an advocate at the bar, and endeavouring to deftroy his credit as a witnefs againft his friend and client. But whatever allowances may be made in general for rhetorical exaggerations ; yet hiftory fhews that in the prefent inftance Cicero's eloquence did not tranfgrefs the limits of truth. For Paterculus has painted the character of Vatinius in the fame difadvantageous colours, and reprefented him as the loweft and moft worthlefs of men. *Orat. in Vatin.* 16. *Vel. Patere.* ii. 69.

L E T T E R   XXIV.

To Cornificius[6].

IT was with great fatisfaction I found by your A.U.701
letter, that you allow me a place in your
thoughts : and it is by no means as doubting the
conftancy of your friendfhip, but merely in com-
pliance with a cuftomary form, that I intreat you
to preferve me ftill in your remembrance.

It is reported that fome commotions have arifen
in Syria : at which I am more alarmed upon
your account than our own, as you are placed fo
much nearer to the confequences. As to affairs
at Rome ; we are enjoying that fort of re-
pofe, which I am fure you would be better
pleafed to hear was interrupted by fome vigorous
meafures for the public welfare. And I hope it

---

[6] Quintus Cornificius, in the year 705, obtained the pro-
confulfhip of Illyricum. In the following year he was re-
moved from thence into fome other province, the name of
which is unknown : but it appears to have been contiguous
to Syria. In this province he refided when the prefent and
twenty-fixth letter of this book were written to him. He was
afterwards appointed governor of Africa : as appears by fe-
veral letters addreffed to him in the next book ; and which
will afford a farther occafion of fpeaking of him. He had
greatly diftinguifhed himfelf in the art of eloquence : and is
fuppofed to have been the author of thofe rhetorical pieces
which are mentioned by Quintilian as written by a perfon of
this name. *Pigh. Annal.* ii. 446. 454. 466. *Quint.* iii. 1.

shortly

 fhortly will : as I find it is Cæfar's intention to concert methods for that purpofe.

Your abfence has infpired me with the courage of engaging in fome compofitions, which other-wife I fhould fcarce have ventured to undertake : tho' there are fome among them which even my judicious friend, perhaps, would not difapprove. The laft that I have finifhed, is upon a fubject, on which I have frequently had occafion to think that your notions were not altogether agreeable to mine : it is an inquiry into the beft fpecies of eloquence [*]. Tho' I muft add, that whenever you have differed from me, it was always with the complaifance of a mafter-artift towards one who is not wholly unfkilled in his art. I fhould be extremely glad that this piece might receive your fuffrage : if not for its own fake, at leaft for its author's. To this end, I fhall let your family know, that, if they think proper, they may have it tranfcribed in order to fend it to you. I ima-gine indeed, altho' you fhould not approve my fentiments, yet that any thing which comes from my hand will be acceptable in your prefent in-active fituation.

When you recommend your character and ho-nours to my protection, it is merely, I dare fay,

[*] This is probably the fame piece, of which an account has been given in rem. 10. on let. 15. B. 10.

for

for the fake of form, and not as thinking it in the A.U. 708.
leaft neceffary. Be affured, the affection which
I am perfuaded mutually fubfifts between us,
would be fufficient to render me greatly zealous
in your fervice. But abftractedly from all motives
of friendfhip, were I to confider only the noble
purpofes to which you have applied your exalted
talents, and the great probability of your attain-
ing the higheft dignity in the commonwealth [8];
there is no man to whom I fhould give the pre-
ference in my good offices, and few that I fhould
place in the fame rank with yourfelf.   Farewel.

L E T T E R   XXV.

C U R I U S [5] to C I C E R O.

I Look upon myfelf as a fort of property, the
poffeffion of which belongs, 'tis true, to At-
ticus; but all the advantage that can be derived
from it is wholly yours. If Atticus therefore
were inclined to difpofe of his right in me, I am
afraid he could only pafs me off in a lot with
fome more profitable commodity : whereas if you
fhould have the fame inclination, how greatly
would it enhance my value to be proclaimed as

---

[8] The confular office.
[5] See rem. 6. p. 361. Vol. II.

one

A.U. 708. one intirely formed into what he is, by your care and kindnefs? I intreat you then to continue to protect the work of your own hands, and to recommend me in the ftrongeft terms to the fuccefsfor of Sulpicius in this province [6]. This will be the fureft means of putting it in my power to obey your commands of returning to you in the fpring: as it will facilitate the fettling of my affairs in fuch a manner, that I may be able by that time to tranfport my effects with fafety into Italy. But I hope, my illuftrious friend, you will not communicate this letter to Atticus: for as he imagines, I am much too honeft a fellow to pay the fame compliment to you both; fuffer him, I befeech you, to remain in this favourable error. Adieu, my dear patron; and falute Tiro in my name.

Oct. the 29th.

LETTER XXVI.

To Cornificius.

I Shall follow the fame method in anfwering your letter, which I have obferved that you great orators fometimes practife in your replies; and begin with the laft article firft. You accufe

[6] Greece.

me then of being a negligent correspondent: but
believe me, I have never once omitted writing,
whenever any of your family gave me notice that
a courier was setting out to you.

I have so high an opinion of your prudence,
that I expected you would act in the manner
your very obliging letter assures me you intend;
and that you would not determine your measures,
till you should know where this paltry Bassus[7]
designed to make an irruption. I intreat you to
continue to give me frequent intelligence of all
your purposes and motions, as well as of
whatever else is going forward in your part of
the world.

It was with much regret that I parted with you,
when you left Italy: but I comforted myself in
the persuasion, that you were not only going into
a scene of profound tranquillity, but leaving one
that was threatened with great commotions. The
reverse, however, has proved to be the fact:
and war has broke out in your quarters, at the
same time that it is extinguished in ours. But
the peace we enjoy is attended, nevertheless, with
many disgusting circumstances: and disgusting
too even to Cæsar himself. It is the certain con-

[7] Cæcilius Bassus was a Roman knight, of the Pompeian
party, who after the battle of Pharsalia fled into Syria: where
he was at this time raising some very formidable commotions
against the authority of Cæsar. *Dio.* xlvii. *p.* 342.

A.U.708. fequence indeed of all civil wars, that the van-
quifhed muft not only fubmit to the will of the
victor, but to the will of thofe alfo who affifted
him in his conqueft.   But I am now become fo
totally callous, that I faw Burfa [8] the other day
at the games which Cæfar exhibited, without the
leaft emotion; and was prefent with equal pati-
ence at the farces of Publius and Laberius [9].   In
fhort, I am fenfible of nothing fo much as of the
want of a judicious friend, with whom I may
freely laugh at what is thus paffing amongft us.
And fuch a friend I fhall find in you, if you will
haften your return hither: a circumftance, which
I look upon to be as much your own intereft, as
I am fure it is mine.   Farewel.

[8] Cicero's inveterate enemy, who had been banifhed fome
years before, but had lately been recalled by Cæfar.   See
rem. 5. p. 263. vol. 1.

[9] For an account of Laberius, fee rem. 1. p. 223. vol. i.
Publius Syrus had likewife diftinguifhed himfelf upon the
Roman ftage in thofe buffoon pieces which they called their
mimes.   But altho' thefe rival poets and actors were both of
them excellent in their way; yet it appears, that their hu-
mour was too low and inelegant to fuit the juft and refined
tafte of Cicero. *Macrob. Saturn.* ii. 7.

LETTER XXVII.

To Dolabella.

I Rejoice to find that Baiæ [z] has changed its nature, and is become on a sudden so wondrous *salutary* [3]. But perhaps it is only in complaisance to my friend, that it thus suspends its usual effects; and will resume its wonted qualities, the moment you depart. I shall not be surprised should this prove to be the case: nor wonder indeed if heaven and earth should alter their general tendencies, for the sake of a man who has so much to recommend him to the favour of both [a].

A.U.708.

[z] See rem. 7. p. 234. vol. ii.

[3] Dolabella had probably informed Cicero in a letter from Baiæ, of the *salutary* effects he experienced from the waters of that place: in answer to which Cicero plays upon the ambiguous meaning of the word *salubres*, and applies in a moral sense what Dolabella had used in a medicinal.

[a] If no other memoirs of these times remained than what might be collected from the letters of Cicero, it is certain they would greatly mislead us in our notions of the principal actors, who now appeared upon the theatre of the Roman republic. Thus, for instance, who would imagine that the person here represented as interesting heaven and earth in his welfare, was in fact a monster of lewdness and inhumanity. But how must the reader's astonishment be raised when he is informed, that it is Cicero himself who tells us so? *Dolabella —a puero pro deliciis crudelitas fuit.* (says our author in one of his Philippic orations) *deinde ea libidinum turpitudo ut in hoc sit semper ipse lætatus, quod ea faceret quæ sibi objici ne ab*

I did

I did not imagine that I had preserved among my papers, the trifling speech which I made in behalf of Deiotarus [+]: however I have found it, and send it to you agreeably to your requeſt. You will read it as a performance, which was by no means of conſequence enough to deſerve much care in the compoſition : and to ſay truth, I was willing to make my old friend and hoſt a preſent of the ſame indelicate kind with his own.

May you ever preſerve a virtuous and a generous mind ! that the moderation and integrity of your conduct, may prove a living reproach to the violence and injuſtice of ſome others amongſt our contemporaries !   Farewel.

inimico quidem poſſent verecundo. If this was a true picture of Dolabella ; what ſhall be ſaid in excuſe of Cicero, for having diſpoſed of his daughter to him in marriage ? Should any too partial advocate of Cicero's moral character, endeavour to palliate this unfavourable circumſtance, by telling us, that he had never inquired into Dolabella's conduct ; might it not juſtly be ſuſpected, that he meant to banter ? Yet this is the very reaſon which Cicero himſelf aſſigns, in the oration from whence the above paſſage is cited. *Et hic, dii immortales ! aliquando fuit meus ! occulta enim erat vitia non* INQUIRENTI. Strange ! that a man who loved his daughter even to a degree of extravagance, ſhould be ſo careleſs in an article wherein her happineſs ————— But I need not finiſh the reſt : where facts ſpeak for themſelves, let me be ſpared the pain of a comment. *Vid. Philip.* xi. 14.

[+] See rem. 2. p. 329. vol. i.

L E T T E R   XXVIII.

Vatinius to Cicero.

I Have not been able to do any thing to the pur- A.U.705.
pofe, with regard to your librarian Diony-
fius [1]: and indeed my endeavours have hitherto
proved fo much the lefs effectual, as the feverity
of the weather which obliged me to retreat out of
Dalmatia, ftill detains me here. However I
will not defift till I have gotten him into my
cuftody. But furely I am always to find fome
difficulty or other in executing your commands:
why elfe did you write to me—I know not what
in favour of Catilius [2]? But avaunt, thou infidious
tempter, with thy dangerous interceffions! And
our friend Servilius too (for *mine* my heart
prompts me to call him, as well as *yours,*) is,
it feems, a joint petitioner with you in this
requeft. Is it ufual then, I fhould be glad to
know, with you orators to be the advocates of
fuch clients, and in fuch caufes? Is it ufual
to plead in behalf of the moft cruel of the

[1] See let. 12. p. 33. of this vol.
[2] This man was quæftor in the year 702; and during the
civil war was intrufted with fome naval command: but it ap-
pears by the prefent letter that he had turned pirate, and
committed great cruelties and depredations upon the coafts of
Illyricum. *Pigh. Annal.* ii. 421.

F 3

'human

A.U. 708. human race? in defence of a man who has mur-
dered our fellow-citizens, plundered their houses,
ravished their wives, and laid whole regions in
defolation? This worthlefs wretch had the info-
lence likewife, to take up arms againft myfelf:
and he is now, 'tis true, my prifoner. But tell
me, my dear Cicero, in what manner can I act
in this affair? I would not willingly refufe any
thing to your requeft: and as far as my own pri-
vate refentment is concerned, I will in compli-
ance with your defires, remit the punifhment I
intended. But what fhall I anfwer to thofe un-
happy fufferers, who require fatisfaction for the
lofs of their effects, and the deftruction of their
fhips? who call for vengeance on the murderer of
their brothers, their children, and their parents?
Believe me, if I had fucceeded to the impudence
as well as to the office of Appius [3], I could not
have the affurance to withftand their cries
for juftice. Neverthelefs, I will do every thing
that lies in my power to gratify your inclinations.

[3] Manutius obferves, that this is not the fame Appius to
whom the letters in the 3d book are addreffed: and refers
to a paffage in Valerius Maximus to prove, that he perifhed
early in the civil wars. But fo he undoubtedly might; and
neverthelefs be the fame perfon here alluded to: for it by no
means appears when, or in what poft it was, that Vatinius
fucceeded to this Appius in queftion. Impudence, it is cer-
tain, was in the number of thofe qualities, which diftin-
guifhed that Appius to whom the letters abovementioned are
written. *Vid. ad At.* iv. 18.

He

He is to be defended at his trial by Volufius: and if his profecutors can be vanquifhed by elo- quence, there is great reafon to expect that the force of your difciple's rhetoric will put them to flight.

I depend upon your being my advocate at Rome, if there fhould be any occafion. Cæſar indeed has not yet done me the juſtice to move for a public thankfgiving, for the fuccefs of my arms in Dalmatia: as if in truth, I were not en- titled to more, and might not juſtly claim the honour of a triumph! But as there are above threefcore cities that have entered into an alliance with the Dalmatians, befides the twenty, of which that country antiently confifted; if I am not to be honoured with a public thankfgiving, till I fhall have taken every one of thefe confiderable towns; I am by no means upon equal terms with the reft of our generals.

Immediately after the fenate had appointed the former thankfgiving for my victories [*], I marched

---

[*] There is fome difficulty in reconciling what Vatinius here fays of a fupplication having been decreed by the fenate, with the complaint he makes above againſt Cæfar, for having delayed to move the houfe for that purpofe. Some of the commentators therefore have fufpected, that this is the be- ginning of a diſtinct letter: and others, that it is a poſtfcript written a confiderable diſtance of time from the body of the epiſtle. But Mr. Rofs has offered, I think, a much better folution, by fuppofing that the thankfgiving, mentioned in the prefent paragraph, was one which had been decreed on

                    into

A.U. 708. into Dalmatia ; where I attacked and made my-
self mafter of fix of their towns.   One of thefe,
which was of very confiderable ftrength, I might
fairly fay that I took four feveral times.   For it
was furrounded by a fortification confifting of
four different walls, which were defended by as
many forts : thro' all which I forced my way to
the citadel, which I likewife compelled to fur-
render.   But the exceffive feverity of the cold,
together with the deep fnows that fell at the fame
time, obliged me to retreat : fo that I had the
mortification, my dear Cicero, to find myfelf
under the neceffity of abandoning my conquefts,
juft as I was upon the point of finifhing the war.
I intreat you then, if occafion fhould require, to
be my advocate with Cæfar, and in every other
refpect to take my intereft under your protection;
in the affurance, that no man poffeffes an higher
degree of affection for you than myfelf.

Narona, Dec. the 15th.

account of fome former fucceffes of Vatinius in his province;
and that the thankfgiving concerning which he complains of
Cæfar's neglect, was one that he was now folliciting in ho-
nour of thofe fucceffes in Dalmatia, of which he here gives
an account.

LETTERS

OF

Marcus Tullius Cicero

TO

Several of his FRIENDS.

BOOK XII.

LETTER I.

TO CURIUS [1].

'TIS true, I once both advised and exhorted you to return into Italy : but I am so far from being in the same sentiments at present, that on the contrary, I wish to escape myself,

To some blest clime remote from Pelop's race [2].

A.U. 709.

---

[1] This is an answer to the 25th letter of the foregoing book.

[2] Alluding to the Cæsarian party. See rem. 7. p. 362. vol. ii.

My

 My heart indeed moſt ſeverely reproaches me, for ſubmitting to be the witneſs of their unworthy deeds. Undoubtedly, my friend, you long ſince foreſaw our evil days approaching, when you wiſely took your flight from theſe unhappy regions : for tho' it muſt needs be painful, to hear a relation of what is going forward amongſt us ; yet far more intolerable it ſurely is, to be the ſad ſpectator of ſo wretched a ſcene. One advantage at leaſt you have certainly gained by your abſence ; it has ſpared you the mortification of being preſent at the late general aſſembly for the election of quæſtors. At ſeven in the morning, the tribunal of Quintus Maximus the conſul, as they called him [3], was placed in the field of Mars [4] : when news being brought of his ſudden death, it was immediately removed. But Cæſar, notwithſtanding he had taken the auſpices [5] as for an aſſembly of the tribes, converted it into

---

[3] Cæſar (as Manutius obſerves) abdicated the conſulſhip upon his late return from Spain, and arbitrarily appointed Quintus Maximus together with Trebonius, conſuls for the remaining part of the year. Maximus therefore not being legally elected, Cicero ſpeaks of him as one whoſe title was acknowledged only by the prevailing faction.

[4] Where the poll for the election of magiſtrates was uſually taken. It was ſituated on the banks of the Tiber.

[5] No aſſembly of the people could be regularly held, nor any public act performed, till the augurs had declared that the omens were favourable for the purpoſe in agitation.

that

that of the centuries [6] : and at one in the after-
noon, declared Caninius duly elected conful.
Be it recorded then, that during the confulate
of Caninius, no man had time to dine; and
yet that there was not a fingle difturbance of
any kind committed : for he was a magiftrate,
you muft know, of fuch wonderful vigilance,
that he never once flept throughout his whole ad-
miniftration. The truth of it is, his adminiftra-
tion continued only to the end of the year; and
both expired the very next morning. But ridi-
culous as thefe tranfactions may appear to you,
who are placed at fo great a diftance from
them; believe me, you could not refrain
from tears, if you were to fee them in all their
true and odious colours. How would you be af-
fected then, were I to mention the numberlefs
inftances of the fame arbitrary kind which daily

[6] The citizens of Rome were caft into three general di-
vifions : into centuries, into curiæ, and into tribes. Some
account of the two latter has been already given in rem. 50.
p. 202. and rem. 7. p. 474. vol. i. The former was an in-
ftitution of Servius Tullius : who diftributed the people
into 193 centuries according to the value of their refpective
poffeffions. Thefe companies had a vote in all queftions,
that came before the people affembled in this manner : and
the majority of voices in each, determined the fuffrage of
that particular century. But as the patricians and the
wealthieft citizens of the republic, filled up 98 of thefe 189
claffes; the inferior citizens were confequently deprived of
all weight in the public deliberations. The prætors, con-
fuls, and cenfors were elected by the people affembled in
centuries : but the quæftors, ediles and tribunes were chofen
in an affembly of the tribes. *Dion. Halicarn.* iv. 20.

occur !

 occur! For my own part, they would be utterly insupportable to me, had I not taken refuge in philosophy; and enjoyed likewise that friend of [7] ours for the companion of my studies, whose *property*, you tell me, you are [8]. However, since you assure me at the same time, that all the benefit which can arise from you, belongs solely to myself; I am perfectly well contented: for what can property give more?

Acilius, who is sent into Greece at the head of some legions as successor to Sulpicius, has great obligations to me: for I successfully defended him in two capital prosecutions, before the commencement of our public troubles. He is a man of a very grateful disposition, and one who upon all occasions, treats me with much regard. Accordingly I herewith send you a letter which I have written to him in your favour, in the strongest terms: and I desire you will let me know what promises he shall give you in consequence of my recommendation. Farewel.

[7] Atticus.

[8] See the beginning of Curius's letter to Cicero, p. 63 of this vol.

L E T T E R II.

To Auctus [*], Proconful.

IN confidence of that fhare you allow me in
your efteem, and of which you gave me fo
many convincing proofs during the time we con-
tinued together at Brundifium [1], I claim a fort
of right of applying to you upon any occafion
wherein I am particularly interefted.   I take the

A.U. 703.

---

 [*] The commentators imagine, that this perfon is the fame
whom Cicero mentions in the foregoing letter to have fuc-
ceeded to Sulpicius in the government of Greece : and that
therefore either inftead of Auctus, the true reading is Acilius,
or that he was called Acilius Auctus. But tho' it is alto-
gether impoffible to determine who the perfon was to whom
this letter is addreffed, or in what year it was written : yet
it feems highly probable that Acilius and Auctus were diffe-
rent men. For Cicero in the preceding epiftle mentions
Acilius as one on whom he had conferred fome very impor-
tant fervices : whereas in the prefent letter, Cicero appears
to have been the perfon obliged. Now it is by no means
credible that our author, if he had ever done any good of-
fices to Auctus, fhould have been totally filent upon a circum-
ftance which would have given him a much higher claim to
the favour he was requefting, than any which he produces.
And the incredibility grows ftill ftronger, when it is remem-
bered that Cicero never fails to difplay his fervices upon all
occafions, in which he can with any propriety mention them.
But on which fide foever of this queftion the truth may lie,
it is a point of fuch very little confequence, that perhaps it
will fcarce juftify even this fhort remark.
 [1] Probably during Cicero's refidence in that city, upon
his return into Italy after the battle of Pharfalia : an account
of which has been given in the foregoing obfervations.

3

liberty

 liberty therefore of writing to you in behalf of
Marcus Curius, a merchant at Patræ, with whom
I am moſt intimately united. Many are the good
offices which have mutually paſſed between
us : and, what indeed is of the greateſt weight,
they reciprocally flowed from the moſt perfect
affection. If then you have reaſon to promiſe
yourſelf any advantage from my friendſhip; if
you are inclined to render the obligations you
have formerly conferred upon me, if poſſible,
even ſtill more valuable; in a word, if you are
perſuaded that I hold a place in the eſteem of
every perſon in your family; let theſe conſidera-
tions induce you to comply with my requeſt in
favour of Curius. Receive him, I conjure you,
under your protection, and preſerve both his
perſon and his property from every injury, and
every inconvenience to which they may be ex-
poſed. In the mean time, I will venture to
aſſure you myſelf, (what all your family will, I
doubt not, confirm) that you may depend upon
deriving great ſatisfaction from my friendſhip,
as well as much advantage from the faithful re-
turns of my gratitude. Farewel.

L E T T E R III.

To Curius.

YOUR letter affords me a very evident proof, that I poſſeſs the higheſt ſhare of your eſteem, and that you are ſenſible how much you are endeared to me in return: both which I have ever been deſirous ſhould be placed beyond a doubt.   Since then we are thus firmly aſſured of each other's affection; let us endeavour to vie in our mutual good offices: a conteſt, in which I am perfectly indifferent on which ſide the ſuperiority may appear.

I am well pleaſed that you had no occaſion to deliver my letter to Acilius [2].   I find likewiſe that you had not much, for the ſervices of Sulpicius; having made ſo great a progreſs, it ſeems, in your affairs as to have curtailed them (to uſe your own ludicrous expreſſion) both of *head* and *feet*.   I wiſh however, you had ſpared the *latter*, that they might *proceed* a little faſter, and give us an opportunity of one day ſeeing you again in Rome.   We want you indeed, in order to preſerve that good old vein of pleaſantry, which is

____

[2] See the latter end of the firſt letter in this book.

2   now,

 now, you may perceive, well-nigh worn out amongst us: infomuch that Atticus may properly enough fay, as he often, you know, ufed, " if it were not for two or three of us, my " friends, what would become of the ancient " glory of Athens !" Indeed, as the honour of being the chief fupport of Attic elegance devolved upon Pomponius [1], when you left Italy; fo in his abfence, it has now defcended upon me. Haften your return then, I befeech you, my friend; left every fpark of wit, as well as of liberty, fhould be irrecoverably extinguifhed with the republic.　Farewel.

LETTER IV.

To CORNIFICIUS.

I Have the fatisfaction to find by your very obliging letter, that my laft was fafely delivered. I doubted not of its affording you pleafure : and therefore was fo much the more uneafy left it fhould lofe its way. You inform me, at the fame time, that a war is broke out in Syria [3], and that Cæfar has given you the government of this province. I wifh you much joy of your command, and hope fuccefs will

[1] Pomponius Atticus.
[3] See rem. 7. on let. 26. of the preceding book.

attend

attend it: as, in full confidence of your wisdom A.U.709.
and vigilance, I am well perfuaded it will.
Neverthelefs I am truly alarmed at what you
mention concerning the invafion which, it is
fufpected, the Parthians are meditating. I find
by your letter, that the number of your forces
is agreeable to what I fhould have conjectured:
I hope therefore, that thefe people will not put
themfelves in motion, till the legions which I
hear are ordered to your affiftance, fhall arrive.
But if you fhould not even with thefe fupplies,
find yourfelf in a condition to face the enemy;
I need not remind you to follow the maxim
of your predeceffor Marcus Bibulus, who, you
know, during the whole time that the Parthians
continued in your province, moft gallantly fhut
himfelf up in a ftrong garrifon [4]. Yet after all,
circumftances will beft determine in what man-
ner it will be proper for you to act: in the mean
time I fhall be extremely anxious, till I receive
an account of your operations.

[4] This feems to be intended as a fneer upon the conduct of
Bibulus. Cicero was governor of Cilicia when Bibulus com-
manded in Syria, and they both follicited at the fame time,
the honour of a public thankfgiving for the fuccefs of their
refpective arms. Cato gave his fuffrage upon this occafion
in favour of Bibulus; but refufed it to Cicero: a preference
which extremely exafperated the latter, and which was pro-
bably the principal caufe of that contempt with which he
fpeaks of Bibulus in the prefent paffage. See vol. ii. p. 50.
rem. 2.

 As I have never omitted any opportunity of writing to you, I hope you will obferve the fame punctually with refpect to me. But above all, let me defire you to reprefent me in your letters to your friends and family as one who is entirely yours. Farewel.

LETTER V.

DECIMUS BRUTUS[5] to MARCUS BRUTUS and CAIUS CASSIUS.

YOU will judge by this letter, in what pofture our affairs ftand. I received a vifit

---

[5] Decimus Brutus, of the fame family with Marcus Brutus, ferved under Cæfar in the wars in Gaul: at the end of which, in the year 703, he returned to Rome, and was chofen one of the city quæftors. It does not appear that he diftinguifhed himfelf by any thing remarkable, till he engaged with Marcus Brutus and Caffius in the confpiracy againft his friend and benefactor. This was executed, as all the world knows, by ftabbing Cæfar in the fenate, on the ides, or the 15th of March: a few weeks before the prefent letter was written. When one confiders the characters of thofe who were the principal actors in this memorable tragedy, it is aftonifhing that they fhould have looked no farther than merely to the taking away of Cæfar's life: as if they imagined, that the government muft necef- farily return into its proper channel, as foon as the perfon who had obftructed its courfe, was removed. They were altogether therefore unprepared for thofe very probable con- tingencies which they ought to have had in view, and which accordingly enfued. Whatever then may be determined as to the patriotifm of the fact itfelf, it was unqueftionably

yefterday

yesterday in the evening from Hirtius [6], who con-
vinced me of Antony's extreme perfidy and ill
intentions towards us.   He assured Hirtius, it
seems, that he could by no means consent I should
take possession of the province, to which I have
been nominated [7]; and that both the army and
the populace were so highly incensed against us,
that he imagined we could none of us continue
with any safety in Rome.   You are sensible, I
dare say, that both these assertions are as abso-
lutely false, as that it is undoubtedly true, what
Hirtius added, that Antony is apprehensive if we
should gain the least increase of power, it will
be impossible for him and his party to maintain

conducted, as Cicero frequently and justly complains, by
the weakest and most impolitic counsels.   Antony, (who
was at this time consul) although he thought proper at first
to carry a fair appearance towards the conspirators, yet
secretly raised such a spirit against them, that they found
it expedient to withdraw from Rome.   Brutus and Cassius
retired to Lanuvium, a villa belonging to the former, about
fifteen miles from the city : at which place they probably
were when Decimus Brutus, who had not yet left Rome,
wrote the following letter.

[6] Hirtius was warmly attached to Cæsar, and extremely re-
gretted his death : but as he was disgusted with Antony, and
perhaps jealous too of his rising power, he seems to have
opposed the cause he approved, merely from a spirit of per-
sonal pique and envy. *Vid. Ad Att.* xiv. 22. xv. 6.

[7] Cæsar, a short time before his death, had nominated
Decimus Brutus to the government of Cisalpine Gaul, and
Antony to that of Macedonia. But as Gaul lay more con-
veniently for Antony's present purposes, his design was to
procure the administration of it for himself.

G 2

their

 their ground. I thought, under thefe difficulties, the moft prudent ftep I could take for our common intereft, would be to requeft that an honourary legation [8] might be decreed to each of us; in order to give fome decent colour to our leaving Rome. Accordingly, Hirtius has promifed to obtain this grant in our favour; tho' I muft add at the fame time, fuch a fpirit is raifed againft us in the fenate, that I am by no means clear he will be able to perform his engagement. And fhould he fucceed, yet I am perfuaded it will not be long ere they declare us public enemies, or at leaft fentence us to banifhment. It appears to me therefore, our wifeft method in the prefent conjuncture, to fubmit to Fortune, and withdraw to Rhodes, or to fome other fecure part of the world. We may there adjuft our meafures to public circumftances, and either return to Rome, or remain in exile, as affairs fhall hereafter appear with a more or lefs inviting afpect: or if the worft fhould happen, we may have recourfe to the laft defperate

---

[8] The fenators could not be long abfent from Rome, without leave of the fenate. When their private affairs therefore required their attendance abroad, it was ufual to apply for what they called a *legatio libera*, which gave a fanction to their abfence, and invefted them with a fort of *travelling title*, that procured them the greater refpect and honours in the countries through which they paffed, and in the place where they propofed to refide.

perate

perate expedient [a].   Should it be afked, " why
" not attempt fomething at prefent, rather than
" wait a more diftant period ?" My anfwer is,
becaufe I know not where we can hope to make
a ftand, unlefs we fhould go either to Sextus Pom-
peius [9], or to Cæcilius Bafius [1].   It is probable in-
deed, that when the news of Cæfar's death fhall be
fpread through their refpective provinces, it may
much contribute to ftrengthen their party : how-
ever it will be foon enough to join them, when
we fhall know the ftate of their forces.

If you and Caffius are defirous I fhould enter
into any engagement on your behalf, I fhall
very readily be your fponfor : and indeed it is a
condition which Hirtius requires.   I defire there-
fore you would acquaint me with your refolution,
as foon as poffible : for I expect before ten

---

[a] That is, (as the commentators explain it) by arming
the flaves, throwing open the prifons, and raifing foreign
nations in their defence.

[9] Sextus Pompeius, the younger fon of Pompey, was in
Corduba when his brother Cneius gave battle to Cæfar.
Cneius attempting to make his efcape after the total defeat
of his army, was killed by fome of the conqueror's foldi-
ers : but Sextus, upon the enemy's approach in order to lay
fiege to Corduba, fecretly abandoned that city, and con-
cealed himfelf till Cæfar's return into Italy.   The latter
had no fooner left Spain, than Sextus collected his broken
forces : and a fhort time after this letter was written, he
appeared at the head of no lefs than fix legions. Hirt. de
Bell. Hifp. Dio. pag. 274.

[1] An account of him has already been given in rem. 7.
p. 65. of this vol.

                              o'clock,

o'clock, to receive an appointment from Hirtius to meet him upon thefe affairs. Let me know at the fame time where I fhall find you.

As foon as Hirtius fhall have given me his final anfwer, I purpofe to apply to the fenate, that a guard may be appointed to attend us in Rome. I do not fuppofe they will comply with this re-queft, as our appearing to ftand in need of fuch a protection, will render them extremely odious. But how fuccefsful foever my demands may prove, I fhall not be difcouraged from making fuch as I think reafonable. Farewel.

LETTER VI.

To Tiro.

NOtwithftanding I wrote this morning by Harpatus, and nothing new has fince occurred; yet I cannot forbear making ufe of this opportunity of conveying a fecond letter to you upon the fame fubject : not, however, as entertaining the leaft diftruft of your care, but becaufe the bufinefs in which I have employed you, is of the laft importance to me [2]. My whole

---

[2] As Cicero was known to favour the confpirators, he did not think it prudent to truft himfelf in Rome after Brutus and Caffius had found it neceffary to withdraw from thence : and accordingly he foon afterwards followed their

design

design indeed in parting with you was, that you A.U. 709. might thoroughly settle my affairs. I desire therefore, in the first place, that the demands of Otillius and Aurelius may be satisfied. Your next endeavour must be, to obtain part at least, if you cannot procure the whole, of what is due to me from Flamma : and particularly insist on his making this payment by the first of January[3]. With regard to that debt which was assigned over to me ; I beg you would exert your utmost dili- gence to recover it : but as to the advance-pay- ment of the other not yet due, I leave you to act as you shall judge proper. And this much for my private concerns. As to those of the public ; I desire you would send me all the certain in- telligence you can collect. Let me know what Octavius[4] and Antony are doing ; what is the

example by retiring into the country. His intention at this time was, to make a tour into Greece for a few months ; and with that view he had dispatched Tiro to Rome, in order to call in the several monies which were due to him, and likewise to discharge some debts which he had himself contracted.

[3] When the new consuls were to enter upon their office : by which time, Cicero proposed to return to Rome.

[4] Octavius, who was afterwards known and celebrated by the name of Augustus Cæsar, was the son of Attia, Julius Cæsar's niece. His uncle, who designed him for the heir both of his power and his fortunes, had sent him, about six months before his death, to Apollonia, a learned seminary of great note in Macedonia. In this place he was to prose- cute his studies and exercises, till Cæsar, who proposed he should accompany him in his intended expedition against

G 4

general

A.U. 709. general opinion of Rome; and what turn you imagine affairs are likely to take. I can scarcely forbear running into the midst of the scene: but I reftrain myfelf, in the expectation of your letter.

Your news concerning Balbus, proves true: he was at Aquinum at the time you were told; and Hirtius followed him thither the next day. I imagine they are both going to the waters of Baiæ: but let me know what you can difcover of their motions.

Do not forget to remind the agents of Dolabella [5]: nor to infift upon the payment of what is due from Papia.   Farewel.

the Parthians, fhould call upon him in his march to that country. But as foon as Octavius was informed of the death of Cæfar, and that he had appointed him his heir; he immediately haftened to Rome: and the eyes of every body, but particularly of Cicero, were now attentively turned towards him, in order to difcover in what manner he would act in this very critical fituation both of his own affairs, and thofe of the republic. *Dio. p.* 271. *Appian. Bell. Civil.* ii.

[5] It appears by the letters written to Atticus at this time, that Cicero had fome confiderable demands upon Dolabella: which arofe, it is probable, from the latter not having yet returned the whole of Tullia's portion, agreeably to the Roman laws in cafes of divorce.

L E T T E R   VII.

To B i t h y n i c u s [6].

I Have many reasons to wish, that the republic A.U.709. may be restored: but, believe me, the promise you give me in your letter, renders it still more ardently my desire.   You assure me if that happy event should take place, you will consecrate your whole time to me: an assurance which I received with the greatest pleasure, as it is perfectly agreeable to the friendship in which we are united, and to the opinion which that excellent man your father [7] entertained of me.   You have received more considerable services, I confess, from the men who are, or lately were, in power, than any that I have been capable of conferring upon you: but in all other respects, there is no person whose connections with you are of a stronger kind than my own. It is with great satisfaction therefore that I find,

[6] This person is supposed by Manutius, to be the son of Quintus Pompeius, who obtained the name of Bithynicus, in honour of his conquests in Bithynia.

[7] Cicero mentions him in his treatise of celebrated orators, as one with whom he had enjoyed a particular friendship.   He attended Pompey in his flight after the battle of Pharsalia, and perished with him in Egypt. *Cic. de clar. orat.* 240.

you

 you not only preferve our friendfhip in your re-
membrance, but are defirous likewife of in-
creafing its ftrength.   Farewel.

LETTER VIII.

To Tiro.

IF you fhould have an opportunity, you may
regifter the money you mention : tho' indeed
it is an acquifition which it is not abfolutely re-
quifite to enroll[s].   However, it may perhaps
be as well.

I have received a letter from Balbus, wherein
he excufes himfelf for not giving me an account
of Antony's intentions concerning the law I in-
quired after ; becaufe he has gotten, it feems, a
violent defluxion upon his eyes.   Excellent ex-
cufe, it muft be owned ! For if a man is not
able to write ; moft certainly, you know, he
cannot dictate ! But let the world go as it will,
fo I may fit down quietly here in the country.

I have written to Bithynicus.——As to what
you mention concerning Servilius ; you who
are a young man may think length of days
a defireable circumftance ; but for myfelf, I have

___

[s] The cenfors every five years numbered the people : at
which time each citizen was obliged to give an exact account
of his eftate.   But if in the interval a man had made any
new acquifition, he was required to enter it before the
prætor.

no such wish [9].   Atticus neverthelefs imagines, A.U. 709. that I am ftill as anxious for the prefervation of my life as he once knew me; not obferving how firmly I have fince fortified my heart with all the ftrength of philofophy.   The truth of it is, he is now feized in his turn with a panic himfelf; and would endeavour to infect me with the fame groundlefs apprehenfions.   But it is my intention to preferve that friendfhip unviolated, which I have fo long enjoyed with Antony [1]: and accordingly I intend writing to him very foon.   I

[9] Servilius Ifauricus died about this time, in an extreme old age: Manutius conjectures therefore, and with great probability, that Tiro in the letter to which the prefent is an anfwer, had given Cicero an account of this event, and at the fame time expreffed his wifhes of living to the fame advanced period.

[1] Both Antony and Cicero feem to have been equally unwilling at this time, to come to an open rupture: but as to a real friendfhip between them, it is highly probable there never had been any.   On the part of Antony at leaft, there were fome very ftrong family-reafons to alienate him from Cicero.   For Antony's father married the widow of Lentulus, whom Cicero had put to death as an accomplice in Catiline's confpiracy; and he himfelf was married to Fulvia, the widow of Clodius, Cicero's moft inveterate enemy. Thefe alliances muft unqueftionably have made impreffions upon Antony's mind, little favourable to fentiments of amity: and probably contributed, among other reafons, to kindle that refentment which terminated in Cicero's deftruction: But whatever the true motive of their enmity towards each other might have been; the firft coolnefs feems to have arifen on the fide of Antony: and if Cicero had refented it with greater moderation, he would have acted perhaps, with more prudence in regard to the public intereft, as well as in refpect to his own. *Vid. Ad Att.* xiv. 19.

shall

 shall defer my letter, however, till your return: but I do not mention this with any design of calling you off from the business you are transacting [2], and which indeed is much more nearly my concern.

I expect a visit from Lepta to-morrow: and shall have occasion for all the sweets of your conversation, to temper the bitterness with which his will be attended. Farewel.

LETTER IX.

To Dolabella, Consul [3].

I Desire no greater satisfaction, my dear Dolabella, than what arises to me from the disinterested part I take in the glory you have lately acquired: however, I cannot but acknowledge, I am infinitely pleased to find, that the world gives me a share in the merit of your late applauded conduct. I daily meet in this place

---

[2] See rem. 2. p. 86. of this vol.

[3] Cæsar had appointed Dolabella to succeed him in the consulship as soon as he should set out upon his Parthian expedition; and accordingly Dolabella upon the death of Cæsar, immediately assumed the administration of that office. His conduct in this critical conjuncture, had rendered it somewhat doubtful which side he was most disposed to favour: but an accident had lately happened which gave the friends of the republic great hopes that he would support the cause of the conspirators. Some of Cæsar's freedmen had erected a sort of altar, upon the spot where his

great

A.U. 709.

great numbers of the firft rank in Rome, who
are affembled here for the benefit of their health,
as well as a multitude of my friends from the
principal cities in Italy : and they all agree in
joining their particular thanks to me, with
thofe unbounded praifes they beftow upon you.
They every one of them indeed tell me, that
they are perfuaded it is owing to your compli-
ance with my counfels and admonitions, that
you approve yourfelf fo excellent a patriot and
fo worthy a conful. I might with ftrict truth
affure them, that you are much fuperior to the
want of being advifed by any man ; and that
your actions are the free and genuine refult of
your own uninfluenced judgment.   But altho' I
do not entirely acquiefce in their compliment,
as it would leffen the credit of your conduct, if
it fhould be fuppofed to flow altogether from
my fuggeftions; yet neither do I wholly reject
it : for the love of praife is a paffion, which I
am apt, you know, fomewhat too immoderately

body had been burnt : at which the populace daily affembled
in the moft tumultuous and alarming manner. Dolabella,
in the abfence of his collegue Antony, interpofed his con-
fular authority in order to fupprefs this mob : and having
caufed the altar to be demolifhed, he exerted a very feafon-
able act of feverity, by commanding the principal ring-
leaders of the riot to be inftantly put to death. It was this
that produced the following letter from Cicero, written from
fome place of public refort, probably from the Baths of
Baiæ. *Dio.* p. 240. 267. *Ad Att.* xiv. 15.

·to

 to indulge.   Yet after all, to take counsel of a
Nestor, as it was an honour to the character
even of that king of kings, Agamemnon him-
self, it cannot surely be unbecoming the dignity
of yours.   It is certainly at least, much to the
credit of mine, that while in this early period
of your life [4], you are thus exercising the su-
preme magistracy with universal admiration and
applause; you are considered as directed by my
guidance and formed by my instructions.

I lately paid a visit to Lucius Cæsar [5] at
Naples; and tho' I found him extremely indis-
posed, and full of pain in every part of his body,
yet the moment I entered his chamber he raised
himself with an air of transport, and without
allowing himself time to salute me, " O my
" dear Cicero, said he, I give you joy of your
" influence over Dolabella, and had I the same
" credit with my nephew, our country might

---

[4] Dolabella was at this time no more than twenty-five
years of age : which was almost twenty years earlier than
he could legally have offered himself as a candidate for the
consular dignity ; the Roman laws having very wisely pro-
vided that no man should be capable of exercising this im-
portant office till he had attained the age of forty-two.

[5] He was a distant relation to Julius Cæsar, and uncle to
Mark Antony.   Upon the celebrated coalition of the tri-
umvirate, he was sacrificed by Antony to the resentment of
Octavius : as in return, Cicero was delivered up to the ven-
geance of Antony.   But Lucius escaped the consequence of
this proscription by the means of Julia, Antony's mother.
Plut. in vit. Ant.

" now

" new be preserved.   But I not only congratu-
" late your friend on his worthy conduct, but
" defire you would return him my particular
" acknowledgments : as indeed he is the fingle
" conful who has acted with true fpirit, fince
" you filled that office." He then proceeded
to enlarge upon your late glorious action ; re-
prefenting it as equal to the moft illuftrious and
important fervice, that ever was rendered to the
commonwealth.   And in this he only echoed
the general voice of the whole republic.   Suffer
me then, to take poffeffion of thofe encomiums
to which I am by no means entitled : and in fome
fort to participate with you in that general ap-
plaufe you have acquired.   To be ferious how-
ever, (for you will not imagine that I make this
requeft in good earneft) I would much rather
refign to you the whole of my own glory, (if
there be any indeed I can juftly claim) than
arrogate to myfelf the leaft portion of that
which is fo unqueftionably your due.   For as
you cannot but be fenfible that I have ever
loved you ; fo your late behaviour has raifed
that affection into the higheft poffible ardour :
as in truth, there cannot be any thing more
engagingly fair, more irrefiftibly amiable, than
the patriot-virtues.   I need not tell you how
greatly the exalted talents and polite man-

ners, together with the fingular fpirit and pro-
bity of Marcus Brutus, had ever endeared him
to my heart. Neverthelefs, his late glorious
atchievement on the ides of March, has won-
derfully heightened that efteem I bore him : and
which I had always looked upon as too exalted
to admit of any farther advance. In the fame
manner, who would have imagined that my
friendfhip towards yourfelf was capable of in-
creafe ? yet it actually has increafed fo very con-
fiderably, that the former fentiments of my heart
feem to have been nothing more than common
affection, in comparifon of that tranfcendent
paffion which I now feel for you.

Can it be neceffary that I fhould either exhort
you to preferve the glory you have acquired,
or agreeably to the ufual ftile of admonition,
fet before your view fome animating examples of
illuftrious merit ? I could mention none for this
purpofe, more forcible than your own : and you
have only to endeavour to act up to the charac-
ter you have already attained. It is impoffible
indeed, after having performed fo fignal a fervice
to your country, that you fhould ever deviate
from yourfelf. Inftead therefore of fending you
any unneceffary exhortations, let me rather con-
gratulate you upon this noble difplay of your
patriotifm. It is your privilege (and a privilege,

perhaps,

perhaps, which no one ever enjoyed before) to A.U. 709.
have exercised the severest acts of necessary justice,
not only without incurring any odium, but with
the greatest popularity : with the approbation of
the lowest, as well as of the best and highest
amongst us.   If this were a circumstance in
which chance had any share, I should congratu-
late your good fortune : but it was the effect of a
noble and undaunted resolution, under the gui-
dance of the strongest and most enlightened
judgment.   I say this, from having read the
speech you made upon this occasion to the people;
and never was any harangue more judiciously
composed.   You open and explain the fact with
so much address, and gradually rise thro' the se-
veral circumstances in so artful a manner, as to
convince all the world that the affair was mature
for your animadversion.   In a word, you have
delivered the commonwealth in general, as well
as the city of Rome in particular, from the dan-
gers with which they were threatened : and not
only performed a singular service to the present
generation, but set forth a most useful example
for times to come.   You will consider yourself
then, as the great support of the republic : and
remember, she expects that you will not only pro-
tect, but distinguish those illustrious persons [5]

[5] Brutus and Cassius, together with the rest of the conspi-
rators.

A.U.709. who have laid the foundation for the recovery of our liberties. But I hope soon to have an opportunity of expreſſing my ſentiments to you more fully upon this ſubject, in perſon. In the mean while, ſince you are thus our glorious guardian and preſerver, I conjure you, my dear Dolabella, to take care of yourſelf for the ſake of the whole commonwealth [7]. Farewel.

[7] Cicero communicated a copy of this letter to Atticus: who appears to have much diſapproved of thoſe encomiums, with which it is ſo extravagantly ſwelled. The hyperbole indeed, ſeems to have been the prevailing figure in Cicero's rhetoric: and he generally dealt it out both to his friends and to his enemies, with more warmth than diſcretion. In the preſent inſtance at leaſt, he was either very eaſily impoſed upon by appearances, or he changed his opinion of Dolabella's public actions and deſigns, according to the colour of his conduct towards himſelf. Perhaps both theſe cauſes might concur, in forming thoſe great and ſudden variations which we find in our author's ſentiments at this period, with reſpect to the hero of the panegyric before us. For in a letter to Atticus, written very ſhortly after the preſent, he ſpeaks of Dolabella with high diſpleaſure; and in another to the ſame perſon a few months later, he exclaims againſt him with much bitterneſs, as one who had not only been bribed by Antony to deſert the cauſe of liberty, but who had endeavoured, as far as in him lay, entirely to ruin it. The accuſation ſeems to have been juſt: but it is obſervable however, that in both the letters referred to, part of Cicero's indignation ariſes from ſome perſonal ill treatment, which he complains of having received from Dolabella. *Vid. Ad At.* xiv. 18. xvi. 15.

L E T T E R X.

To Trebonius [8].

I Have recommended my *Orator* (for that is the title which I have given to the treatise I promifed to fend you) to the care of your freedman Sabinus. I was induced to truft it in his charge, from the good opinion I entertain of his countrymen : if indeed I may guefs at his country by his name [9], and he has not, like an artful candidate at an election, ufurped an appel-

[8] Some account has already been given of Trebonius in rem. 4. p. 181. vol. ii. Cæfar upon his return from Spain in the preceding year, appointed him conful with Quintus Fabius Maximus : but this and other favours of the fame kind, were not fufficient to reftrain him from entering into the confpiracy which was foon afterwards formed againft Cæfar's life. At the fame time therefore that Brutus and Caffius found it expedient to leave Rome, Trebonius fecretly withdrew into Afia Minor, which had before been allotted to him as his proconfular province : and he was on his way to that government, when the prefent letter was written. *Dio.* p. 236, 247. *Ad At.* xiv. 10.

[9] Cicero fuppofes that Sabinus was fo called, as being a native of Sabinia ; a country in Italy, the inhabitants of which were celebrated for having long retained an uncorrupted fimplicity of manners. *Hanc olim veteres vitam coluere Sabini,* is Virgil's conclufion of that charming defcription which he gives of the pleafing labours and innocent recreations of rural life. *Georg.* ii. 532.

H 2

lation

A.U. 709. lation to which he has no right [1]. However,
there is such a modesty in his countenance,
and such an air of sincerity in his conversation,
that I am much deceived if he does not possess,
in some degree at least, the true Sabine simpli-
city.   But not to suffer him to take up any more
of my paper: I will now turn, my dear Tre-
bonius, to yourself.   As there were some cir-
cumstances attending your departure, that in-
creased the affection I bear towards you; let
me intreat you, in order to sooth the uneasiness
I feel from your absence, to be as frequent a
correspondent on your part, as you shall certain-
ly find me on mine.   There are two reasons in-
deed, why you ought to be more so : the first is,
that as the republic can now no longer be consi-
dered as in Rome, but removed with its glorious
defenders; we who remain here must expect to
receive from our provincial friends, what we used
to transmit to them; an account, I mean, of
the commonwealth.   The next reason is, because
I have many other opportunities in your absence,
besides that of writing, to give you proofs of my

[1] It was an artifice sometimes practised by the candidates
for offices, in order to recommend themselves to the good
graces of their constituents, to pretend a kindred to which
they had no right, by assuming the name of some favourite
and popular family. *Manut.*

friendship :

friendſhip : whereas you have none, I think, A.U. 709.
of teſtifying yours, but by the frequency of your
letters.   As to all other articles, I can wait ; but
my firſt and moſt impatient deſire is, to know
what ſort of journey you have had ; where you
met Brutus[2] ; and how long you continued toge-
ther.   When you are advanced farther towards
your province, you will acquaint me, I hope,
with your military preparations, and with what-
ever elſe relates to our public affairs : that I may
be able to form ſome judgment of our ſituation.
I am ſure at leaſt, I ſhall give no credit to any
intelligence, but what I receive from your hands.
In the mean time, take care of your health, and
continue to allow me the ſame ſingular ſhare
of your affection which I have always enjoyed.
Farewel.

[2] Brutus had not left Italy when Trebonius ſet out for
Aſia, nor did he leave it till ſeveral months afterwards : ſo
that the inquiry which Cicero here makes, muſt relate to
ſome interview which he ſuppoſed that Trebonius might have
had with Brutus before the former embarked. *Vid. Ad At.*
xiv. 10.

LETTER XI.

TREBONIUS to CICERO [3].

A.U. 709. I Arrived at Athens on the 22d of this month;
where, agreeably to my wishes, I had the satis-
faction of finding your son in the pursuit of
the nobleft improvements, and in the higheft
efteem for his modeft and ingenuous behaviour [4].
As you perfectly well know the place you poffefs
in my heart, you will judge, without my telling
you, how much pleafure this circumftance af-
forded me. In conformity indeed to the un-
feigned friendfhip which has fo long been ce-
mented between us, I rejoice in every advantage
that can attend you, be it ever fo inconfiderable;
much more therefore in one fo important to your
happinefs. Believe me, my dear Cicero, I do
not flatter you when I fay, there is not a youth
in all this feminary of learning more ardently
devoted to thofe refined and elevated arts,
which are fo peculiarly your paffion, or who in
every view of his character is more truly ami-
able, than our young man. I call him *ours:* for

---

[3] This letter feems to have been written, before the pre-
ceding epiftle had reached the hands of Trebonius.

[4] See the remarks on let. 37. of this book.

be

be affured, I cannot feparate myfelf from any A. U. 709.
thing with which you are connected. It is with
great pleafure therefore, as well as with ftrict
juftice, I congratulate both you and myfelf,
that a youth for whom we ought to have fome
affection whatever his difpofition might be, is of
a character to deferve our higheft. As he inti-
mated a defire of feeing Afia, I not only invited,
but preffed him to take the opportunity of vifit-
ing that province whilft I prefided there: and you
will not doubt of my fupplying your place in
every tender office of paternal care. But that
you may not be apprehenfive this fcheme
will prove an interruption of thofe ftudies, to
which, I know, he is continually animated by
your exhortations; Cratippus [5] fhall be of our
party. Nor fhall your fon want my earneft in-
citements to advance daily in thofe fciences, into
which he has already made fo fuccefsful an en-
trance.

I am wholly ignorant of what is going for-
ward at Rome; only I hear fome uncertain
rumours of commotions amongft you. But I
hope there is no foundation for this report; that
we may one day fit down in the peaceful poffef-
fion of our liberties, retired from the noife and
buftle of the world: a privilege which hitherto

[5] See rem. 3. p. 171. of this vol.

A.U.709. it has not been my fortune to enjoy. However, having had a fhort relaxation from bufinefs during my voyage to this place, I amufed myfelf with putting together a few thoughts, which I always defigned as a prefent to you. In this performance I have inferted that lively obfervation which you formerly made fo much to my honour, and have pointed out by a note at the bottom, to whom I am indebted for the compliment. If in fome paffages of this piece, I fhould appear to have taken great liberties; I fhall be juftified, I perfuade myfelf, by the character of the man at whom my invective is aimed[6]: and you will undoubtedly excufe the juft indignation I have expreffed againft a perfon of fuch infamous principles.   Why, indeed, may I not be indulged in the fame unbounded licence as was allowed to honeft Lucilius[7]? He could not be animated with greater abhorrence of the vices, which he has fo freely attacked; and certainly they were not more worthy of fatyr than thofe againft which I have inveighed.

I hope you will remember your promife, and take the firft opportunity of introducing me as a party in fome of your future dialogues. I doubt not if you fhould write any thing upon the fub-

* Probably at Antony,
[7] See rem. 8. p. 319. vol. ii.

ject

ject of Cæsar's death, that you will give an in-
stance of your friendship and your justice, by
ascribing to me no inconsiderable share of that
glorious transaction.

I recommend my mother and family to your
good offices, and bid you farewel.

Athens, May the 25th.

L E T T E R XII.

To Matius [8].

I Know not whether it is with greater pain or
pleasure, that I reflect on the visit which I
lately received from our very good friend, the
well-natur'd Trebatius. He called upon me the

---

[8] It is principally owing to this and the following letter,
that the name and character of Matius are known to poste-
rity : as he is no where mentioned by any of the antient hi-
storians of this memorable period. His inviolable and disin-
terested affection to Cæsar, together with the generous cou-
rage with which he avowed that attachment when Cæsar
was no more; as they strongly mark out the virtues of his
heart, so they will best appear by his own spirited reply
to the present epistle. But Matius was as much distin-
guished by his genius as his virtues : and he was perfectly
well accomplished in those arts, which contribute to the
innocent pleasure and embellishment of human life. Gar-
dening and poetry, in particular, seem to have been his
favourite amusements : in the former of which, his coun-
trymen were indebted to him for some useful improve-
ments ; as they likewise were in the latter, for an elegant
translation of the Iliad. *Columel.* xii. 44. *Aul. Gel.* vi. 6.
ix. 4.

next

 next morning after my arrival at Tufculum: and as he was by no means fufficiently recovered from his late indifpofition, I could not forbear reproving him for thus hazarding his health. He interrupted me with faying, that nothing was of more importance to him than the bufinefs which brought him to my houfe: and upon my inquiry if any thing new had occurred; he immediately entered into an account of your complaints againft me. But before I give them a particular anfwer, let me begin with a few previous reflections.

Amongft all my acquaintance, I cannot recollect any man with whom I have longer enjoyed a friendfhip, than with yourfelf: and altho' there are feveral for whom my affection commenced as early, there are few for whom it has rifen fo high. The truth of it is, I conceived an efteem for you from the firft moment I faw you: and I had reafon to believe, that you thought of me in the fame favourable manner. But your long abfence from Rome, which immediately fucceeded our firft acquaintance, together with that active courfe of life wherein I was engaged, and which was fo entirely different from yours, did not at that time, admit of our improving this mutual difpofition, by a more frequent intercourfe. Neverthelefs, even fo long ago as when

Cæfar

Cæsar was in Gaul, and many years before the A.U. 709.
commencement of the civil war, I experienced
your friendly inclinations towards me. For as you
imagined that my union with Cæsar would be
greatly advantageous on my fide, and not alto-
gether unferviceable on his; you generoufly re-
commended me to his favour, and was the caufe
of his cultivating my friendfhip. I forbear to
mention feveral inftances which occurred at that
period, of the unreferved manner in which we
both converfed and correfponded together: as
they were followed by others of a more impor-
tant nature. At the opening of the civil war,
when you were going to meet Cæfar at Brundi-
fium, you paid me a vifit in my Formian villa.
This fingle favour, had it been attended with no
other, was, at fuch a critical juncture, an ample
teftimony of your affection. But can I ever
forget the generous advice you fo kindly gave
me at the fame time: and of which Trebatius,
I remember, was himfelf a witnefs? Can I ever
forget the letter you afterwards wrote to me,
when you went to join Cæfar in the diftrict, if I
miftake not, of Trebula? It was foon after this,
that either by gratitude, by honour, or perhaps by
fate, I was determined to follow Pompey into
Greece: and was there any inftance of an obliging
zeal, which you did not exert in my abfence both

for

 for me and for my family ? was there any one, in ſhort, whom either they or I had more reaſon to eſteem our friend? But I returned to Brundiſium : and can I forget (let me aſk once more) with what an obliging expedition you haſtened, as ſoon as you heard of my arrival, to meet me at Tarentum ? How friendly were your viſits ; how kind your endeavours to reaſon me out of that dejection, into which the dread of our general calamities had ſunk me ! At length, however, I returned to Rome : where every proof of the greateſt intimacy, and upon occaſions too of the moſt important kind, mutually paſſed between us. It was by your directions and advice, that I learned to regulate my conduct with reſpect to Cæſar : and as to other inſtances of your friendſhip ; where was the man, except Cæſar himſelf, at whoſe houſe you more frequently viſited, or upon whom you beſtowed ſo many agreeable hours of your converſation ? in ſome of which, you may remember, it was, that you encouraged me to engage in my philoſophical writings. When Cæſar afterwards returned from compleating his victories, it was your firſt and principal endeavour to eſtabliſh me again in his friendſhip : and it was an endeavour, in which you perfectly well ſucceeded. But to what purpoſe, you will aſk, perhaps, this long detail ? Longer indeed I muſt ac-

know-

knowledge it is, than I was myfelf aware: how- A.U.709.
ever, the ufe I would make of thefe feveral circum-
ftances, is to fhew you how much reafon I have
to be furprifed, that you, who well know the
truth of them, fhould believe me capable
of having acted inconfiftently with fuch power-
ful ties.   But befides thefe motives of my attach-
ment to you ; motives known and vifible to the
whole world ; there are others of a far lefs
confpicuous kind : and which I am at a lofs
to reprefent in the terms they deferve. Every
part indeed of your character I admire : but
when I confider you as the wife, the firm, and
the faithful friend ; as the polite, the witty, and
the learned companion ; thefe, I confefs, are the
ftriking points amidft your many other illuftrious
qualifications, with which I am particularly
charmed. But it is time to return to the com-
plaints you have alledged againft me. Be affured
then, I never once credited the report of your
having voted for the law you mentioned to Tre-
batius : and indeed if I had, I fhould have been
well perfuaded that you were induced to concur
in promoting it, upon fome very juft and rational
motive. But as the dignity of your character
draws upon you the obfervation of all the world;
the malevolence of mankind will fometimes give
feverer conftructions to your actions, than moft

certainly

A.U. 709. certainly they merit. If no inftances of this
kind have ever reached your knowledge, I know
not in what manner to proceed in my juftifica-
tion. Believe me, however, I have always de-
fended you upon thefe occafions with the fame
warmth and fpirit, with which I am fenfible you
are wont to oppofe, on your part, the calumnies
that are thrown out upon myfelf. Thus with
regard to the law I juft now mentioned ; I have
always peremptorily denied the truth of the
charge : and as to your having been one of the
managers of the late [9] games ; I have conftantly
infifted, that you acted agreeably to thofe pious
offices that are due to the memory of a departed
friend. In refpect to the latter, however ; you
cannot be ignorant, that if Cæfar was really a
tyrant, (as I think he was [1]) your zeal may be

[9] At the time when Cæfar was killed, he was preparing,
agreeably to a vow which he had made at the battle of
Pharfalia, to exhibit fome games in honour of Venus : a di-
vinity, from whom he affected to be thought a defcendant.
Octavius foon after his return to Rome, upon the death of
Cæfar, celebrated thefe games at his own expence : and
Matius undertook to be one of the managers. As this was
a public mark of refpect paid to the memory of Cæfar, and
might tend to inflame the minds of the populace againft the
confpirators ; it gave much difguft to the friends of the re-
public : and Cicero, 'tis probable, was in the number of
thofe who had openly fpoken of it with difpleafure. He
did fo at leaft, in a letter to Atticus. *Vid. Ad At.* xv. 2.
Appian. Bel. Civil. ii. 407.

[1] " It is with injuftice (faid the celebrated queen of Swe-
den) " that Cæfar is accufed of being a tyrant, if to go-

considered in two very different views. It may A.U. 709.
be faid, (and it is an argument which I never fail
to urge in your favour) that you fhewed a very
commendable fidelity, in thus difplaying your af-
fection to a departed friend. On the other hand,
it may be alledged (and in fact it is alledged) that
the liberties of our country ought to be far pre-
ferable even to the life itfelf of thofe whom we
hold moft dear. I wifh you had been informed
of the part I have always taken, whenever this
queftion has been ftarted. But there are two cir-
cumftances that reflect the brighteft luftre upon
your character, and which none of your friends
more frequently or more warmly commemorate,
than myfelf; I mean your having always moft
ftrongly recommended pacific meafures to Cæfar,
and conftantly advifed him to ufe his victory
with moderation : in both which, the whole

" vern Rome, was the moft important fervice he could
" have performed to his country." 'Tis certain, that the
republic was well-nigh reduced to a ftate of total anarchy,
when Cæfar ufurped the command : but it is equally certain
that he himfelf had been the principal author and fomenter
of thofe confufions, which rendered an abfolute authority the
only poffible expedient for reducing the commonwealth into
a ftate of tranquillity and good order. If this be true, it
feems no very intricate queftion to determine, what verdict
ought to be paffed upon Cæfar. But furely it is difficult to
know by what principles Cicero can be acquitted, who
reviled that man when dead, whom he was the firft to flatter
when living.

world

 world is agreed with me in acknowledging your merit.

I think myself much obliged to our friend Trebatius, for having given me this occasion of justifying myself before you. And you will credit the professions I have here made, unless you imagine me void of every spark both of gratitude and generosity : an opinion, than which nothing can be more injurious to my sentiments, or more unworthy of yours. Farewel.

LETTER XIII.

MATIUS TO CICERO.

I Received great satisfaction from your letter, as it assured me of my holding that rank in your esteem, which I have ever wished and hoped to enjoy. Indeed I never doubted of your good opinion : but the value I set upon it, rendered me sollicitous of preserving it without the least blemish. Conscious, however that I had never given just offence to any candid and honest mind, I was the less disposed to believe, that you, whose sentiments are exalted by the cultivation of so many generous arts, could hastily credit any reports to my disadvantage : especially as you were one for whom I had

at

at all times difcovered much fincere good will. A.U.709.
But as I have the pleafure to find, that you think
of me agreeably to my wifhes; I will drop this
fubject, in order to vindicate myfelf from thofe
calumnies, which you have fo often and with fuch
fingular generofity oppofed.   I am perfectly
well apprifed of the reflections that have been
caft upon me fince Cæfar's death.   It has been
imputed to me, I know, that I lament the lofs
of my friend, and think with indignation on the
murderers of the man I loved.   " The welfare
" of our country, fay my accufers, (as if they
had already made it appear, that the deftruction
of Cæfar was for the benefit of the common-
wealth) " the welfare of our country is to be
" preferred to all confiderations of amity." It
may be fo: but I will honeftly confefs, that I
am by no means arrived at this elevated ftrain of
patriotifm.   Neverthelefs, I took no part with
Cæfar in our civil diffentions: but neither did
I defert my friend, becaufe I difliked his mea-
fures.   The truth is, I was fo far from approv-
ing the civil war, that I always thought it
unjuftifiable; and exerted my utmoft endeavours
to extinguifh thofe fparks by which it was
kindled. In conformity to thefe fentiments, I did
not make ufe of my friend's victory to the grati-
fication of any lucrative or ambitious purpofes

A.U.709. of my own: as fome others moft shamefully did, whose intereft with Cæfar was much inferior to mine. Far, in truth, from being a gainer by his fuccefs, I fuffered greatly in my fortunes by that very law which faved many of thofe who now exult in his death, from the difgrace of being obliged to fly their country[2]. Let me add, that I recommended the vanquifhed party to his clemency, with the fame warmth and zeal as if my own prefervation had been concerned. Thus defirous that all my fellow-citizens might enjoy their lives in full fecurity, can I reprefs the indignation of my heart againft the affaffins of that man, from whofe generofity this privilege was obtained: efpecially as the fame hands were lifted up to his deftruction, which had firft drawn upon him all the odium and envy of his adminiftration? Yet I am threatened, it feems, with their vengeance, for daring to condemn the deed. Unexampled infolence! that fome fhould glory in the perpetration of thofe crimes, which others fhould not be permitted even to deplore! The meaneft flave has ever been allowed to indulge without controle, the fears, the forrows, or the joys of his heart:

[2] The law alluded to, is probably that which Cæfar enacted for the relief of thofe who had contracted debts before the commencement of the civil war: of which fee rem. 11. p. 260. vol. II.

but

but thefe our affertors of *liberty*, as they call
themfelves, endeavour to extort from me by
their menaces, this common privilege of every
creature.   Vain and impotent endeavours! no
dangers fhall intimidate me from acting up to
the generous duties of friendfhip and humanity;
perfuaded as I have ever been, that death in an
honeft caufe ought never to be fhunned, and
frequently to be courted.   Yet why does it thus
move their difpleafure, if I only wifh that they
may repent of what they have perpetrated? for
wifh, I will acknowledge I do, that both they
and all the world may regret the death of Cæfar.
" But as a member, fay they, of the common-
" wealth, you ought above all things to defire
" its prefervation." Now that I fincerely do fo,
if the whole tenor of my paft conduct, and all
the hopes I can reafonably be fuppofed to enter-
tain, will not fufficiently evince; I fhall not
attempt to prove it by my profeffions.   I conjure
you then to judge of me, not by what others may
fay, but by the plain tendency of my actions: and
if you believe I have any intereft in the tran-
quillity of the republic, be affured that I will
have no communication with thofe, who would
impioufly difturb its peace.   Shall I renounce
indeed thofe patriot principles I fteadily purfued
in my youth, when warmth and inexperience

I 2

might

A.U.709. might have pleaded fome excufe for errors? Shall I in the fober feafon of declining age, wantonly unravel at once the whole fair contexture of my better days? Moft affuredly not: nor fhall I ever give any other offence than in bewailing the fevere cataftrophe of a moft intimate and illuftrious friend! Were I difpofed to act otherwife, I fhould fcorn to deny it: nor fhould it be ever faid, that I covered my crimes by hypocrify, and feared to avow what I fcrupled not to commit.

But to proceed to the other articles of the charge againft me: it is farther alledged that I prefided at thofe games which the young Octavius exhibited in honour of Cæfar's victories. The charge, I confefs, is true: but what connection has an act of mere private duty, with the concerns of the republic? It was an office not only due from me to the memory of my departed friend, but which I could not refufe to that illuftrious youth, his moft worthy heir. I am reproached alfo with having been frequent in paying my vifits of compliment to Antony: Yet you will find that the very men who impute this as a mark of difaffection to my country, appeared much more frequently at his levee, either to follicit his favours or to receive them. But after all, can there be any thing, let me

aík,

ask, more insufferably arrogant than this accu- A. U. 709.
sation ? Cæsar never opposed my associating with
whomsoever I thought proper, even tho' it were
with persons whom he himself disapproved : and
shall the men who have cruelly robbed me of
one friend, attempt likewise by their malicious
insinuations, to alienate me from another ? But
the moderation of my conduct will, I doubt
not, discredit all reports that may hereafter be
raised to my disadvantage : and I am persuaded
that even those who hate me for my attachment
to Cæsar, would rather choose a friend of my
disposition, than of their own. In fine, if my
affairs should permit me, it is my resolution to
spend the remainder of my days at Rhodes. But
if any accident should render it necessary for me
to continue at Rome; my actions shall evince,
that I am sincerely desirous of my country's wel-
fare. In the mean time, I am much obliged to
Trebatius for supplying you with an occasion
of so freely laying open to me the amicable
sentiments of your heart; as it affords me an
additional reason for cultivating a friendship with
one whom I have ever been disposed to esteem.
Farewel.

LETTER XIV.

MARCUS BRUTUS and CAIUS CASSIUS, Prætors[3],
to MARK ANTONY, Conful.

A.U. 709. IF we were not perfuaded of your honour and friendfhip, we fhould not trouble you with the prefent application : which in confidence of both, we doubt not of your receiving in the moft favourable manner.

We are informed that great numbers of the veteran troops are already arrived in Rome, and that many more are expected by the firft of June. Our fentiments would be extremely changed indeed, if we entertained any fears or fufpicions with regard to yourfelf. However as we refigned ourfelves entirely to your direction, and in compliance with your advice, not only publifhed an edict, but wrote circular letters in order to difmifs our friends who came to our affiftance from the municipal towns ; we may juftly look upon ourfelves as worthy of being admitted into a fhare of your councils : efpecially in an article

[3] They had been appointed prætors for the prefent year, by Cæfar. The reader has already been informed, that Brutus and Caffius finding it neceffary foon after the affaffination of Cæfar, to withdraw from Rome, retired to a villa of the former at Lanuvium : from whence this letter was probably written.

wherein

wherein we are particularly concerned. It is our
joint requeſt therefore, that you would explicitly
acquaint us with your intentions, and whether
you imagine we can poſſibly be ſafe amidſt ſuch
a multitude of veteran troops, who have even
ſome deſign, we are told, of replacing the altar [4]
which was erected to Cæſar: a deſign ſurely
which no one can wiſh may meet with your
approbation, who has any regard to our credit
or ſecurity [5]. It has ſufficiently appeared, that
from the beginning of this affair, we have had a
view to the public tranquillity, and have aimed
at nothing more than the recovery of our com-
mon liberties. No man except yourſelf has it
in his power to deceive us; becauſe we never
have truſted, nor ever will truſt, any other: and
moſt certainly you have too much integrity to
betray the confidence we have repoſed in you.
Our friends, however, notwithſtanding that they
have the ſame reliance upon your good-faith,
are greatly alarmed for our ſafety; as they think
ſo large a body of veterans may much more
eaſily be inſtigated to violent meaſures by ill-
deſigning men, than they can be reſtrained by

[4] See rem. 3 p. 92. of this vol.

[5] Becauſe the ſuffering of divine honours to be paid to
Cæſar, would neceſſarily impreſs the higheſt ſentiments of
him upon the minds of the populace; and conſequently
tend to incenſe them againſt thoſe who were concerned in
taking away his life.

I 4

your

A.U.709. your influence and authority.   We intreat you therefore, to return us a full and satisfactory anfwer.   To tell us that you ordered thefe troops to march to Rome, as intending to move the fenate in June next, concerning their [6] affairs; is amufing us with a very idle and trifling reafon: for as you are affured that we fhall not attempt to obftruct this [7] defign; from what other quarter can you poffibly fufpect that it will be oppofed?   In a word, it cannot be thought that we are too anxious for our own prefervation, when it is confidered, that no accident can happen to our perfons without involving the whole republic in the moft dangerous commotions.   Farewel.

[6] Antony's *pretended* reafon for drawing together this body of veteran troops, was in order to procure a ratification from the fenate of thofe grants of lands which had been made to them by Cæfar, as a reward of their fervices : but his *true* reafon was to ftrengthen his hands againft thofe who fhould attempt to oppofe his meafures.

[7] The confpirators had given public affurances to the veteran troops, that they would not endeavour to annul the grants which Cæfar had made in their favour.   *Dio.* p. 257.

L E T T E R XV.

To Caius Cassius.

BELIEVE me, my Caffius, the republic is the perpetual fubject of my meditations; or to exprefs the fame thing in other words, you and Marcus Brutus are never out of my thoughts. It is upon you two, indeed, together with Decimus Brutus, that all our hopes depend. Mine are fomewhat raifed by the glorious conduct of Dolabella, in fuppreffing the late infurrection [8]: which had fpread fo wide and gathered every day fuch additional ftrength, that it feemed to threaten deftruction to the whole city. But this mob is now fo totally quelled, that I think we have nothing farther to fear from any future attempt of the fame kind. Many other fears, however, and very confiderable ones too, ftill remain with us: and it entirely refts upon you, in conjunction with your illuftrious affociates, to remove them. Yet where to advife you to begin for that purpofe, I muft acknowledge myfelf at a lofs. To fay truth, it is the tyrant alone, and not the tyranny, from which we feem to be delivered: for altho' the man indeed

____
[8] See rem. 3. p. 92. of this vol.

A.U. 709. is deſtroyed, we ſtill ſervilely maintain all his deſpotic ordinances. We do more: and under the pretence of carrying his deſigns into execution, we approve of meaſures which even he himſelf would never have purſued [9]. And the misfortune is, that I know not where this extravagance will end. When I reflect on the laws that are enacted, on the immunities that are granted, on the immenſe largeſſes that are diſtributed, on the exiles that are recalled, and on the fictitious decrees that are publiſhed; the only effect that ſeems to have been produced by Cæſar's death is, that it has extinguiſhed the ſenſe of our ſervitude, and the abhorrence of that deteſtable uſurper: as all the diſorders into which he threw the republic, ſtill continue. Theſe are the evils therefore, which it is incumbent upon you and your patriot coadjutors to redreſs: for let not my

[9] A few days after Cæſar's death, Antony aſſembled the ſenate in the temple of Tellus, in order to take into conſideration the ſtate of public affairs. The reſult of their deliberations was, to decree a general act of oblivion of what was paſt, and to confirm the ſeveral nominations to magiſtracies, and other grants, which had been made by Cæſar. This was a very prudent and neceſſary meaſure, in order to preſerve the public tranquillity: and it was principally procured by the authority and eloquence of Cicero. But Antony ſoon perverted it to his own ambitious purpoſes: for being appointed to inſpect the papers of Cæſar, he forged ſome, and modelled others as beſt ſuited his own deſigns; diſpoſing of every thing as he thought proper, under the authority of this decree. *Dio.* p. 250. 256.

friends

friends imagine, that they have yet compleated A.U.709.
their work. The obligations, it is true, which
the republic has already received from you, are
far greater than I could have ventured to hope:
ftill however her demands are not entirely fatif-
fied; and fhe promifes herfelf yet higher fervices
from fuch brave and generous benefactors. You
have revenged her injuries, by the death of her
oppreffor: but you have done nothing more.
For tell me, what has fhe yet recovered of her
former dignity and luftre? Does fhe not obey
the will of that tyrant now he is dead, whom fhe
could not endure when living? And do we not,
inftead of repealing his public laws, authenticate
even his private memorandums? You will tell
me, perhaps, (and you may tell me with truth)
that I concurred in paffing a decree for that pur-
pofe. It was in compliance, however, with pub-
lic circumftances: a regard to which is of much
confequence in political deliberations of every
kind. But there are fome however, who have
moft immoderately and ungratefully abufed the
conceffions we found it thus neceffary to make.

I hope very fpeedily to difcufs this and many
other points with you in perfon. In the mean
time be perfuaded, that the affection I have
ever borne to my country, as well as my parti-
cular friendfhip to yourfelf, renders the advance-

ment

A.U. 709. ment of your credit and esteem with the public,
extremely my concern.   Farewel.

LETTER XVI.

TO OPPIUS[2].

THE sentiments and advice which your let-
ter has so freely given me in relation to
my leaving Italy[3], together with what you said
to Atticus in a late conversation upon this sub-
ject, have greatly contributed, he can bear me
witness, to dispel those doubts that occurred on
which-ever side I viewed this question.   I have
ever thought indeed, that no man was more ca-
pable of forming a right judgment, nor more
faithful in communicating it, than yourself: as
I am sure I very particularly experienced, in the
beginning of the late civil wars.   For when I
consulted you in regard to my following Pompey,
or remaining in Italy ; your advice, I remem-
ber, was, that " I should act as my honour
" directed."   This sufficiently discovered your
opinion : and I could not but look with admira-

---

[2] The MSS. vary in the name of the person to whom
this letter is addressed, some writing it *Appius*, and others
Oppius.   If the latter be the true reading, perhaps he is the
same of whom some account has been given in rem. 9.
p. 134. vol. ii.

[3] See rem. 2. p. 85. of this vol.

tion

tion on fo remarkable an inftance of your fince-
rity.   For notwithftanding your ftrong attach-
ment to Cæfar, who, you had reafon to think,
would have been better pleafed if I had purfued
a different conduct; yet you rather chofe I fhould
act agreeably to my honour, than in conformity
to his inclination.   My friendfhip for you, how-
ever, did not take its rife from this period: for I
was fenfible that I enjoyed a fhare in your efteem
long before the time of which I am fpeaking. I
fhall ever remember indeed, the generous fer-
vices you conferred both upon myfelf and my
family, during the great misfortunes which I
fuffered in my exile: and the ftrict intimacy
in which we converfed with each other after my
return, as well as the fentiments which upon all
occafions I profeffed to entertain of you, are cir-
cumftances which none who were inclined to ob-
ferve them, could poffibly overlook.   But you
gave me a moft diftinguifhing proof of the good
opinion you had conceived of my conftancy and
fidelity, by the unreferved refignation of your
heart to me, after the death of Cæfar.   I fhould
think myfelf therefore a difgrace to human na-
ture, if I did not juftify thefe your favourable
fentiments, by every kind of good office in my
power, as well as by the return of my warmeft
affection.   Continue yours to me, my dear Op-
pius,

A.U.709. pius, I intreat you : a requeſt however, which
I prefer more in compliance with the cuſtomary
form, than as thinking it in the leaſt neceſſary.
I recommend all my affairs in general to your
protection, and leave it to Atticus to inform
you in what particular points I deſire your ſer-
vices. When I ſhall be more at leiſure, you
may expect a longer letter. In the mean time
take care of your health, as the moſt agreeable
inſtance you can give me of your friendſhip.
Farewel.

LETTER XVII.

To Trebatius.

I Am the more enamoured with this city [4],
becauſe I find you are much the favourite of
every body in it. But I know not, in truth,
where you are otherwiſe : and I ſhould rather
have told you, that even the abſence of your
freed-man Rufio is no leſs regretted among them,

---

[4] Cicero, after much debate with himſelf concerning the
voyage which he mentions in the preceding letter ; at
length fixed his reſolution and embarked. He ſailed along
the weſtern coaſt of Italy towards Rhegium : but came
aſhore every night in order to lodge at the villa of ſome
friend. He was in this manner purſuing his voyage into
Greece, when he wrote the preſent letter, from Velia : a
ſea-port town on the coaſt of Lucania.

than

than if he were a perfon of as much confequence
as you and I. However I by no means difap-
prove of your having called him from hence,
in order to fuperintend the buildings you are
carrying on in the Lupercal [5]. For notwith-
ftanding your houfe at Velia is altogether as agree-
able as that which you have in Rome; yet I
fhould prefer the latter to all the poffeffions you
enjoy here. Neverthelefs, if you fhould take
the opinion of a man whofe advice you feldom
reject, you will not part with your patrimony
on the banks of the noble Heles, nor forfake a
villa which had once the honour of belonging
to Papirius : an intention which the citizens of
Velia are in fome fear left you fhould entertain.
But altho' it be incommoded indeed by the great
concourfe of ftrangers who vifit the adjoining
grove; yet that objection may eafily be removed
you know, by cutting down [6] this impertinent

[5] A range of buildings in Rome, fo called from an antient
temple of the fame name which had been formerly erected
upon that fpot to the god Pan. *Dion. Halicarn.* l. 24.

[6] Groves were generally confecrated to fome divinity; as
this feems to have been, by the number of ftrangers who
probably frequented it on a religious account. Inftead of
lucum therefore, which is the reading adopted by Manutius,
and followed in the tranflation, fome of the commentators
have thought it fhould be *lotum*; becaufe, if it were a con-
fecrated grove, it could not be cut down without commit-
ting an act of impiety. But this objecti n is founded upon
the miftake that Cicero fpoke in a ferious fenfe, what he
feems plainly to have intended in a ludicrous one.

plantation :

 plantation: which will prove a very confiderable advantage likewife both to your pocket and your profpect. To fpeak ferioufly; it is a great convenience, efpecially in fuch diftracted times as the prefent, to be poffeffed of an eftate which affords you a refuge from Rome, in a pleafant and healthy fituation, and in a place where you are fo univerfally beloved. To thefe confiderations I will add, my dear Trebatius, that, perhaps, it may be for my advantage alfo that you fhould not part with this villa. But whatever you may determine, take care both of yourfelf and my affairs: and expect to fee me, if the gods permit, before the end of the year.

I have purloined from Sextius Fadius, one of Nico's difciples, a treatife which the latter has written concerning the pleafures of the palate. Agreeable phyfician! how eafily will he make me a convert to his doctrine! Our friend Baffus was fo jealous of this treafure, that he endeavoured to conceal it from me: but I imagine, by the freedom of your table-indulgencies, that he has been lefs referved in communicating the fecrets of it to you.——The wind has juft now turned to a favourable point, fo that I muft bid you farewel.

Velia, July the 20th.

L E T T E R   XVIII.

To the Same.

YOU see the influence you have over me: A.U. 709. tho' indeed it is not greater than what you are juftly entitled to, from that equal return of friendfhip you make to mine. I could not therefore be eafy in the reflection, I will not fay of having abfolutely refufed, but of not having complied however with the requeft you made me, when we were lately together. Accordingly, as foon as I fet fail from Velia, I employed myfelf in drawing up the treatife you defired, upon the plan of Ariftotle's topics [7] : as indeed I could not look upon a city in which you are fo generally beloved, without being reminded of my friend. I now fend you the produce of my meditations : which I have endeavoured to exprefs with all the perfpicuity that a fubject of this nature will admit. Neverthelefs, if fome paffages fhould appear dark; you muft do me

[7] The treatife here mentioned, is ftill extant among Cicero's works : and appears to be a fort of epitome of what Ariftotle had long before publifhed upon the fame fubject. The principal defign of it is, to point out the feveral fources from whence arguments upon every queftion may be derived.

A.U.709. the juftice to remember, that no fcience can be rendered perfectly intelligible, without the affift-ance of a mafter to explain and apply its rules. To fend you no farther for an inftance, than to your own profeffion: could a knowledge of the law be acquired merely from books? Un-doubtedly it could not: for altho' the treatifes which have been written upon that fubject, are extremely numerous; yet they are by no means of themfelves fufficient inftructors, without the help of fome learned guide to enlighten their obfcurities. However, with refpect to the ob-fervations in the prefent performance; if you give them a frequent and attentive perufal, you will certainly be able to enter into their mean-ing: but the ready application of them, can only be attained by repeated exercife. And in this exercife I fhall not fail to engage you, if I fhould return fafe into Italy, and find the repub-lic in a ftate of repofe. Farewel.

Rhegium [*], July the 28th.

[*] A fea-port upon the weftern point of Calabria, oppofite to Sicily: it is now called *Regio*.

L E T T E R XIX.

Brutus and Cassius, Prætors [9], to Antony,
Conful.

THE letter we have received from you, A.U. 709.
is altogether agreeable to your late con-
tumelious and menacing edict, and by no means
becoming *you* to have written to *us*.   We have
in no fort, Antony, given you any juft provo-
cation : nor could we have imagined, that you
would look upon it as any thing extraordinary,
if invefted as we are with the high authority of
prætors, we thought proper in a public manifefto
to fignify our requefts to the conful.   But if it
raifes your indignation that we prefumed to take
this liberty as prætors, allow us to lament, that
you fhould not indulge us in it at leaft as
friends.

We receive it as an inftance of your juftice,
that you deny ever having complained of our

---

[9] The prætors could not legally abfent themfelves from
Rome for above ten days, unlefs they obtained a fpecial dif-
penfation from the fenate for that purpofe.   Brutus and
Caffius therefore not thinking it fafe to truft themfelves in the
city, publifhed a fort of manifefto directed to Antony as
conful, requefting him to move the fenate for this licenfe in
their favour.   Antony, inftead of complying with their re-
queft, feems to have anfwered it by publifhing a manifefto
on his part, which was followed likewife by a private letter
that produced the prefent epiftle.

K 2 levying

 levying troops and contributions, and making
applications to the armies both at home and
abroad to rife in our defence : a charge, which
we likewife difavow in every particular. We
cannot but wonder, however, fince you were
filent upon this head, that you fhould be fo little
able to command yourfelf upon another, as to
reproach us with the death of Cæfar.

We leave it to your own reflections to de-
termine what fentiments it ought to create in us,
that the prætors of Rome, in order to preferve
the tranquillity and liberties of the common-
wealth, cannot publifh a manifefto declaring
their defire of retiring from the execution of their
office, without being infulted by the conful. 'Tis
in vain, however, that you would intimidate us
by your arms : for it would ill become the fpi-
rit we have fhewn, to be difcouraged by dangers
of any kind. As little fhould Antony attempt
to ufurp an authority over thofe, to whom he is
himfelf indebted for the liberty he enjoys. To
the free and independent, the menaces of any
man are perfectly impotent. Had we a defign
therefore of having recourfe to arms ; your
letter would be altogether ineffectual to deter us
from our purpofe. But you are well convinced,
that no confideration can prevail with us to re-
kindle the flames of a civil war : and perhaps
you

you artfully threw out thefe menaces, in order
to perfuade the world that our pacific meafures
are the effect, not of choice, but timidity.

To fpeak plainly our fentiments; we wifh to
fee you raifed to the higheft honours: but to ho-
nours that are conferred by a free republic.   It is
our defire likewife not to engage with you in any
contefts: but we muft add, that the poffeffion of
our liberties is of far higher value in our efteem
than the enjoyment of your friendfhip.   Well
confider what you undertake, and how far you
may be able to carry it into execution; reflect-
ing, not how many years Cæfar was permitted
to live, but how fhort a period he was fuffered
to reign [1].   In the mean while, we implore the
gods to infpire you with fuch counfels as may
tend to the advantage both of yourfelf, and of
the commonwealth.   But fhould they prove
otherwife, we wifh that the confequence may be
as little detrimental to your own intereft, as fhall
be confiftent with the dignity and fafety of the
republic.

Auguft the 4th.

[1] Cæfar did not continue longer than five months in the
peaceable enjoyment of his ufurpation: for he returned to
Rome from the conqueft of Pompey's fons in Spain, in the
month of October 708, and was affaffinated in the March
following. *Vel. Paterc.* ii. 56.

K 3

LETTER XX.

To Plancus [2].

A.U. 709.

I Had left Rome, and was actually on my voy-age to Greece, when I was recalled by the general voice of the republic [3]: but the conduct of Marc Antony ever since my return, has not

[2] Some general account of Plancus has already been given in rem. 6. p. 221. vol. ii.   In the beginning of the present year he was appointed by Cæsar, governor of the farther Gaul: where he now was, at the head of three legions. He is said, during his residence in that province, to have founded the city of Lions.   Upon the death of Cæsar, to whom he had been warmly attached, Cicero employed all his art to engage him on the side of the senate: and Plancus after much hesitation at length declared himself accordingly. But this declaration seems to have been entirely the effect of a belief, that the rupture between Antony and the senate was upon the point of being accommodated: it is certain at least, that it was not sincere. For Plancus soon afterwards betrayed the cause he had thus professed to support, and went over with his troops to Antony.   *Pigh. Annal.* ii. 465.   *Senec. Ep.* 91. *Vel. Paterc.* ii. 63.   See note 11. p. 384. of this vol.

[3] The principal motive of Cicero's intended voyage into Greece, was in order to avoid the danger of taking part in a civil war, which he apprehended would soon break out between Antony and young Pompey; the latter being ex-pected from Spain, at the head of a considerable army. But as his leaving Italy at so critical and important a conjuncture, might justly expose him to the censure of unworthily desert-ing the republic; he was long and greatly embarrassed between the desire of preserving his character on the one side, and of securing his person on the other: the two points which seem throughout his whole life to have held him in perpetual sus-pence.   However, he at length embarked: but he no sooner sailed than he repented, as usual, of the step he had taken.

permitted

permitted me to enjoy a moment of repofe. The
ferocity (for to call it pride would be imputing
a vice to him which is nothing uncommon) the
ferocity of his temper is fo exceffive, that he can-
not bear a word, or even a look, which is animat-
ed with the leaft fpirit of liberty.   It is this that
fills my heart with a thoufand difquietudes : but
difquietudes, in which my own prefervation is by
no means concerned. No, my friend, I have nothing
farther to wifh with refpect to myfelf; whether I
confider the years to which I am arrived[*], the ac-
tions that I have performed, or the glory (if that
may be mentioned as of any value in the account)
with which they have been crowned.   All my
anxiety is for our country alone ; and the more
fo, my dear Plancus, as the time appointed for

Neverthelefs he purfued his voyage, and arrived in Sicily :
from whence he propofed to ftretch over into Greece : but in
attempting this paffage, he was blown back by contrary
winds on the coaft of Italy.   Upon his going afhore in order
to refrefh himfelf, he was informed by fome of the principal
inhabitants of that part of the country who were juft arrived
from Rome, that there were great hopes Antony would accom-
modate affairs to the general fatisfaction of all parties. This
news was followed by a letter from Atticus preffing him to
renounce his intended voyage, as alfo by an interview with
Brutus, who likewife expreffed his difapprobation of that
fcheme.   Upon thefe confiderations therefore he gave up all
farther thoughts of Greece, and immediately returned to
Rome. *Vid. Ad At.* xiv. 13, 22. xv. 19, 20, 21, 33.
xvi. 6, 7.

[*] Cicero was at this time in his 63d year.

K 4   your

A.U. 709. your fucceffion to the confular office [5], is fo re-
mote, that it is rather to be wifhed, than ex-
pected, that we fhould be able to preferve our li-
berties fo long alive. What rational hopes indeed
can poffibly be entertained, where a commonwealth
is totally oppreffed by the arms of the moft violent
and outrageous of men; where neither the fenate,
nor the people have any authority; where neither
laws nor juftice prevail: and in one word, where
there is not the leaft trace or fhadow of civil
government remaining? But as you receive, I
imagine, the public accounts of what is tranf-
acted amongft us; I need not defcend into a detail
of particulars. Let me rather, in confequence of
that affection I bear you, and which has been ftill
increafing from our earlieft youth; let me rather
remind and exhort you, to turn all your thoughts
and cares towards the republic. If it fhould not
be utterly deftroyed ere you enter upon the con-
fular office, it may without difficulty be fteered
right: Tho' I will add, that much vigilance as
well as great good fortune muft concur, in order
to preferve it to that defirable period. But I
hope we may fee you here, fomewhat before that

---

[5] Plancus was in the number of thofe whom Cæfar had
named to the confulate, in that general defignation of ma-
giftrates which he made a fhort time before his death. But
as Plancus ftood laft in the lift, his turn was not to commence
till the year 711.

                              time

time ſhall arrive.   Mean while, beſides the in-
ducements that ariſe to me from my regard to the
well-being of the republic, you may be aſſured
that from my particular attachment likewiſe to
yourſelf, I ſhall exert my utmoſt efforts for the
advancement of your credit and honours.   By
theſe means I ſhall have the ſatisfaction to diſ-
charge at once the duties I owe, both to my
country and to my friend : to that country which
is the object of my warmeſt affections, and to
that friend whoſe amity I would moſt religiouſly
cultivate.

I am extremely rejoiced, though by no means
ſurpriſed, to find that you treat Furnius [6] agree-
ably to his rank and merit.   Be aſſured that
whatever favours you ſhall think proper to confer
upon him, I ſhall conſider them as ſo many im-
mediate inſtances of your regard to myſelf.
Farewel.

[6] He was lieutenant to Plancus in Gaul.

LETTER XXI.

DECIMUS BRUTUS, Conful ' elect, to CICERO.

A.U. 709. IF I entertained the leaft doubt of your incli-
nations to ferve me, I fhould be extremely
copious in my follicitations for that purpofe : but
I have ftrongly perfuaded myfelf, that my intereft
is already a part of your care.

I led my army againft the moft interior inha-
bitants of the Alps, not fo much from an am-
bition of being faluted with the title of *impe-
rator* [8], as in order to comply with the martial
fpirit of my troops, and to ftrengthen their at-
tachment to our caufe. In both thefe views, I
have, I think, fucceeded : as the foldiers have had
an opportunity by this meafure of experiencing the

[7] Decimus Brutus was nominated by Cæfar to be collegue
with Plancus : of whofe appointment to the confular office,
mention has been made in rem. 5. on the preceding epiftle.
Soon after the reft of the confpirators found it neceffary to
leave Rome, Decimus withdrew into Cifalpine Gaul, in order
to take poffeffion of that province which had been allotted
to him by Cæfar, and to put himfelf in a pofture of defence
againft the attempts which Antony was meditating. Shortly
after his arrival in that province, he employed his troops in
an expedition againft certain inhabitants of the neighbouring
mountains : and having happily executed this fcheme, he
wrote the following letter to requeft Cicero's fuffrage in pro-
curing him thofe diftinctions which the fenate ufually de-
creed to their fuccefsful generals.

[8] See vol. i. p. 1. rem. 1.

courage

courage and the generofity of their general. I
was engaged with the moft warlike of thefe peo-
ple: and have taken and deftroyed great num-
bers of their forts. In fhort, I thought the
action fufficiently confiderable, to fend an ac-
count of it to the fenate. I hope therefore you
will fupport my pretenfions with your fuffrage:
as it will at the fame time be greatly contribut-
ing to the credit of the common caufe. Fare-
wel.

L E T T E R XXII.

To Decimus Brutus, Conful elect.

IT is of much confequence to the fuccefs of
this epiftle, whether it reaches you in an
anxious, or an eafy hour. Accordingly, I have
directed the bearer to watch the favourable mo-
ment of delivering it into your hands: as there is
a time, my friend, when a letter, no lefs than
a vifit, may prove extremely unfeafonable. But
if he fhould obferve the caution I have injoined
him; and this fhould find you, as I hope it will,
in a ftate of mind perfectly ferene and undifturb-
ed; I doubt not of your ready compliance with
the requeft I am going to make.

Lucius

 Lucius Lamia offers himself as a candidate, at the enfuing election of prætors. There is no man with whom I live in an equal degree of familiarity: as we are intimately indeed united by a long acquaintance. But what greatly likewife recommends him to me is, that nothing affords me more entertainment than his company. To this I muft add, the infinite obligations I received from him in my affair with Clodius. He was at that time at the head of the equeftrian order; and he entered with fo much fpirit into my caufe, that the conful Gabinius commanded him to withdraw from Rome; an indignity never offered before to any citizen of the republic. As the world has not forgoten what he thus fuffered upon my account; I am fure it would be the higheft reproach upon my character if I did not remember it myfelf: and therefore, my dear friend, be well affured that the good or ill fuccefs of Lamia in his prefent purfuit, will no lefs fenfibly affect me, than if I were perfonally concerned. Notwithftanding therefore the illuftrious character which Lamia bears, together with the great popularity he has acquired by the magnificence of the games he exhibited when he was Ædile, yet I am labouring with as much affiduity to promote his intereft, as if he had none of thefe advantages to recommend him.

If

If then I poffefs that fhare in your affection, which A.U. 709. I am well perfuaded I enjoy; let me intreat you to write to Lupus to fecure the votes of thofe equeftrian centuries, over which you bear an un- limited fway. But not to detain you with a mul- tiplicity of words, I will conclude all with moft fincerely affuring you, that altho' there is no- thing, my dear Brutus, which I have not reafon to expect from your friendfhip; yet you can in no inftance more effectually oblige me, than by complying with my prefent requeft. Farewel.

L E T T E R XXIII.

To the Same [9].

THERE is none of my friends with whom I live in fo ftrict an intimacy, as with La- mia. To fay that I am much indebted to his good offices, would not be fpeaking of them in the terms they deferve: for the truth is, (and it is a truth of which the whole republic is fenfible) he has conferred upon me the higheft and moft generous obligations. Lamia, after having paf- fed thro' the office of Ædile with the greateft fplen- dor and magnificence, now offers himfelf as a can-

[9] This letter feems to have been a kind of duplicate of the former; as it is written to the fame perfon, and upon the fame occafion.

didate

A.U.709. didate for the prætorſhip : and it is univerſally acknowledged, that he wants neither intereſt nor dignity to ſupport his pretenſions. However, the oppoſition he is likely to meet with from his competitors is ſo ſtrong, that I have many fears for the event : and therefore think myſelf obliged to be his general ſollicitor upon this occaſion. I well know how much it is in your power to ſerve me in this affair : and I have no doubt of your inclination.　Be aſſured then, my dear Brutus, that you cannot more ſenſibly oblige me, than by aſſiſting Lamia in his preſent purſuit : and it is with all the warmth of my heart that I intreat you to exert your utmoſt intereſt for that purpoſe.　Farewel.

LETTER XXIV.

To Caius Cassius.

IT gives me great pleaſure to find, that my late ſpeech [1] has received your approbation.　If I could more frequently enforce the

---

[1] Upon Cicero's return to Rome, (ſee rem. 3. p. 134. of this vol.) he received a ſummons from Antony to attend a meeting of the ſenate, which was to be holden the next morning : but as the buſineſs of this meeting was to decree certain divine honours to the memory of Cæſar, our author excuſed himſelf from being preſent.　The following day however, Antony being abſent, Cicero ventured to appear in the ſenate : when he delivered the ſpeech to which he here

ſame

fame fentiments, the liberties of the republic might eafily be recovered. But that far more defperate and deteftable fcoundrel [a] than he [b] at whofe death you faid, " the worft of all villains is " expired," is watching for a pretence to begin his murderous purpofes : and his fingle view in charging me with having advifed the killing of Cæfar, is merely to excite the veteran foldiers againft my life. But this is a danger which I am not afraid to hazard, fince he gives me a fhare with you in the honour of that glorious deed. Hence it is, however, that neither Pifo who firft ventured to inveigh againft the meafures of Antony, nor myfelf who made a fpeech to the fame purpofe about a month [z] afterwards, nor Publius Servilius who followed my example, can any of us appear with fafety in the fenate. For this inhuman gladiator has evidently a defign upon our lives : and he hoped to have rendered me the firft victim of his cruel vengeance. With this fanguinary view he entered the fenate on the 19th of September, having feveral days before retired to the villa of Metellus, in order to prepare an inflammatory fpeech againft me [s]. But

alludes, and which is the firft of thofe that are called his *Philippics*.   See life of Cic. iii. 81.

  [a] Antony.   [b] Cæfar.

  [z] The fpeech mentioned in the preceding remark.

  [s] It was in anfwer to this fpeech that Cicero compofed his fecond Philippic ; which however he did not deliver. For,

who

 who shall reconcile the silent meditations of eloquence with the noisy revels of lewdness and debauchery? Accordingly it was the opinion of all his audience, (as I have already, I believe, mentioned to you in a former letter,) that he could not so properly be said to have delivered a speech, as to have discharged, with his usual indecency, the horrid fumes of his scandalous intemperance.

You are persuaded, you tell me, that my credit and eloquence will be able to produce some good effect. And some indeed they have produced; considering the sad situation of our affairs. They have rendered the people sensible, that there are three persons of consular rank, who because they are in the interest of the republic, and have spoken their sentiments in the senate with freedom, cannot attend that assembly without the danger of being assassinated. And this is all the good you are to expect from my oratory.

A certain relation of yours * is so captivated with his new alliance, that he no longer concerns himself in the success of your games; but on the contrary is mortified to the last degree at those peals of applause with which your brother was

by the advice of his friends, he absented himself from this meeting of the senate, as they did not think it safe for him to be present. *Manut.*

* Lepidus is supposed to be the person here meant: as he was related to Cassius by his own marriage, and had lately married his son to Antony's daughter.

di-

diftinguifhed [5].   Another of your family [6] has A.U. 709. been foftened by fome grants, which it is pretended that Cæfar had defigned to confer upon him. This however, might be borne with patience: but is it not utterly beyond all indurance, that there fhould be a man who da˜es openly avow that he fupports the meafures of that fcoundrel Antony, with the hopes that his fon will be chofen conful when you and Brutus are intitled to be candidates for that office? As to our friend Lucius Cotta, a fatal defpair (for fo he terms it himfelf) has almoft entirely driven him from the fenate.   Lucius Cæfar, that firm and excellent patriot, is prevented from coming thither by his ill ftate of health: and Servius Sulpicius, who is a true friend to the caufe of liberty, and whofe authority might be of infinite fervice in the prefent conjuncture, is unhappily abfent from Rome.   After having mentioned thefe, I muft take the liberty to fay, that I cannot add any others, excepting the confuls elect, who may be juftly deemed as well-wifhers to the republic. The truth is, thefe are the only perfons upon whofe

[5] Brutus and Caffius were obliged as prætors, to exhibit certain games in honour of Apollo, with which the public were annually entertained on the 3d of July: but as they had withdrawn themfelves from Rome, thefe games were conducted by the brother of Caffius.

[6] It is not known to whom Cicero alludes in this place, nor in the period immediately following.

 advice and authority the commonwealth can
depend.   And fmall indeed would their number
be, even in the beft of times : how unequal then
muft their ftrength be found, to combat againft
the worft ? All our hopes therefore reft entire-
ly upon you and Brutus; I mean, if you have
not withdrawn from us with a view only to your
own prefervation : for if that fhould be the cafe,
we have nothing, alas! to hope neither from Bru-
tus, nor from you.   But if, on the contrary, you
are forming fome glorious enterprife, worthy of
your exalted characters ; I doubt not that the re-
public by your affiftance, will foon recover her
liberties : and I have only to wifh, that I may
not be deftroyed ere that happy day fhall arrive.
In the mean time, my beft fervices neither are,
nor fhall be wanting to your family : and whe-
ther they fhould apply to me for that purpofe,
or not, I fhall never fail to give them proofs of
my friendfhip towards you.   Farewel.

LETTER XXV.

To Plancus.

A.U. 709.

Agreeably to the friendship which subsists between us, my services should not have been wanting to advance your dignities [7], if I could have been present in the senate consistently with my honour or my safety. But no man can freely deliver his opinion in that assembly, without being exposed to the violences of a military force, that are licensed to commit their outrages with full impunity: and it would ill become my rank and character to speak upon public affairs in a place, where I am more attentively observed, and more closely surrounded by soldiers, than by senators. In any instance of private concern, my best offices shall not be wanting to you: nor shall they indeed even in those of a public nature, whatever hazard I may run, where my appearance is absolutely necessary to promote your interest. But where it may be equally advanced without my concurrence; suffer me, I intreat you, to pay a proper regard to my own dignity and preservation. Farewel.

[7] The occasion on which Plancus had applied to Cicero for his services in the senate, does not appear.

                    LET-

LETTER XXVI.

TO CAIUS CASSIUS.

A.U. 709. THE malignant spirit of your friend [a], breaks out every day with greater and more open violence. To inftance, in the firft place, the ftatue which he has lately erected near the roftrum, to Cæfar : under which he has infcribed, To THE EXCELLENT FATHER OF HIS COUNTRY ; intimating, that you and your heroic affociates are to be confidered, not only as affaffins but parricides. In which number I am likewife included : for this outrageous man reprefents me as the principal advifer and promoter of your moft glorious enterprife.   Would to Heaven the charge were true ! for had I been a party in your councils, I fnould have put it out of his power thus to perplex and embarrafs our affairs [s].   But this was a point

---

[a] Antony.

[s] Cicero frequently reproaches the confpirators, with having committed a capital miftake in fparing Antony when they deftroyed Cæfar: an error which our author would have prevented, it feems, had they admitted him into their councils. But it may be affirmed, (and upon the authority of Cicero himfelf) that nothing could have been more unjuftifiable, than to have rendered Antony a joint victim with Cæfar.   'Tis true, there was an antient law fubfifting, by which every one was authorifed to lift up his fword againft the man, who fhould difcover any defigns of invading the public liberties.   But Antony was fo far from having

which

which depended upon yourfelves to determine : A.U. 709.
and fince the opportunity is now over, I can only
wifh that I were capable of giving you any ef-
fectual advice. But the truth is, I am utterly
at a lofs in what manner to act myfelf: for to
what purpofe is refiftance, where one cannot op-
pofe force by force?

It is evidently the intent of Cæfar's party, to
revenge his death. And accordingly Antony
being on the 2d of October laft prefented to
the people by Canutius[9], mentioned the gene-
rous deliverers of our country in terms, that
traitors alone deferve. He fcrupled not to affert
likewife, that you had acted intirely by my ad-
vice ; and that Canutius alfo was under the fame
influence. He had the mortification however
to leave the roftrum with great difgrace. In a
word, you may judge what are the defigns of this
faction by their having feifed the appointments
of your lieutenant[1] : for does not their conduct
in this inftance fufficiently declare, that they
confidered this money as going to be remitted .

given indications of this kind at Cæfar's death, that Cicero
in a letter written to Atticus foon afterwards, tells him, he
looked upon Antony as a man too much devoted to the
indulgencies of a luxurious life, to be inclined to form any
fchemes deftructive of the public repofe : *quem quidem ego* (fays
he) *epularum magis arbitror rationem habere, quam quidquam
mali cogitare.* Plut. in vit. Publicol. Ad Att. vi. 3.

[9] He was one of the tribunes for the prefent year.

[1] As proconful of Syria : to which province Caffius was
probably on his way, when this letter was written.

L 3

to

 to a public enemy? Wretched condition indeed! that we who fcorned to fubmit to a mafter, fhould more ignobly crouch to one of our fellow flaves! Neverthelefs, I am ftill inclined to flatter myfelf, that we are not quite deprived of all hopes of being delivered by your heroic efforts. But where then, let me afk, are your troops? And with this queftion I will conclude my letter: as I had rather leave the reft to be fuggefted by your own reflections, than by mine. Farewel.

LETTER XXVII.

TO CORNIFICIUS.

STratorius has given me an ample account of the fad fituation of affairs in your province [z]. Oh, my friend, what infufferable outrages are committed, in every part of the Roman dominions! But thofe which have been offered to yourfelf are fo much the lefs to be borne, as they are aggravated by the fuperior veneration which is due to your illuftrious rank and character. Notwithftanding therefore, that your great and generous fpirit may incline you to look upon thefe infults with calmnefs, and perhaps

___
[z] Of Africa. See rem. 6. p. 61. of this vol.

with

with indifference, yet you ought by no means to
suffer them to pass unchastised.

The news of Rome, I well know, is regularly
transmitted to you : otherwise I would take upon
myself to be your informer; and particularly of
the late attempt of Octavius [1]. The fact laid to
his charge, is considered by the populace as a mere
fiction of Antony, in order to gain a pretence to
seise upon the young man's estate. But the more
penetrating and better sort, not only credit the
report, but highly approve the design. Indeed,
the hopes of the republic are greatly turned
towards Octavius: as there is nothing which
his generous thirst of glory, 'tis believed, will
not animate him to perform. My friend An-
tony at the same time is so sensible of his being
generally detested, that altho' he discovered the

[1] " Octavius, in order to maintain by stratagem what he
" could not gain by force, formed a design against Antony's
" life, and actually provided certain slaves to assassinate
" him : who were discovered and seised with their poignards
" in Antony's house." Thus far Dr. Middleton : who might
have added (as a learned critic has remarked) that Cicero
himself, together with his nephew Quintus, were charged by
Antony with being accomplices in this plot: and that the
charge appears to have been true. For tho' in the present
letter indeed, Cicero talks of this affair, as if he was no
otherwise acquainted with it than by common report; yet in
a speech which he afterwards made in the senate, when An-
tony had retired into Gaul, taking notice of the above-men-
tioned accusation, he avows and glories in the charge. *Life
of Cic.* iii. 89. *Tunstal's observ. on the letters between Cic. and
Brut.* p. 142. *Philip.* iii. 7, 8.

L 4

assassins

A.U. 709.

 affaffins in his houfe, yet he would not venture to make the affair public. He fet out for Brundifium on the 9th of October, in order to meet the four legions [4] that are returning from Macedonia: he hopes by bribing them over to his intereft to conduct them to Rome, and with their affiftance to fix the yoke upon our necks. Thus you fee the fituation of the republic! if a republic indeed it may with any propriety be called, where all is in a ftate of inteftine war. I frequently lament your fortune in having been born fo late, as never to have tafted the happinefs of living in a found and well-regulated commonwealth. You remember the time, however, when there was a profpect at leaft, of better days: but now that profpect is no more! How in truth fhould it any longer fubfift, after Antony dared to declare in a general affembly of the people, that " Canutius affected to rank himfelf with " thofe [5] who could never appear in Rome, fo " long as he preferved his life and authority." But thanks to philofophy for having taught me to indure this and every other mortification, which human nature can poffibly fuffer: and indeed it has not only cured me of all my difquie-

---

[4] Thefe were part of that army which Cæfar intended to lead againft the Parthians; and which he had fent before him into Macedonia, to wait his arrival for that purpofe.

[5] The confpirators.

tudes,

tudes, but armed my breaft againſt every future A.U. 709. aſſault of fortune. And let me adviſe you to fortify yourſelf with the ſame reſolution; in the full perfuaſion, that nothing but guilt deſerves to be conſidered as a real evil. But theſe are reflections which you know much better how to make, than I can inſtruct you.

Stratorius has always been highly in my eſteem: but he has rendered himſelf more particularly ſo by the great diligence, fidelity and judgment he diſcovers in the management of your affairs.— Take care of your health, as the moſt pleaſing inſtance you can give me of your friendſhip. Farewel.

LETTER XXVIII.

To the Same.

MY very intimate and moſt accompliſhed friend Caius Anicius, has obtained a titular legation ⁶ into Africa, in order to tranſact ſome buſineſs relating to his private concerns in that province. Let me therefore intreat your beſt offices to him upon all occaſions, and that you would give him your aſſiſtance for the more eaſy and expeditious diſpatch of his affairs. But above all (as it is ſuperior to all in my friend's

⁶ See rem. 8. p. 84. of this vol.

eſti-

A.U.709. eſtimation) I recommend the dignity of his rank and character to your peculiar regard : and accordingly I make it my requeſt, that you would appoint lictors to attend him. This is a compliment which I always ſpontaneouſly paid during my own proconſulate, to thoſe of ſenatorial rank who came into my province ; and which I have ever likewiſe myſelf received upon the ſame occaſions : as indeed it is what I have both heard and obſerved to have been generally practiſed by proconſuls of the greateſt diſtinction. You will act then in the ſame manner, my dear Cornificius, in the preſent inſtance, if I have any ſhare in your affection ; and in all other reſpects will conſult the honour and intereſt of my friend : aſſuring yourſelf that you cannot confer upon me a more acceptable ſervice. Farewel.

LETTER XXIX.

To Tiro.

I See into your ſcheme : you have a deſign that *your* letters as well as mine [7] ſhould make their appearance in public. But tell

[7] It appears from an epiſtle to Atticus, that Cicero had formed a deſign about this time of publiſhing a collection of his letters. It is probable however that the greater part of thoſe which are now extant, were ſent into the world at dif-

me

me how happened it, that you who are wont A.U.709.
to be the fupreme judge and critic of my writ-
ings, fhould be guilty of fo inaccurate an ex-
preffion as to defire me " *faithfully* [s] to preferve
" my health ?" That adverb furely can have
no bufinefs there : as its proper employment is to
attend upon fome word that imports a moral
obligation.   In figurative language its ufe indeed
is various : as it may be applied even to inani-
mate and intellectual objects, provided (as Theo-
phraftus obferves) the metaphor be not too bold
and unnatural.   But we will referve this for a
converfation when we meet.

Demetrius has been here : but I had the
addrefs to avoid both him and his retinue.

---

ferent times, and by different hands, after his deceafe: as
there are many of them which one can fcarce fuppofe that
either himfelf, or any friend who had a regard to his memo-
ry, would have fuffered to come abroad. *Vid. Ad At.*
xvi. 5.

[s] It is impoffible, perhaps, to determine precifely, where-
in the impropriety of this expreffion confifted : as it does not
appear from the original whether Tiro fpoke of his own health
or of Cicero's.   In the tranflation however it is applied to the
latter : as it feems to render the expreffion lefs critically juft.
For as Tiro was Cicero's flave, the care of his health was a
duty which the former owed to the latter, as a neceffary
means of enabling him to perform thofe fervices to which Ci-
cero had a right.   According therefore to our author's own
remark concerning the literal ufe of the word *fidelis,* Tiro
might very properly have applied it in the fenfe here men-
tioned.   But there was no fuch duty owing from the mafter
to the flave : and confequently Tiro could not in ftrict pro-
priety have applied it to Cicero.

Doubtlefs,

A.U. 709. Doubtlefs, you will regret that you loft the opportunity of feeing him. It is an opportunity however which you may ftill recover: for he returns, it feems, to-morrow. Accordingly I purpofe to leave this place the next morning.

I am extremely uneafy about your health: and intreat you not to omit any means that may contribute to its re-eftablifhment. It is thus that you will render me infenfible of your abfence, and abundantly difcharge all the fervices I require at your hands.

I am obliged to your good offices towards Cufpius; for I greatly intereft myfelf in the fuccefs of his affairs. Adieu.

LETTER XXX.

To CORNIFICIUS.

QUintus Turius, who was an African merchant of great probity, as well as of an honourable family, is lately dead. He has appointed Cneius Saturninus, Sextus Aufidius, and Caius Anneius, together with Quintus Confidius Gallus, Lucius Servilius Pofthumus, and Caius Rubellius, all of them men of the fame worthy character as himfelf, his joint heirs. I find you have already treated them in fo generous a manner,

ner,

ner, that they have more occasion for my ac- A.U. 709.
knowledgments to you than my recommenda-
tion : and indeed the favours they gratefully pro-
fess to have received from your hands, are more
confiderable than I fhould have ventured per-
haps to requeft. Neverthelefs, as I perfectly
well know the regard you pay to my recommen-
dation, I will take courage; and intreat you to
add to thofe fervices which you have already,
without my follicitation, fo liberally conferred
upon them.   But what I am particularly to defire
is, that you would not fuffer Eros Turius, the
teftator's freedman, to continue to embezzle his
late patron's effects.   In every other inftance alfo
I recommend their intereft to your protection;
affuring you that you will receive much fatisfac-
tion from the regard and attachment of thefe my
illuftrious friends.   Again and again therefore I
very earneftly recommend them to your good
offices.   Farewel.

LETTER XXXI.

To Decimus Brutus, Conful elect.

A.U. 709.

WHEN our friend Lupus arrived with your difpatches, I had retired from Rome [9], to a place where I thought I could be moft fecure from danger. For this reafon, notwithftanding he took care that your letter [1] fhould be delivered into my hands, and continued fome days in the city, yet he returned without receiving my anfwer. However, I came back hither on the 9th of this month [2], when I immediately, as my firft and principal concern, paid a vifit to Panfa [3]: from whom I had the fatisfaction of hearing fuch an account of you, as was moft agreeable to my wifhes. As you wanted not any exhortations to engage you

[9] Soon after Cicero's late return to Rome, (fee rem. 3. p. 134. of this vol.) he came to an open rupture with Antony. He found it neceffary therefore for his fecurity to remove from the city to fome of his villas near Naples. *Life of Cic.* iii. 87.

[1] The fame probably which ftands the 21ft in the prefent book, p. 138.

[2] December. Antony had juft before left Rome, in order to march his army into Cifalpine Gaul. Upon the news of this retreat Cicero immediately returned to the city. *Life of Cic.* iii. 98.

[3] Conful elect for the enfuing year.

in

in the nobleſt enterpriſe [4] that ſtands recorded A.U.709.
in hiſtory; ſo I am perſuaded they are alto-
gether unneceſſary in the preſent conjuncture.
It may not be improper, neverthelefs, juſt to
intimate that the whole expectations of the Ro-
man people, and all their hopes of liberty, are
intirely fixed upon you. If you conſtantly bear
in mind (what I well know is ever in your
thoughts) the glorious part you have already
atchieved, moſt undoubtedly you can never for-
get how much there ſtill remains for you to per-
form. In fact, ſhould that man to whom I
always declared myſelf a friend till he openly
and forwardly took up arms againſt the re-
public; ſhould Antony poſſeſs himſelf of your
province [5], I ſee not the leaſt poſſibility of our
preſervation. I join my earneſt interceſſions
therefore, with thoſe of the whole republic,
that you would finiſh what you have ſo happily
begun, and deliver us for ever from the tyranny
of a deſpotic government. This patriot-taſk
belongs particularly to yourſelf: and Rome, or
to ſpeak more properly, every nation throughout
the world, not only expects but requires their
deliverance at your hands. But I am ſenſible
(as I have already ſaid) that you need no exhor-

[4] The killing of Cæſar.
[5] Ciſalpine Gaul.

tations

 tations to animate you for this purpofe. I will fpare my admonitions therefore, and rather affure you (what indeed is more properly my part) that my moft zealous and active fervices fhall always be exerted for your intereft. Be well perfuaded then, that not only for the fake of the republic, which is dearer to me than my life, but from my particular regard likewife to your-felf, I fhall omit no opportunity of forwarding your glorious defigns, and of promoting thofe honours you fo juftly deferve. Farewel.

LETTER XXXII.

To Cornificius.

THERE is no man that cultivates my friendfhip with greater marks of efteem than Sextus Aufidius: nor is there any of equef-trian rank, who bears a more diftinguifhed cha-racter. The ftrictnefs of his morals is fo hap-pily tempered with the fweetnefs of his difpofi-tion, that he unites the fevereft virtue with the eafieft and moft engaging addrefs. I recom-mend his affairs in Africa to you, with the ut-moft warmth and fincerity of my heart. You will extremely oblige me therefore by fhewing

him

him that you pay the higheſt regard to my re- A.U.709.
commendation : and I very earneſtly intreat you,
my dear Cornificius, to comply with this requeſt.
Farewel.

L E T T E R XXXIII.

To Decimus Brutus, Conſul elect.

MArcus Seius has, I ſuppoſe, informed you,
what my ſentiments were at the confe-
rence which Lupus held at my houſe with Libo,
your relation Servilius, and myſelf : as he was
preſent during the conſultation. And though
Greceius immediately followed him, he can give
you an account of all that paſſed after Seius ſet
out [6].

The grand and capital point, which I could
wiſh you to be well convinced of, and ever to
bear in your mind is, that in acting for the ſecurity
of our common liberties, you ought by no means
to wait the ſanction of the ſenate : as that aſſem-
bly is not yet ſufficiently free and uncontroled
in its deliberations. To conduct yourſelf by a

[6] The principal intent of this conſultation ſeems to have
been to determine, whether Decimus Brutus ſhould venture
without the expreſs ſanction of the ſenate, to act offenſively
againſt Antony : who was at this time on his march to diſ-
poſſeſs Brutus of Ciſalpine Gaul.

A.U. 709. contrary principle, would be to condemn the first glorious steps you took for the deliverance of the commonwealth; and which were so much the more illustrious, as they were unsupported by the formal suffrage of public authority. It would be to declare, that the measures of young Cæsar are rash and ill-considered: who in the same unauthorifed manner, has undertaken the important cause of the commonwealth [7]. In a word, it would be to shew the world that you thought those brave and worthy veterans your fellow-soldiers, together with the fourth and martial legions [8], had judged and acted irrationally in deeming their consul an enemy to his country, and confecrating their arms to the service of the

[7] When Antony set out for Brundifium in order to meet the legions which were returning from Macedonia, as has been related in the 27th letter of this book, Octavius went amongst those veteran foldiers to whom Cæfar had granted settlements in Campania. From thefe he drew together, at his own expence and by his private authority, a very confiderable body of troops to oppofe Antony, if he had thought proper to have made any attempts upon Rome with the Macedonian legions. *Philip*. ii. 2. 12. *Ad Att*. xvi. 8.

[8] The Roman legions were originally named according to the order in which they were raifed, as the *first*, the *fecond*, &c. But as thofe legions which were occafionally raifed in the provinces, were diftinguifhed likewife in the fame manner, it was ufual to add to this numeral defignation fome other, for the fake of avoiding confufion. This latter denomination was generally taken either from the country in which they ferved, as the *legio Parthica*, or from the name of the general who levied them, as the *legio Augufta*; or from the name of fome divinity, as in the prefent inftance, the *legio Martia*. *Rofin. de Antiq. Rom*. p. 966.

republic.

republic [9]. To purfue meafures which are agree-
able to the general fenfe of the fenate, may be
well confidered as acting under their exprefs au-
thority; when it is fear alone that reftrains them
from fignifying their approbation in a formal
manner.   In fine, you can no longer hefitate
whether you fhould be guided by the principle I
am recommending, as you have in two ftrong in-
ftances, been governed by it already: firft on the
ides of March, and lately when you raifed your
troops.   Upon the whole then, you ought to be
both difpofed and prepared to act, not merely as
you fhall be commanded, but in fuch a manner as
to render your atchievements the fubject of uni-
verfal admiration and applaufe.   Farewel.

L E T T E R XXXIV.

To the Same.

OUR friend Lupus very punctually deli-
vered your commands and your letter to
me, the next morning after his arrival in Rome:
which was in fix days from his leaving Mutina [1].

[9] Thefe two legions (part of thofe which arrived from
Macedonia) refufed the offers which Antony made to them
at Brundifium, and afterwards joined themfelves with
Octavius. *Ad Att.* xvi. 8. *Philip.* iii. 3.

[1] A city in Cifalpine Gaul, where Decimus Brutus was
fhortly afterwards befieged by Antony. It is now called
Modena.

M 2   I cannot

A.U.709. I cannot but confider you as recommending my
own honours to my protection, when you requeſt
me to be the guardian of yours : for be aſſured
they are equally my concern.   It will give me
great pleaſure therefore to find, that you doubt.
not of my promoting them upon every occaſion
to the beſt of my zeal and judgment.   Accord-
ingly, altho' I had purpoſed not to appear in the
ſenate before the firſt of January next, yet the
tribunes of the people having on that very day on
which your manifeſto [2] was publiſhed, iſſued out
a proclamation for a meeting of the ſenate on the
20th of this month [3], in order to move that a
guard might be appointed for the ſecurity of the
conſuls elect [4]; my affection towards you induced
me to change my reſolution, and I determined
to attend.   I thought indeed it would be a moſt
unpardonable omiſſion, if the ſenate ſhould be
holden without taking notice of your ineſtimable
ſervices to the republic ; as it unqueſtionably
would have been if I had not attended : or that
I ſhould not be preſent to ſupport any decree
that might happen to be propoſed for the ad-

[2] The purport of this manifeſto of Decimus Brutus, was
to declare his reſolution of endeavouring to preſerve the
province of Ciſalpine Gaul, over which he preſided, in its
allegiance to the republic. *Philip.* iii. 4.

[3] December.

[4] Hirtius and Panſa.

vancement

vancement of your honours. For this reason A.U. 709.
I came early into the senate: and my presence
brought together a great number of the members.
I will leave it to your other friends to inform you
what I there said to your advantage; as well as
of the speech which I afterwards made to the
same purpose, in a very numerous assembly of
the people [s]. In the mean time, let me intreat
you to believe, that I shall most zealously em-
brace every opportunity of contributing to the
increase of those dignities you already possess:
and altho' I am sensible I shall meet with many
rivals in my good offices for this purpose; yet
I will venture to claim the first rank in that ho-
nourable list. Farewel.

[s] These two speeches are the third and fourth of the
Philippics. The senate, amongst other decrees which they
passed upon this occasion, approved and ratified the mea-
sures which Decimus Brutus had taken in Cisalpine Gaul
for the defence of that province. *Philip.* iv. 4.

LET-

LETTER XXXV.

TO CORNIFICIUS.

A.U. 709.

I Am waging war here againſt that moſt iniqui-
tous of all ſanguinary ruffians, my collegue [6]
Antony : but by no means, however, upon equal
terms ; as I have nothing but my tongue to
oppoſe to his arms. He ventured in a ſpeech
which he lately made to the people, to throw
out ſome bitter invectives againſt you. But his
inſolence did not paſs unchaſtiſed : and he ſhall
have ſtill farther reaſon to remember, againſt
whom it is that he has thus pointed his injurious
attacks. But as your other friends, I imagine,
ſupply you with accounts of our tranſactions, I
ſhould rather inform you what turn affairs are
likely to take : and indeed it is a point of no
very difficult conjecture. The republic labours
under a total oppreſſion : her friends are without
a leader, and our glorious tyrannicides are diſ-
perſed into different and diſtant quarters. Panſa
means well to the commonwealth, and delivers
his ſentiments with great ſpirit and freedom.
Hirtius recovers but ſlowly [7] : and in truth, I

---

[6] Antony and Cicero were collegues as members of the
college of Augurs.

[7] Panſa and Hirtius, as has already been noted, were
conſuls elect for the approaching year. The latter about

know

know not what to think of him. Our only hope A.U. 709.
is, that the people at laſt will be awakened from
their lethargy, and act with a ſpirit becoming the
deſcendants of their heroic anceſtors. For myſelf
at leaſt, I will never be wanting to my country;
and whatever misfortune may attend the com-
monwealth after I have exerted my beſt efforts
to prevent it, I ſhall bear it with perfect equani-
mity.   You may depend likewiſe upon my ſup-
porting you in your rank and dignities, to the
utmoſt of my power.   Accordingly in an aſſem-
bly of the ſenate which was holden on the 20th of
this month [8], I propoſed (among other neceſſary
and important articles which I carried by a great
majority) that the preſent proconſuls ſhould be
continued in their reſpective governments ; and
that they ſhould be ordered not to reſign them
into other hands, than thoſe which the ſenate
ſhould appoint.   I made this motion, not only
as thinking it highly expedient for the intereſt of
the republic, but with a particular view alſo of
preſerving you in your provincial command [9].

this time was attacked by a moſt dangerous ſickneſs : and
his health was eſteemed of ſo much importance at this
juncture to the commonwealth, that public vows were put
up for his recovery. *Philip.* vii. 4.

  [8] December.

  [9] Antony, a ſhort time before he left Rome in order to
march againſt Decimus Brutus, had procured an illegal di-
ſtribution of the provinces among his friends : by which

M 4   Let

A.U. 709. Let me exhort you then for the fake of our country, and let me conjure you by your regard to myfelf, not to fuffer any man to ufurp the leaft part of your authority: but in every inftance to maintain the dignity of your rank and character, as a poffeffion which nothing can countervail.

To deal with you agreeably to that fincerity which our friendfhip requires; I muft tell you, that all the world would have highly applauded your conduct, if you had complied with my advice in regard to Sempronius. But the affair is now over: and in itfelf indeed, it was a matter of no great importance. It is of the utmoft, however, that you fhould employ, as I hope you will, every poffible mean to retain your province in its allegiance. I would add more, but your courier preffes me to difpatch: I muft intreat you therefore to make my excufes to Cherippus, for not writing to him by this opportunity. Farewel.

Caius Calvifius was appointed to fucceed Cornificius in Africa. *Philip.* iii. *Pigh. Annal.* ii. p. 465.

LETTER XXXVI.
Quintus Cicero to Tiro.

YOUR letter brought with it a very ftrong, A.U.709. tho' filent, reproof for my having thus long omitted writing to you. I could not indeed but be fenfible how much I had loft by my negligence, when I obferved that thofe points which my brother (from tendernefs, perhaps, or hafte) had but flightly touched in his letter, were faithfully reprefented in yours in all their genuine colours. This was particularly the cafe in refpect to what you mentioned concerning the confuls elect[a]. I know indeed that they are totally funk in floth and debauchery: and if they fhould not recede from the helm, we are in the utmoft danger of being irrecoverably loft. I was myfelf a witnefs during a fummer's campaign with them in Gaul, that they were guilty of fuch actions, and within fight too of the enemy's camp, as are almoft beyond all belief: and I am well perfuaded, unlefs we fhould be better fupported than we are at prefent, that the fcoundrel Antony will gain them over to his party, by admitting them as affociates in his licentious pleafures. The truth of it is, the re-

----

[a] Panfa and Hirtius.

public

A.U.709. public muft neceffarily either throw herfelf under the protection of the tribunes, or employ fome private hand to defend her caufe : for as to thefe noble confuls of ours ; one of them is fcarce worthy to prefide over Cæfena[1], and I would not truft the other with fuperintending the paltry hovels of Coffutius[2].

I hope to be with you towards the latter end of this month. In the mean while, let me repeat what I have often faid, that I tenderly love you. My impatience to fee you is indeed fo immoderate, that if our firft meeting were to happen in the midft of the forum, I fhould not forbear to tranfgrefs the rules of good breeding, and moft warmly embrace you in the prefence of the whole affembly. Farewel.

[1] " An obfcure town in Italy fituated upon the Papis : " a river which empties itfelf into the Adriatic between " Ufens and the Rubicon." Mr. *Rofs*.

[2] Who this perfon was, is unknown. Pique and prejudice feem to have had a confiderable hand in the draught, which Quintus has here delineated of the two confuls. That Panfa and Hirtius were infected with the fafhionable vices of the age, is altogether probable : but that they wanted either fpirit or capacity for action, is by no means true ; as will evidently appear in the farther progrefs of thefe letters.

L E T T E R XXXVII.

Cicero the Son [1], to his deareſt Tiro.

AFTER having been in daily and earneſt expectation of your couriers, they are at length, to my great ſatisfaction, arrived; having performed their voyage in forty-ſix days from the time they left you. The joy I received from my dear father's moſt affectionate letter, was crowned by the very agreeable one which attended it from yourſelf. I can no longer repent therefore of having neglected writing to you; as it has proved a mean of furniſhing me with an ample proof of your good-nature: and it is with much pleaſure I find, that you admit the apology I made for my ſilence.

That the advantageous reports you have heard of my conduct, were perfectly agreeable, my deareſt Tiro, to your wiſhes, I can by no means doubt: and it ſhall be my conſtant endeavour

A.U. 709.

---

[1] He was at this time purſuing his ſtudies at Athens under the direction of Cratippus, one of the moſt celebrated philoſophers of the peripatetic ſect. If young Cicero had not the talents of his father; his genius however ſeems by no means to have been contemptible: and the preſent letter, written when he was but nineteen years of age, is a full confutation of thoſe who have charged him with a want of ſenſe even to a degree of ſtupidity. See p. 320. of this vol.

 to confirm and increase the general good opinion
which is thus arising in my favour.   You may
venture therefore with great confidence to be,
what you obligingly promise, the herald of my
fame.   Indeed, I reflect with so much pain and
contrition of mind on the errors into which my
youth and inexperience have betrayed me, that
I not only look upon them with abhorrence,
but cannot bear even to hear them mentioned:
and I am well convinced, that you take a part
in the uneasiness which I suffer from this cir-
cumstance.   It is no wonder you should be
sollicitous for the welfare of a person, whom
both interest and inclination recommend to your
good wishes: as I have ever been desirous you
should partake of all the advantages that attend
me.   But if my conduct has formerly given you
pain; it shall henceforward, be assured, afford
you reason to think of me with double satis-
faction.

I live with Cratippus rather as his son, than
his pupil : and not only attend his lectures with
pleasure, but am extremely delighted with the
peculiar sweetness of his conversation.   Accord-
ingly I spend whole days in his company, and
frequently indeed, the most part of the night:
as I intreat him to sup with me as often as his
engagements will permit. Since the introduction

of

of this cuftom, he every now and then unex-   A.U. 709.
pectedly fteals in upon us while we are at table;
and laying afide the feverity of the philofopher,
enters with great good humour into all the mirth
and pleafantry of our converfation.   Let me re-
queft you then to haften hither as foon as pof-
fible, in order to enjoy with us the fociety of
this moft agreeable and excellent man.   As to
Bruttius, I never fuffer him to be abfent from
me a fingle moment.   His company is as enter-
taining, as his conduct is exemplary: and he
perfectly well knows how to reconcile mirth and
good humour with the ferious difquifitions of
philofophy.   I have taken a houfe for him near
mine; and affift his narrow fortunes as far as
my flender finances will admit [5].

I have begun to declaim in Greek under Caf-
fius; as I choofe to employ myfelf in Latin ex-
ercifes of that kind with Bruttius.   I live in
great familiarity alfo with thofe learned and ap-
proved friends of Cratippus, whom he brought
with him from Mitylene: and pafs much of my
time likewife with Epicrates, one of the moft
confiderable perfons in Athens, together with
Leonides, and feveral others of the fame rank

---

[5] The allowance which Cicero made to his fon during
his refidence at Athens, was about 700 _l._ a year. _Vid. Ad
Att._ xvi. 1.

and

 and merit. Thus I have given you a general sketch of my life.

As to what you mention concerning Gorgias; notwithstanding that he was of service to me in my oratorical exercises, yet my father's commands were superior to all other confiderations: and as he peremptorily wrote to me that I fhould immediately difmifs him [6], I have obeyed his injunctions. I would not fuffer myfelf indeed to hefitate a moment; left my reluctance fhould raife any fufpicions in my father to my difadvantage. Befides, I thought it would ill become me, to take upon myfelf to be a judge of the propriety of his orders. I am extremely obliged to you however, for the friendly advice you give me in this affair.

I very readily admit the excufe you make on account of your want of leifure; perfectly well knowing how much your time is generally engaged. I am extremely glad to hear that you have bought a farm: and wifh you much joy of the purchafe. But you muft not wonder that I deferred my congratulations to this part of my letter; for you will remember it was about

---

[6] This unworthy tutor had encouraged his pupil in a paffion for drinking: a vice, in which the young Cicero, how fincere foever he might have been in his prefent refolves, moft fhamefully fignalifed himfelf in his more mature years. *Plut. in vit. Cic. Plin. Hift. Nat.* xiv. 22.

the

the fame place in yours that you communicated A.U. 709.
to me the occafion of them. You have now a
retreat from all the fatiguing ceremonies of the
city, and are become a Roman of the true old
rural kind [7]. I take pleafure in figuring you to
myfelf in the midft of your country-employ-
ments, buying your tools of hufbandry, dealing
out your orders to your bailiff, and carefully
treafuring up the fruit-feeds from your defert.
To be ferious; I fincerely join with you in re-
gretting, that I could not be of fervice to you
upon this occafion. But be affured, my dear
Tiro, I fhall not fail to affift you, if ever for-
tune fhould put it in my power: efpecially as I
am fenfible you made this purchafe with a view
to my ufe as well as your own.

I am obliged to your care in executing my
commiffion. I defire you would fee that I have
a writer fent to me who underftands Greek: as I
lofe much time in tranfcribing my lectures. But
above all, I intreat you to take care of your
health, that we may have the pleafure of enjoy-
ing together many philofophical converfations.
I recommend Antherus to your good offices, and
bid you farewel.

[7] Alluding, perhaps, to thofe celebrated Romans in the
earlier ages of the republic, who after having been called
forth from their farms to the fervice of their country, dif-
charged with glory the functions of the ftate, and then re-
turned to their ploughs.

LET.

LETTER XXXVIII.

From the SAME, to TIRO.

A.U.709. **T**HE reasons you assign for the intermission of your letters, are perfectly just: but I hope, that these excuses will not very frequently recur. 'Tis true, I receive intelligence of public affairs from particular expresses, as well as from general report; and am continually assured likewise of my father's affection, by his own hand; yet I always take great pleasure in reading a letter from yourself, be it upon ever so trifling a subject. I hope, therefore, since I am thus earnestly desirous of hearing from you, that you will not for the future send me apologies instead of epistles.   Farewel.

LETTER XXXIX.

BITHYNICUS [8] to CICERO.

IF we were not mutually attached to each other by many singular good offices, I should remind you of that friendship which formerly subsisted between our parents: but I leave arguments of this kind to those, who have neglected to im-

* See rem. 6. p. 89. of this vol.

prove

prove their hereditary connections.   For myfelf, A.U.709.
I am well fatisfied with going no farther for my
claim to your fervices, than to our own perfonal
amity.   In confidence of which let me intreat
you, if you believe that none of your favours will
be thrown away upon me, that you would upon
all occafions during my abfence [9] take my inte-
refts under your protection.   Farewel.

[9] In Sicily: to which province he fucceeded as governor
at the expiration of his prætorfhip. *Pigh. Annal.* iii. p. 476.

LETTERS

OF
Marcus Tullius Cicero
TO
Several of his FRIENDS.

BOOK XIII.

LETTER I.

TO CORNIFICIUS [1].

I Neglect no opportunity (and indeed if I did A.U.710. I should fail in what you have a full right to expect from me) not only of celebrating your merit, but of promoting those honours it so justly deserves. But I choose you should be informed of my zealous endeavours for this

[1] See rem. 6. p. 61. of this vol.

purpose,

A.U.710. purpofe, by the letters of your family, rather than by my hand.   Let me employ it in exhorting you to turn all your care and your attention upon the republic.   This is an object worthy of your fpirit, and your talents: as it is agreeable likewife to thofe hopes which you ought to entertain, of ftill rifing in the dignities of your country.   But this is a topic I will enlarge upon another time.   In the mean while, I will inform you that the public affairs are totally in fufpence ; as the commiffioners are not yet returned, whom the fenate deputed to Antony; not to fue for peace indeed, but to denounce war, unlefs he fhall immediately pay obedience to the orders with which they are charged [2].

I feifed the firft occafion that offered of refuming my former fpirit, in ftanding forth as the protector both of the fenate and the people : and

[2] Thefe injunctions were, that Antony fhould inftantly quit the fiege of Modena, and defift from all hoftilities in Gaul.   Cicero ftrongly oppofed the fending this deputation ; as it was below the dignity of the fenate to enter into any fort of treaty with a man whom they had already in effect, declared a public enemy ; as it would have the appearance of fear ; and as the only method of bringing Antony to his duty would be by an immediate and vigorous profecution of the war.   But thefe reafons, and others of the fame tendency which Cicero urged with great warmth and eloquence, were over-ruled by the friends of Antony : and it was ordered that Servius Sulpicius, Lucius Pifo, and Lucius Philippus, all of them perfons of confular rank, fhould carry this meffage from the fenate to Antony. *Vid.* *Philip.* v.

from

from the moment I thus declared myfelf the ad-
vocate of liberty, I have not loft the leaft favour-
able opportunity for the defence of our com-
mon rights.   But this likewife is an article for
which I choofe to refer you to the information of
others.

It is with all poffible warmth and earneftnefs
that I recommend Titus Pinarius to your favour,
as one who, not only from a fimilitude of tafte
and ftudies, but as he is poffeffed alfo of every
amiable virtue, engages my ftrongeft affection.
He comes into your province in order to fuper-
intend the affairs of Dionyfius : who as he is
much, I am fenfible, in your efteem, fo no man
ftands higher in mine.   Unneceffary therefore as
I know it to be to recommend his interefts to
your protection, yet I cannot forbear doing fo :
and I doubt not of your giving occafion to the
very grateful Pinarius of fending me a letter of
acknowledgment for your good offices both to
himfelf and to Dionyfius.   Farewel.

LETTER II.

TO DECIMUS BRUTUS, Consul elect.

A.U. 710.   POLLA[3] sends me word that an opportunity offers of conveying a letter to you: but at present I have nothing material to write. All public business indeed is intirely suspended, till we shall hear what success the deputies[4] have met with: from whom we have not yet received any intelligence. I will take this occasion however of telling you, that the senate and the people are greatly anxious concerning you; not only as their own preservation depends upon yours, but as they are extremely sollicitous that you should acquit yourself with glory. The truth is, you are in a very remarkable degree the general affection of the whole republic; which confidently hopes, that as you lately delivered us from one tyrant[5], so you will now free us from the danger of another[6].

We are raising troops[7] in Rome and throughout all Italy, if that term may with any propriety

---

[3] The wife of Decimus Brutus.
[4] Those mentioned in the preceding letter.
[5] Cæsar.
[6] Antony.
[7] The senate did not suspend their preparations for war, notwithstanding the deputation they had sent to Antony.

be

be employed, where every man eagerly preſſes A.U.710.
to enter into the ſervice: ſo warmly are the
people animated with a paſſion of recovering
their liberties, and ſuch is their abhorrence of
the ſlavery they have thus long ſuſtained!

We now expect ſoon to receive an account from
you, not only of your own operations, but of
thoſe likewiſe of our common friend Hirtius, and
of Cæſar, whom I muſt particularly call *mine:*
I hope ſhortly to ſee you all three united in the
general honour of one common victory. For
the reſt, I have only to add (what I had rather
you ſhould learn however from the letters of
your family, and what I hope they are ſo juſt
as to aſſure you) that I neither do, nor ever ſhall
neglect any opportunity of contributing to the
advancement of your public honours. Farewel.

On the contrary, Hirtius and Octavius marched into Gaul
at the head of a conſiderable army, while Panſa remained
in Italy, in order to complete the additional troops with
which he purpoſed to join them. *Life of Cir.* iii. 121.

LETTER III.

To Plancus [8].

A.U. 710. THE visit I lately received from Furnius [9] afforded me great satisfaction, not only upon his own account, but more particularly on yours; as he painted you so strongly to my mind that I could not but fancy during the whole conversation, that you were actually present. He represented to me the heroism you display in the military affairs of your province; the equity of your civil administration; the prudence which distinguishes every part of your conduct in general; together with what I was by no means indeed a stranger to before, the charms of your social and friendly qualities. To this he did not forget to add likewise, the singular generosity which you have shewn in your behaviour towards himself. Every one of these articles I heard with pleasure: and for the last I am much obliged to you [1].

The friendship I enjoy with your family, my dear Plancus, commenced somewhat before you

---

[8] See rem. 2. p. 134. of this vol.

[9] He was one of the lieutenants of Plancus.

[1] Furnius had been particularly recommended by Cicero to the favour of Plancus. See let. 20. of the preceding Book.

were

were born: and as the affection which I conceived
for you, begun from your childhood, so in your
more mature years it was mutually improved
into the strictest intimacy.   These are considerations which strongly engage me to favour your
interests: which I look upon indeed as my own.
Merit in conjunction with fortune have crowned
you, even thus early in your life, with the highest
distinctions: as the diligent exertion of your
superior talents, has frustrated the opposition of
those many envious antagonists, who vainly endeavoured to obstruct your way.   And now, if
you will be influenced by the advice of a man
who greatly loves you, and who from a long
connection with you has an equal claim to your
regard with the oldest of your friends; you will
receive all the future honours of your life from
the republic in its best and most constitutional
form.   There was a season, you know, (for
nothing surely could have escaped your discernment) there was a season [a] when the world
thought you too compliant with the prevailing
faction of the times: and I should have
thought so too, if I had imagined that your
approbation was to be measured by your submission.   But as I knew the sentiments of your

---

[a] During Cæsar's usurpation.

heart,

A.U.710. heart, I was perfuaded you had prudently con-
fidered the extent of your power. Public
affairs however are at prefent in a far different
fituation; and you may now freely act in every
point as your judgment fhall direct. The time
is fhortly approaching, when in confequence of
your prefent defignation, you will enter upon
the confular office[1]: and you will enter upon it,
my friend, in the prime of your years; with the
advantage of poffefling the nobleft and moft
commanding eloquence; and at a period too
when there is the utmoft fcarcity of fuch il-
luftrious citizens as yourfelf. Let me conjure
you then by the immortal gods, moft earneftly
to purfue thofe meafures that will infure the
higheft glory to your character. Now there
is but one poffible method of acting towards
the republic with this advantage to your reputa-
tion: at leaft there is but one in the prefent con-
juncture, as the commonwealth has for fo many
years[+] been difturbed by our inteftine commo-
tions.

When I write to you in this ftrain, it is rather
in compliance with the dictates of my affection,
than as fuppofing that you ftand in need either of
precepts or admonitions. I am fenfible that

[1] See rem. 5. p. 136. of this vol.
[+] The civil wars had now continued about feven years.

you

you are sufficiently supplied with reflections of A.U. 710.
this nature, from the same source whence I derive
them myself: it is time therefore to put an end
to what I designed, not as an ostentation of my
wisdom, but merely as an instance of my friend-
ship. I will only add, that you may depend
upon the most zealous of my services upon every
occasion, wherein I shall imagine your credit
and character is concerned.   Farewel.

L E T T E R IV.

Plancus to Cicero.

I Am exceedingly obliged to you for your
letter [s] : a favour, for which I am indebted,
I perceive, to the account that Furnius gave
of me in the conversation you mention. If I
have not written to you sooner, you must impute
it to my being informed that you were set
out upon your expedition into Greece: and I
was not apprised of your return till a very short
time before I learned it from your letter. I
mention this because I should think myself de-
serving of the highest reproach, if I were inten-
tionally guilty of an omission even in the slightest

[s] The preceding epistle.

office

 office of friendſhip towards you.   The intimacy
indeed which was contracted between you and my
father; the early eſteem I conceived of your
merit, together with thoſe inſtances of affection
I have received from you; ſupply me with many
powerful reaſons for not failing in the regards I
owe you.   Be aſſured therefore, my dear Cicero,
there is no man whom I am ſo much diſpoſed to
revere as yourſelf: as indeed the great diſparity
of our ages, may well juſtify me in looking up
to you with all the ſacred reſpect of filial vene-
ration.   I received your admonitions therefore,
as ſo many dictates of the moſt conſummate
wiſdom ; at the ſame time that I conſidered them
as inſtances likewiſe of your unfeigned ſincerity :
for in this reſpect I judge of *your* heart by what
I feel in my *own*.   If I had any doubt then what
meaſures to purſue, or were inclined to adopt
others than thoſe you recommend; I ſhould
moſt certainly be determined by your judgment,
or reſtrained by your advice : but in my preſent
ſituation, can there poſſibly be an inducement to
draw me from thoſe paths you point out? The
truth is, that whatever honourable diſtinctions I
have acquired either by my own induſtry, or by
the favours of fortune, tho' far inferior to what
your affection repreſents them; yet they want no
other luſtre perhaps, but that of having been

attain...

attained with the general approbation of the com- A.U. 710. monwealth : and this even the moſt inveterate of my enemies acknowledge.   Be aſſured then, that the whole of my power, my prudence and my authority, ſhall ever be exerted in the ſervice of the republic.   As I am no ſtranger to your ſentiments, I am well perſuaded that mine would never diſagree with yours, if I had the happineſs of having you ſo near me as to be able to conſult them.   But tho' I cannot enjoy this very deſirable advantage, yet I truſt you will never have occaſion to condemn my conduct.

I am extremely impatient to learn what is tranſacting in the nearer Gaul [6], as well as what effect the preſent month [7] may produce in regard to affairs at Rome.   In the mean time, I am earneſtly labouring to prevent the people of this province from purſuing the example of their neighbours, by taking advantage of the public diſturbances to throw off their allegiance. And ſhould my endeavours be attended with the ſucceſs they deſerve, I doubt not of being approved, not only by every friend of liberty in general, but,

[6] Where Decimus Brutus commanded, who at this time was actually beſieged in Modena by Mark Antony : a circumſtance, to which Plancus, 'tis probable, was no ſtranger, though he thought proper to affect ignorance.

[7] January : when the new conſuls always entered upon their office.   The conſuls for the preſent year were Hirtius and Panſa.

what

A.U.710. what I am moft ambitious of, by yourfelf in particular. Farewel, my dear Cicero, and love me with an equal return of that affection I bear you.

LETTER V.

To Plancus.

THE duplicate you fent me of your letter [*] was an inftance of your obliging care left I fhould be difappointed of what I fo impatiently wifhed to receive. The contents afforded me a double fatisfaction; and I am at a lofs to determine whether the friendfhip you profefs for myfelf, or the zeal you difcover for the republic, rendered it moft truly acceptable. To fpeak my own opinion indeed, the public affections are altogether noble and fublime; but furely there is fomething more amiably fweet in thofe of the private kind. Accordingly that part of your letter where you remind me of the intimacy in which I lived with your father, of the early difpofition you found in yourfelf to love me, together with other paffages to the fame friendly purpofe, filled my heart with the moft exquifite pleafure; as

[*] The foregoing.

                                    the

the sentiments you profess with regard to the A.U. 710.
commonwealth, raised in me the highest satis-
faction: and to say truth, I was so much the
more pleased with the latter, as they were ac-
companied at the same time with the former.

To repeat what I said in the letter to which
you have returned so obliging an answer, let me
not only exhort, but intreat you, my dear Plan-
cus, to exert your utmost powers in the service
of the commonwealth. There is nothing that
can more contribute to the advancement of your
glory: for amongst all human honours, none
most certainly is superior to that of deserving
well of one's country. Your great good sense
and good nature will suffer me, I know, to speak
my sentiments to you with the same freedom
that I have hitherto used. Let me again observe
then, that the honours you have already acquired,
tho' you could not indeed have attained to them
without merit, yet they have principally been
owing to fortune, in conjunction with the par-
ticular circumstances of the times. But whatever
services you shall perform for the republic in this
very critical conjuncture, will reflect a lustre upon
your character that will derive all its splendour
from yourself alone. It is incredible how odious
Antony is become to all sorts of people, except

those

A.U. 710. thofe only of the fame difhoneft views with him-
felf: but the great hopes and expectations of the
republic, are fixed upon you and the army you
command. Let me conjure you then in the
moft folemn manner, not to lofe fo important
an opportunity of eftablifhing yourfelf in the
efteem and favour of your fellow-citizens, or in
other words, of gathering immortal praife. Be-
lieve me, it is with all the tendernefs of a father
that I thus admonifh you; that I enter into your
interefts with as much warmth as if they were my
own; and that my exhortations proceed from
the zeal I bear for the glory of my friend, and
for the welfare of my country. Adieu.

LETTER VI.

To Caius Cassius.

OH, that you had invited me to that glo-
rious feaft you exhibited on the ides of
March! Be affured I would have fuffered none
of it to have gone off untouched [9]. Whereas
the part you unhappily fpared, occafions me,
above all others, more trouble than you can
well imagine. I muft acknowledge at the fame

[9] Alluding to the confpirators having fpared Antony when
they deftroyed Cæfar. See rem. 8. p. 148. of this vol.

time,

time, that we have two moſt excellent conſuls [a] : A.U. 710. but as to thoſe of conſular rank, there is not one of them who does not merit the higheſt reproach. The ſenate in general however, exert themſelves with ſpirit : as the lower order of magiſtrates diſtinguiſh themſelves by their ſingular reſolution and zeal. In a word, it is impoſſible to ſhew a better or more vigorous diſpoſition than appears in the populace, not only of Rome, but throughout all Italy. But Philippus and Piſo, on the contrary, whom the ſenate deputed with peremptory orders to Antony [b], have executed their commiſſion in a manner that raiſes our higheſt indignation. For notwithſtanding that Antony refuſed to comply with every ſingle article of the ſenate's injunctions; yet theſe unworthy deputies had the meanneſs to charge themſelves with bringing back the moſt inſolent demands [c]. This behaviour of theirs has occaſioned all the world to

[a] Hirtius and Panſa.
[b] See rem. 2. on let. 1. of this book.
[c] " The purport of them was, that the ſenate ſhould aſſign
" lands and rewards to all his troops, and confirm all the
" other grants which he and Dolabella had made in their
" conſulſhip : that all his decrees from Cæſar's books and
" papers ſhould be confirmed : that no account ſhould be
" demanded of the money taken from the temple of Opis, &c.
" On theſe terms he offered to give up Ciſalpine Gaul, pro-
" vided, that he might have the greater Gaul in exchange
" for five years, with an army of ſix legions, to be completed
" out of the troops of Decimus Brutus." *Life of Cic.* iii.
123.

 have recourse to my assistance, and I am become extremely popular, in a way wherein popularity is seldom acquired: I mean by supporting a good cause.

I am altogether ignorant in what part of the world you are at present, as well as of what schemes you are either executing or meditating. A report prevails that you are gone into Syria: but for this we have no certain authority. We can a little more depend upon the accounts we receive of Brutus, as his distance from us is less remote [3].

It has been remarked here by men of some pleasantry, and much indignation against Dolabella, that he has shewn himself in too great haste to be your *successor*: as he is most uncivilly set out to take *possession* of your government when you have enjoyed it scarce a single month [4]. 'The case is clear therefore, say they, that Cassius should by no means give him admittance.' But

---

[3] Marcus Brutus when he found it necessary to leave Italy, withdrew into Macedonia, where he was at this time employed in raising forces in support of the republican cause.

[4] The province of Syria had been intended by Cæsar for Cassius: but Mark Antony, after the death of Cæsar, had artfully procured it to be allotted to Dolabella. Accordingly the latter left Rome, a short time before the expiration of his consulship the last year, in order to be beforehand with Cassius in getting possession of this government: and it is in allusion to this circumstance that the humour of the present passage, such as it is, consists.

to be ferious: both you and Brutus are men- A.U.710.
tioned with the higheft applaufe; as it is gene-
rally fuppofed that each of you has drawn toge-
ther an army far beyond our expectations.——
I would add more, if I knew with certainty the
fituation of yourfelf and your affairs: but I
hazard this letter merely upon the doubtful cre-
dit of common fame.   It is with great impa-
tience therefore that I wait for better intelligence
from your own hand.   Farewel.

L E T T E R   VII.

To Trebonius[5].

WOULD to Heaven you had invited me to
that noble feaft which you made on the
ides of March: no remnants, moft affuredly,
fhould have been left behind[6].   Whereas the
part you unluckily fpared gives us fo much per-
plexity, that we find fomething to regret even in
the godlike fervice which you and your illuftri-
ous affociates have lately rendered to the republic.
To fay the truth, when I reflect that it is owing
to the favour of fo worthy a man as yourfelf, that
Antony now lives to be our general bane; I am

<hr>

[5] He was at this time in Afia Minor: of which province
he was governor.   See rem. 8. p. 99. of this vol.

[6] See rem. 9. on the preceding letter.

O 2

fome-

A.U. 710. sometimes inclined to be a little angry with you for taking him aside when Cæsar fell [7] : as by this mean you have occasioned more trouble to myself in particular, than to all the rest of the whole community. From the very first moment indeed that Antony's ignominious departure from Rome [8], had left the senate uncontrouled in its deliberations, I resumed the spirit which you and that inflexible patriot your father were wont to esteem and applaud. Accordingly, the tribunes of the people having summoned the senate to meet on the 20th of December, upon other matters; I seised that opportunity of taking the whole state of the republic into consideration [9] : and more by the

[7] As it had been resolved in a council of the conspirators, that Antony's life should be spared, they did not choose he should be present when they executed their design upon Cæsar; probably lest he should attempt to assist his friend, and by that means occasion them to spill more blood than they intended. For this reason Trebonius held Antony in discourse at the entrance into the senate, till the rest of the conspirators had finished their work. *Dio. p.* 249. *Plut. in vit. Brut.*

[8] Upon the news that two of the four legions from Brundisium [see rem. 4. p. 152. of this vol.] had actually declared for Octavius and posted themselves in the neighbourhood of Rome, Antony left the city with great precipitation; and putting himself at the head of his army, marched directly in order to wrest Cisalpine Gaul out of the hands of Decimus Brutus. Cicero, who was at this time in the country, took the opportunity of Antony's absence to return to Rome: where he arrived on the 9th of December in the preceding year, about a month or two, 'tis probable, before he wrote the present letter. *See Life of Cic.* iii. 97.

[9] It was upon this occasion that Cicero spoke his third Philippic.

zeal than the eloquence of my fpeech, I revived
the drooping fpirits of that oppreffed affembly,
and awakened in them all their former vigour. It
was owing to the ardour with which I thus con-
tended in the debates of this day, that the people
of Rome firft conceived a hope of recovering their
liberties : and to this great point all my thoughts
and all my actions have ever fince been perpetual-
ly directed.   Thus important however as my oc-
cupations are, I would enter into a full detail of
our proceedings, if I did not imagine that pub-
lic tranfactions of every kind are tranfmitted to
you by other hands.   From them therefore you
will receive a more particular information;
whilft I content myfelf with giving you a fhort
and general fketch of our prefent circumftances
and fituation.   I muft inform you then, we have
a fenate that acts with fpirit ; but that as to thofe
of confular dignity, part of them want the cou-
rage to exert themfelves in the manner they
ought, and the reft are ill-affected to the repub-
lic.   The death of Servius [1] is a great lofs to
us.   Lucius Cæfar [2], tho' he is altogether in

---

[1] Servius Sulpicius : to whom feveral letters in the fore-
going part of this collection are addreffed. He was one,
and the moft confiderable, of the three confulars whom the
fenate had lately deputed to Antony : but very unfortunate-
ly for that embaffy, he died juft as he arrived in Antony's
camp. *Phil.* ix. 1.

[2] See rem. 5. p. 94. of this vol.

A.U. 710. the intereſt of liberty, yet in tenderneſs to his
nephew [3] does not concur in any very vigo-
rous meaſure.   The conſuls [4] in the mean time
deſerve the higheſt commendations : I muſt
mention Decimus Brutus likewiſe with much ap-
plauſe.   The conduct of young Cæſar alſo is
equally laudable : and I perſuade myſelf that
we have reaſon to hope he will complete the work
he has begun.   This at leaſt is certain, that if
he had not been ſo extremely expeditious in
raiſing the veteran forces [a], and if two legions
had not deſerted to him from Antony's army,
there is nothing ſo cruel or ſo flagitious which
the latter would not have committed.——But as
theſe are articles which I ſuppoſe you are already
appriſed of, I only juſt mention them in order to
confirm them.

You ſhall hear farther from me, whenever
I can find a more leiſure moment.   Farewel.

[3] Antony.
[4] Hirtius and Panſa.
[a] See rem. 7. p. 162. of this vol.

L E T T E R VIII.

To Caius Cassius.

IT is owing, I imagine, to the difficulty of for- A.U. 710.
warding any difpatches during the winter
feafon, that we have yet received no certain in-
telligence of what you are doing, nor even know
in what part of the world you are placed.   It is
univerfally reported however (tho' more I believe
from what people wifh, than from what they
have fufficient grounds to affert) that you have
raifed an army and are actually in Syria : a re-
port which the more eafily gains credit, as it ap-
pears to be extremely probable.

Our friend Brutus has acquired great honour by
his late glorious and unexpected atchievements [5];
not only as being in themfelves extremely de-
firable to the friends of liberty, but from the
wonderful expedition likewife with which he per-
formed them.   If it be true therefore that you
are in poffeffion of thofe provinces we imagine;
the republic is very powerfully fupported : as

---

[5] He had lately fent an account to the fenate of his fuccefs
againft Caius the brother of Mark Antony; having forced
him to retire with a few cohorts to Apollonia, and fecured
Macedonia, Illyricum, and Greece, together with the feve-
ral armies in thofe countries, to the intereft of the republic.
Vid. Philip. x.

O 4

that

 that whole tract of country which extends from the neareſt coaſt of Greece as far as Egypt, is upon this ſuppoſition in the hands of two the moſt faithful friends of the commonwealth. Neverthelefs if my judgment does not deceive me, the event of this war depends entirely upon Decimus Brutus : for if he ſhould be able to force his way out of Mutina, (as we have reaſon to hope) it will in all probability be totally at an end. There are now indeed but few troops employed in carrying on that ſiege : as Antony has ſent a large detachment to keep poſſeſſion of Bononia [6]. In the mean while our friend Hirtius is poſted at Ciaterna [7], and Cæſar at Forum-Cornelii [8], each of them at the head of a very conſiderable army : at the ſame time that Panſa is raiſing at Rome a large body of Italian troops. But the ſeaſon of the year has hitherto prevented their entering upon action : and indeed Hirtius appears by the ſeveral letters I have received from him, to be determined to take all his meaſures with the utmoſt precaution.

Both the Gauls, excepting only the cities of Bononia, Regium, and Parma, are zealouſly affected to the republic : as are alſo your clients

[6] Bologna.
[7] Quaderna.
[8] Imola.

on the other side the Po.   The senate likewise is A.U. 710.
firm in the cause of liberty : but when I say the
senate, I must exclude all of consular rank, ex-
cept Lucius Cæsar, who indeed is faithfully at-
tached to the interest of the commonwealth. The
death of Servius Sulpicius has deprived us of a
very powerful associate.   As for the rest of the
consulars ; part of them are ill-affected to the re-
public, others want spirit to support its cause,
and some there are who look with envy on those
patriot citizens whose conduct they see distin-
guished by the public applause.   The populace
however, both in Rome and throughout all Italy,
are wonderfully unanimous in the common cause.
—I have nothing farther, I think, to add, but
my wishes that your heroic virtues may shine out
upon us from yon eastern regions, in all their
enlivening warmth and lustre.   Farewel.

L E T T E R IX.

To Lucius Papirius Pætus [7].

I Have received a second letter from you, con-
cerning your friend Rufus : and since you in-
terest yourself thus warmly in his behalf, you
might depend upon my utmost assistance, even if

[7] See rem. 1. p. 15. vol. ii.

he

A.U. 710. he had done me an injury.   But I am perfectly
senfible from thofe letters of his which you com-
municated to me, as well as from your own, how
much my welfare has been his concern.   I cannot
therefore refufe him my friendly offices, not only
in regard to your recommendation, which has all
the weight with me it ought, but in compliance
alfo with my own inclinations.   I muft acknow-
ledge that it was his and your letters, my dear
Pætus, which firft put me upon my guard againft
the defigns that were formed to deftroy me[8].   I
afterwards indeed received intelligence from fe-
veral other hands to the fame effect, and particu-
larly of the confultations that were held concern-
ing me both at Aquinium and Fabrateria[9] : of
which meetings, I find, you were likewife ap-
prifed.   One would imagine that this party had
forefeen how much I fhould embarrafs their
fchemes, by the induftry they employed in order
to compafs my deftruction : and as I had not the
leaft fufpicion of their purpofes, I might incau-

[8] This probably alludes to fome defign of the veteran fol-
diers againft Cicero's life : as it appears from a letter to At-
ticus written foon after Cæfar's death, that our author had
been cautioned not to truft himfelf in Rome on account of
the danger to which he would be expofed from the infolence
of thofe troops. *Vid. Ad At.* xv. 5.

[9] Thefe towns were fituated in Latium, or what is now
called the Campagna di Roma.   They ftill fubfift under the
names of *Aquino* and *Fabratera.*

tioufly

tioufly have fallen into their fnares, if it had not been for the admonitions you fent me in confequence of the information you had received from Rufus.   Your friend therefore wants no advocate with me for my good offices : and I wifh the republic may be in fo happy a fituation, as to afford me an opportunity of giving him the moft fubftantial proofs of my gratitude.

But to difmifs this fubject: I am forry you no longer frequent the feftive tables of your friends; as you cannot renounce thefe parties of good chear, without depriving yourfelf of a very exquifite gratification.   And to tell you the truth, I am forry likewife upon another account: as I am afraid you will lofe the little knowledge you had acquired in the art of cookery, and be abfolutely at a lofs how to fet forth a tolerable fupper.   For as you made no very confiderable improvements in this fafhionable fcience, even when you had many curious models for your imitation; what ftrange aukward things muft your entertainments prove now, that you enjoy no longer the fame advantages ? When I informed Spurinna [1] of this wonderful revolution in the fyftem of your affairs, he fhook his prophetic head, and declared that it portended fome

A.U.710.

[1] A celebrated diviner : who is faid to have forewarned Cæfar of the ides of March. *Suet. in Jul.* 81.

terrible

A.U.710. terrible difafter to the commonwealth; unlefs, said he, this extraordinary phænomenon be occafioned by the prefent cold weather, and your friend fhould return with the zephyrs to his accuftomed train of life. But without a joke, my dear Pætus, I would advife you to fpend your time in the chearful fociety of a fet of worthy and agreeable friends: as there is nothing, in my eftimation, that more effectually contributes to the happinefs of human life. When I fay this, I do not mean with refpect to the fenfual gratifications of the palate, but with regard to that pleafing relaxation of the mind which is beft produced by the freedom of focial converfe, and which is always moft agreeable at the hour of meals. For this reafon the Latin language is much happier, I think, than the Greek, in the term it employs to exprefs affemblies of this fort. In the latter they are called by a word which fignifies *compotations*; whereas in ours they are more emphatically ftiled *convivial* meetings: intimating that it is in a communication of this nature, that life is moft truly enjoyed. You fee I am endeavouring to bring philofophy to my affiftance in recalling you to the tables of your friends: and indeed I prefcribe them as the beft recipe for the re-eftablifhment of your health.

Do

Do not imagine, my friend, from my writing A.U.710.
in this ſtrain of pleaſantry, that I have renounced
my cares for the republic. Be aſſured, on the
contrary, that it is the ſole and unintermitted buſi-
neſs of my life to ſecure to my fellow-citizens the
full poſſeſſion of their liberties: to which end
my admonitions, my labours, and the utmoſt
powers of my mind, are upon all occaſions un-
weariedly employed. In a word, it is my firm
perſuaſion, that if I ſhould die a martyr to theſe
patriot-endeavours, I ſhall finiſh my days in the
moſt glorious manner. Again and again I bid
you farewel.

L E T T E R X.

Caius Cassius, Proconſul, to Cicero.

I Am to inform you of my arrival in Syria:
where I have joined the generals Lucius
Murcus and Quintus Criſpus [2]. Theſe brave and
worthy citizens, having been made acquainted
with what has lately paſſed in Rome, immediate-
ly reſigned their armies to my command: and
with great zeal and ſpirit co-operate with me in

[2] " They had been prætors, A. U. 708. Cæſar ſent the
" former into Syria, and the latter into Bithynia, with pro-
" conſular authority." *Dio.* xlvii. *Appian.* iii. Mr. *Roſs.*

the

A.U. 710. the fervice of the republic. Aulus Allienus has
delivered to me the four legions which he brought
from Egypt [5]: the legion which was commanded
by Cæcilius Baffus [4] has likewife ·joined me.
And now it is unneceffary, I am perfuaded, that I
fhould exhort you to defend the intereft both of
myfelf and of the commonwealth to the utmoft
of your abilities : but it may animate your zeal
and your hopes to be affured, that a powerful ar-
my is not wanting to fupport the fenate and its
friends, in the caufe of liberty. For the reft, I
refer you to Lucius Cartéius, whom I have di-
rected to confer with you upon my affairs. Fare-
wel.

From my camp at Tarichea [5], March the 7th.

[3] " Allienus was lieutenant to Dolabella, by whom he
" was fent into Egypt in order to conduct thofe legions
" into Syria. He accordingly executed his commiffion :
" but inftead of delivering thefe troops to Dolabella, he went
" over with them to Caffius." *Quartier.*

[4] See rem. 7. p. 65. of this vol.

[5] Situated upon the lake of Genefaret in Galilee.

LETTER XI.

Asinius Pollio[6], to Cicero.

YOU muft not wonder that you have heard A.U.710. nothing from me in relation to public affairs, fince the breaking out of the war. Our couriers have always found it difficult to pafs unmolefted through the foreft of Caftulo[7]: but it is now more than ever infefted with robbers. Thefe banditti however, are by no means the principal obftruction to our intercourfe with Rome: as the mails are perpetually fearched and

[6] Afinius Pollio was in every refpect, one of the moft accomplifhed perfons among his contemporaries. His extenfive genius was equal to all the nobler branches of polite literature, and he gave the moft applauded proofs of his talents as a poet, an orator, and an hiftorian. He united the moft lively and pleafing vein of wit and pleafantry, with all that ftrength and folidity of underftanding which is neceffary to render a man of weight in the more ferious and important occafions of life: in allufion to which uncommon affemblage of qualities it was faid of him, that he was a man *omnium horarum*. It is to be regretted that a character fo truly brilliant on the intellectual fide, fhould fhine with lefs luftre in a moral view. 'Tis evident however from the prefent epiftle, that in taking part with Cæfar againft Pompey, private confiderations were of more force with him than public utility, and determined him to fupport a caufe which his heart condemned. This letter was written from the farther Spain : of which province Cæfar a fhort time before his death had appointed Pollio governor.

[7] A city antiently of great note : at prefent it is only a fmall village called *Cazorla*, in the province of New Caftile n Spain.

detained

A.U. 710. detained by the foldiers that are pofted for that purpofe by both parties in every quarter of the country. Accordingly if I had not received letters by a fhip which lately arrived in this river [8], I fhould have been utterly ignorant of what has been tranfacted in your part of the world. But now that a communication by fea is thus opened between us, I fhall frequently, and with great pleafure, embrace the opportunity of correfponding with you.

Believe me, there is no danger of my being influenced by the perfuafions of the perfon you mention [9]. As much as the world abhors him, he is far from being detefted to that degree which I know he deferves: and I have fo ftrong an averfion to the man, that I would upon no confideration bear a part in any meafures wherein he is concerned [1]. Inclined both by my temper and my ftudies to be the friend of tranquillity and freedom, I frequently and bitterly lamented our late unhappy civil wars. But as the for-

----

[8] The Quadalquivir: upon which the city of Corduba, from whence this letter is dated, was fituated.

[9] Antony; as Manutius conjectures: tho' fome of the commentators, with greater probability, fuppofe that he means Lepidus. *Vid. Epift. Famil.* x. 11. & 15.

[1] Nothing could be more infincere, it fhould feem, than thefe profeffions: as it is probable that Pollio was at this time determined to join Antony. It is certain at leaft that he did fo foon afterwards, and carried with him the troops under his command. *Patercul.* ii. 63.

midable

midable enemies which I had among both par-
ties, rendered it altogether unfafe for me to re-
main neuter; fo I would not take up arms on
that fide where I knew I fhould be perpetually
expofed to the infidious arts of my capital adver-
fary [z].   But tho' my inclinations were not with
the party I joined; my fpirit however would not
fuffer me to ftand undiftinguifhed among them:
in confequence of which I was forward to engage
in all the dangers of the caufe I had efpoufed.
With refpect to Cæfar himfelf, I will confefs
that I loved him with the higheft and moft in-
violable affection: and indeed I had reafon. For
notwithftanding his acquaintance with me com-
menced fo late as when he was in the height of
his power; yet he admitted me into the fame
fhare of his friendfhip, as if I had been in the
number of thofe with whom he had lived in the
longeft intimacy.   Neverthelefs, as often as I
was at liberty to follow my own fentiments, I
endeavoured that my conduct fhould be fuch as
every honeft man muft approve: and whenever
I was obliged to execute the orders I received,
it was in a manner that evidently difcovered how

[z] The perfon hinted at is, perhaps, Cato: as Pollio had
early diftinguifhed his enmity towards that moft illuftrious
of Romans by a public impeachment. *Vid. Dial. de Cauf.
Corrupt. Eloquen:*. 34.

 much my actions were at variance with my heart. The unjust odium, however, that I incurred by these unavoidable compliances, might well teach me the true value of liberty, and how wretched a condition it is to live under the government of a despotic power. If any attempts therefore are carrying on to reduce us a second time under the dominion of a single person, whoever that single person may be, I declare myself his irreconcileable enemy. The truth is, there is no danger so great that I would not chearfully hazard for the support of our common liberties. But the consuls have not thought proper to signify to me either by any decree of the senate, or by their private letters, in what manner I should act in the present conjuncture. I have received indeed only one letter from Pansa since the ides of March: by which he advised me to assure the senate, that I was ready to employ the forces under my command in any service they should require. But this would have been a very imprudent declaration at a time when Lepidus had professed in his public speeches, as well as in the letters he wrote to all his friends, that he concurred in Antony's measures. For could I possibly, without the consent of the former, find means to subsist my army in their march thro'

his

his provinces ? But granting that I could have A.U.710.
furmounted this difficulty, I muft have conquered
another and a ftill greater : as nothing lefs than
a pair of wings could have rendered it practi-
cable for me to have croffed the Alps, whilft
every pafs was guarded by the troops of Lepidus.
Add to this, that I could by no means convey
any difpatches to Rome : as the couriers were
not only. expofed in a thoufand different places to
the danger of being plundered, but were detained
likewife by the exprefs orders of Lepidus [1]. It is
well known, however, that I publicly declared at
Corduba, that it was my refolution not to refign
this province into any other hands than thofe
which the fenate fhould appoint : not to mention
how ftrenuoufly I withftood all the applications
that were made to me for parting. with the thir-
tieth legion.   I could not indeed have given it
up, without depriving myfelf of a very confider-
able ftrength for the defence of the republic : as
there are no troops in the whole world that are
animated with a braver or more martial fpirit
than thofe of which this legion is compofed.
Upon the whole, I hope you will do me the
juftice to believe, in the firft place, that I am
extremely defirous of preferving the public tran-
quillity ; as there is nothing I more fincerely wifh

[1] Lepidus was governor of that part of Spain which lay
neareft to Italy.   See rem. [2] on letter 14. of this book.

P 2   than

A.U. 710. than the fafety of all my fellow-citizens : and in the next place, that I am determined to vindicate my own and my country's rights.

It gives me greater fatisfaction than you can well imagine, that you admit my friend into a fhare of your intimacy. Shall I own neverthelefs, that I cannot think of him as the companion of your walks, and as bearing a part in the pleafantry of your converfation, without feeling fome emotions of envy? This is a privilege, believe me, which I infinitely value : as you fhall moft affuredly experience by my devoting the whole of my time to your company, if ever we fhould live to fee peace reftored to the republic.

I am much furprifed that you did not mention in your letter, whether it would be moft fatiffactory to the fenate that I fhould remain in this province, or march into Italy. If I were to confider only my own eafe and fafety, I fhould certainly continue here : but as in the prefent conjuncture the republic has more occafion for legions than for provinces, (efpecially as the lofs of the latter may with great eafe be recovered) I have determined to move towards Italy with my troops. For the reft, I refer you to the letter I have written to Panfa : a copy of which I herewith tranfmit to you. Farewel.

Corduba, March the 16th.

L E T-

L E T T E R XII.

To Caius Cassius.

YOU will receive a full account of the present situation of affairs from Tidius Strabo: a person of great merit, and extremely well-affected to the republic. Need I add how strong his attachment likewise is to yourself, when it thus evidently appears by his leaving his family and his fortunes in order to follow you? For the same reason I forbear to follicit your good offices in his behalf: as I am perfuaded you will think his coming to you a fufficient recommendation to your favour.

If any misfortune fhould attend our arms, be affured that the friends of the republic have no other refource left than in you and Marcus Brutus. We are at this juncture indeed in the moft imminent danger: as it is with great difficulty that Decimus Brutus ftill holds out at Mutina. However, if he fhould be fpeedily relieved, we may look upon victory as our own: if not, let me repeat it again, every friend of liberty will fly for refuge to Brutus and to you. May you ftand ready then with all that fpirit which is neceffary for the full and complete

P 3   deli-

A.U. 710. deliverance of our diftreffed country ! Fare-
wel.

LETTER XIII.

TO PLANCUS.

THE account that Furnius gave us of your
difpofition towards the republic, afforded
the higheft fatisfaction both to the fenate and the
people. But your letter which was afterwards
read in the fenate, feemed by no means to com-
port with thofe fentiments our friend had thus re-
prefented you as entertaining. At the very time
indeed when your illuftrious collegue is fuftaining
a fiege from a lawlefs crew of the moft worthlefs
villains, you do not fcruple to advife us to peace.
But if peace is their fincere defire, let them im-
mediately lay down their arms, and fue for it in
a proper manner : otherwife they muft expect to
obtain it, not by treaty, be affured, but by the
fword alone. But I leave it to Furnius and your
worthy brother to acquaint you with the recep-
tion which your letter upon this fubject, as well
as that of Lepidus, met with from the fenate.
Mean while, notwithftanding you are well quali-
fied to be your own advifer, and that it will foon
be in your power likewife to have recourfe to the
faithful

faithful and friendly counfels of Furnius and A.U. 710. your brother; yet, in compliance with that af-fection to which you have fo many powerful claims, I cannot forbear fending you a few ad-monitions.   Believe me then, my dear Plancus, whatever honours you have hitherto acquired, (and you have acquired in truth the higheft) they will be confidered as fo many vain and empty titles, unlefs you dignify them by joining in the defence both of the liberties of the people, and the authority of the fenate.   Let me conjure you therefore to feparate yourfelf from thofe affociates with whom you have hitherto been united, not by choice indeed but by the general attraction of a prevailing party.   It has been the fortune of many, as it will probably be yours, to exercife the fupreme magiftracy during times of public commotions: but not one of this number ever derived to himfelf that efteem and veneration which naturally flows from the confular dignity, who had not diftinguifhed his adminiftration by an active and zealous regard for the interefts of the commonwealth.   To this end it is neceffary, that you renounce the fociety of thofe impious citizens, whofe principles are far different from your own; that you fhew yourfelf the friend, the guide, and the protector of all thofe who are faithfully attached to our

P 4

con-

 conftitution; and in fine, that you be well per-
fuaded that the re-eftablifhment of the public
tranquillity confifts, not merely in laying down
our arms, but in being fecure from all reafonable
apprehenfion of their ever being refumed to en-
flave us again.   Thus to think and thus to act,
will render your character both as a conful and
a confular, moft truly illuftrious : but if you
fhould fteer yourfelf by other maxims and by
other meafures, you will poffefs thofe exalted
diftinctions, not only without honour, but with
the utmoft difgrace.

And now, if I have expreffed my fentiments
with fomewhat more than ordinary ferioufnefs,
impute it to the zeal of my affection towards you ;
affuring yourfelf at the fame time, that you will
undoubtedly find my advice is founded on truth,
if you make the experiment in a manner worthy
of your character.   Farewel.

March the 20th.

L E T T E R   XIV.

To Lepidus[a].

THE singular regard I bear you, renders it greatly my concern that you should be distinguished with the highest dignities of the re-

A.U. 710.

---

[a] Marcus Æmilius Lepidus was descended from one of the noblest and most antient families in Rome : and he was himself distinguished with some of the most honourable posts in the republic. He stood high in the confidence and friendship of Julius Cæsar : who when he was dictator named him for the master of the horse ; when he was consul, in the year 707, declared him his collegue ; and who a short time before his death appointed him governor of the nearer Spain. One of the most elegant of the Roman historians has represented Lepidus, as void of all military virtues, and in every view of his character as altogether unworthy of that high station to which fortune had exalted him. Accordingly he is described by Shakespear in the tragedy of Julius Cæsar, as,

> —— *a slight unmeritable man,*
> *Meet to be sent on errands.*

But tho' the poet has been strictly true to history ; it may be questioned, perhaps, whether the historian has been equally faithful to truth. For when one considers the great trust which Cæsar reposed in Lepidus ; his address in prevailing with young Pompey, who had made himself master almost of all Spain, to renounce his conquests ; together with the share he had in forming that celebrated league between Antony, Octavius and himself, which gave him a third part in the division of the whole Roman dominions ; is it credible that his talents were destitute of lustre ? History, perhaps, may be more reasonably relied upon in what it has delivered concerning his moral character: and it is probable that Lepidus was strongly infected with avarice, ambition and vanity. This at least is certain, that he acted towards the senate in the present conjuncture, with great dissimulation

public.

A.U.710. public.   I cannot therefore but regret, that you omitted to pay your acknowledgments to the senate for those extraordinary honours they lately conferred upon you [b].

I am glad you are desirous of composing those unhappy dissentions that destroy the tranquillity of our country : and if you can effect this good work consistently with the enjoyment of our liberties, it will be greatly to your own credit, as well as to the advantage of the commonwealth. But if the peace you propose, is to re-establish a most oppressive tyranny ; be well assured there is not a man in his senses who will not rather renounce his life than thus suffer himself to be made a slave. I should think therefore, that your wisest way would be to avoid engaging as the mediator of a peace which is neither approved by the senate, or the people, nor indeed by any lover of his country in the whole republic. But as this is a truth which you will undoubtedly learn from others; I will only add, that I hope

and treachery. At the time when this letter was written, he was at the head of a very considerable army in the Narbonensian Gaul, which Cæsar had annexed to the province of Spain, in favour of Lepidus. *Pigh. Annal.* ii. 451. *Vel. Patercul.* ii. 63. 80. *Dio.* xlv. 275.

[b] The senate had lately decreed, that the statue of Lepidus should be erected in the forum with an inscription, in honour of the services he had performed to his country by prevailing with young Pompey to lay down his arms. *Philip.* xvi. 4.

you

you will confider with your ufual prudence, in A.U.710.
what manner it will be beft and moft advifeable
for you to act.   Farewel.

L E T T E R XV.

To Caius Cassius.

I Will not tell you with how much zeal I lately
ftood forth, both in the fenate and before the
people, an advocate for the advancement of your
honours [4]; as it is a circumftance which I had
rather you fhould learn from the letters of your
family, than from my own hand. I fhould eafily
have carried my point in the former, if I had
not met with a ftrenuous oppofition from Panfa.
Neverthelefs, after having enforced my fenti-
ments in the fenate, I made a fpeech to the fame
purpofe in an affembly of the people : to which
I was introduced by Marcus Servilius the tri-
bune.   I urged upon this occafion, (and with a
warmth and vehemence fuitable to a popular

* Dolabella having entered into Afia Minor, and com-
mitted great outrages and hoftilities in that province, was
declared, by a general vote of the fenate, a public enemy :
in confequence of which a debate arofe concerning the
perfon to whom the war to be carried on againft Dolabella
fhould be entrufted. Cicero moved that a commiffion fhould
be granted to Caffius for that purpofe, with the moft ho-
nourable and extenfive powers. But his motion was over-
ruled by the fuperior intereft of Panfa, who feems to have
been fecretly defirous of obtaining this command for him-
felf. *Vid. Philip.* xi.

audience)

 audience) all that I moſt juſtly might in your favour : and my ſpeech was received with a louder and more univerſal applauſe than ever was known before. I hope you will pardon me that I took theſe ſteps contrary to the perſuaſions of your mother-in-law : who was apprehenſive they might give offence to Panſa. He did not indeed, forget to avail himſelf of theſe fears : and he aſſured the people, that even your own family were averſe to my making this motion. I was by no means, I confeſs, governed by their ſentiments in the caſe : as I acted entirely with a view to an intereſt which I have always endeavoured to promote; the intereſt I mean of the republic in general; as well as with a regard to the advancement of your glory in particular.

There is one article upon which I very largely expatiated in the ſenate, as I afterwards repeated it likewiſe in my ſpeech to the people : and I hope your conduct will fully juſtify what I then ſaid. I undertook to aſſure the public, that you would not wait for the ſanction of our decrees; but agreeably to your uſual ſpirit, would upon your own ſingle authority, take ſuch meaſures as ſhould appear expedient to you for the defence of the commonwealth. I went even farther; and almoſt ventured to affirm, that you had already acted in this manner. The truth of it is, altho' I

was not at that time certainly informed either in
what part of the world you were, or what number
of troops you were furnished with; yet I was
confident, I said, that every legion in Asia [5] had
submitted to your command, and that you had
recovered that province to the republic. I have
only to add my wishes, that in every enterprise
you shall undertake, you may still rise above
yourself with superior glory.   Farewel.

L E T T E R   XVI.

Plancus to Cicero.

I Should employ this letter in giving you a full
explanation of my measures, if I had no other
method of convincing you, that I have in every
respect conducted myself towards the republic
agreeably to my own promises and to your per-
suasions. I have ever been ambitious indeed of
obtaining your esteem, as well as your friend-
ship: and if I have wished to secure you for my
advocate where I have acted wrong; I have been
no less desirous of giving you occasion to applaud
me for acting right. But I was going to say,
that I shorten this letter for two reasons: the first
is, because I have entered into an ample detail

---

[5] Asia Minor.

A.U.710. of every thing in my public manifesto [6]; and the next, becaufe you will receive a circumftantial account of all that relates to me from Marcus Varifidius, a Roman knight and my particular friend, whom I have directed to wait upon you. In the mean time, let me proteft, that it was not without much concern that I faw others anticipate me in the good opinion of the republic: but I forebore to declare myfelf, till I fhould be in a condition to effect fomething worthy of thofe expectations the fenate has conceived of me, and of that high office [7] I fhall fhortly bear. And fhould fortune fecond my endeavours, I hope to render fuch confiderable fervices to the republic, that not only the prefent age fhall feel the advantage of my affiftance, but that it fhall be remembered likewife in times to come. Mean while, that I may purfue thefe endeavours with the greater alacrity, let me intreat your fuffrage in procuring me thofe honours which your letter fets before my view as incitements of my patriotifm: and your intereft for this purpofe is equal, I well know, to your inclination. Take care of your health, and give me your friendfhip in the fame degree that I fincerely give you mine.

[6] See the next letter.
[7] The confulate: upon which Plancus was to enter the following year.

LET-

L E T T E R   XVII.

PLANCUS, Conful elect, to the Confuls, the
Prætors, the Tribunes, the Senate, and
the Commons of Rome.

BEFORE I make any profeffions with A.U.710.
refpect to my future conduct, I deem it
neceffary to juftify myfelf to thofe who may
think that I have held the republic too long in
fufpence concerning my defigns [s]. For I would
by no means have it imagined that I am atoning
for my paft behaviour, when in fact, I am only
feifing the firft favourable opportunity of publicly
declaring a refolution, which I have long formed.
I was in no fort ignorant however, that at a time
of fuch general and alarming confufions, a lefs
deliberate difcovery of my intentions would have
proved moft to my own private advantage: as I
was fenfible that feveral of my fellow-citizens
had been diftinguifhed with great honours, by a
more hafty explication of their purpofes. But
as fortune had placed me in fuch a fituation,
that I could not be earlier in teftifying mine
without prejudicing that caufe which I could
better ferve by concealing them; I was willing

[s] See rem. 2. p. 134. of this vol.

to

A.U. 710. to fuffer for a feafon in the good opinion of the
world: as I preferred the intereft of the public
to that of my own reputation. That this was
the genuine motive of my proceedings, cannot
reafonably, I truft, be queftioned. For can it
be fuppofed, that a man in my profperous cir-
cumftances, and of my well-known courfe of life,
whofe utmoft hopes too were upon the very point
of being crowned [9], could be capable either of
meanly fubmitting to the deftructive ambition
of another, or impioufly cherifhing any danger-
ous fchemes of his own? But it required fome
time, as well as much pains and expence, to
render myfelf able to perform thofe affurances I
purpofed to give to the republic, and to every
friend of her caufe; that I might not approach
with mere empty profeffions to the affiftance of
my country, but with the power of performing
an effectual fervice. To this end, as the army
under my command had been ftrongly and fre-
quently follicited to revolt, it was neceffary to
perfuade them that a moderate reward conferred
by the general voice of the commonwealth, was
far preferable to an infinitely greater from any
fingle hand. My next labour was to convince
thofe many cities which had been gained the

[9] Alluding to his being to enter the next year on the
confular office.

laft

last year by largesses and other donations, that A.U. 710.
these were obligations of no validity, and that
they should endeavour to obtain the same bene-
factions from a better and more honourable quar-
ter.   I had still the farther task, to prevail with
those who commanded in the neighbouring pro-
vinces, to join with the more numerous party in
a general association for the defence of our com-
mon liberties, rather than unite with the smaller
number in hopes of dividing the spoils of a
victory that must prove fatal to the whole world.
Add to this, that I was obliged to augment my
own troops and those of my auxiliaries; that I
might have nothing to fear whenever I should
think proper, contrary to the inclination of some
about me, openly to avow the cause which it was
my resolution to defend.   Now I shall never be
ashamed to acknowledge, that in order to bring
their several schemes to bear, I submitted, tho'
very unwillingly indeed, to the mortification of
dissembling the intentions I really had, and of
counterfeiting those which I certainly had not :
as the fate of my collegue [1] had taught me how

[1] Decimus Brutus. To what particular circumstance of
his conduct Plancus alludes, the history of these times does
not discover. Perhaps he may only mean in general, that
Decimus had imprudently drawn upon himself the siege of
Modena, before he had made the proper dispositions against
an attack.

A.U.710. dangerous it is for a man who means well to his country, to divulge his refolutions ere he is fufficiently prepared to carry them into execution. For this reafon it was that I directed my brave and worthy lieutenant Caius Furnius, to reprefent to you more fully than I thought prudent to explain in my difpatches, thofe meafures which feemed neceffary for the prefervation both of this province and of the republic in general; as being the more concealed method of conveying my fentiments to you upon that fubject, as well as the fafer with refpect to myfelf.

It appears then, that I have long been fecretly attentive to the defence of the commonwealth. But now that by the bounty of the gods I am in every refpect better prepared for that purpofe, I defire to give the world, not only reafon to hope well of my intentions, but clear and undoubted proofs of their fincerity.

I have five legions in readinefs to march; all of them zealoufly attached to the republic, and difpofed by my liberalities to pay an entire obedience to my orders. The fame difpofition appears in every city throughout this province: and they earneftly vie with each other in giving me the ftrongeft marks of their duty. Accordingly they have furnifhed me with as confiderable a body of auxiliary forces both horfe and foot, as they could
poffibly

possibly have raifed for the fupport of their own national liberties. As for myfelf, I am ready either to remain here in order to protect this province, or to march wherefoever elfe the republic fhall demand my fervices. I will offer yet another alternative; and either refign my troops and government into any hands that fhall be appointed, or draw upon myfelf the whole weight of the war: if by thefe means I may be able to eftablifh the tranquillity of my country, or even retard thofe calamities with which it is threatened.

If at the time that I am making thefe declarations, our public difturbances fhould happily be compofed; I fhall rejoice in an event fo advantageous to the commonwealth, notwithftanding the honour I fhall lofe by being too late in the tender of my fervices [2]. But on the contrary, if I am early enough in my offers to bear a full part in all the dangers of the war; let me recommend it to every man of juftice and candour to vindicate me againft the malevolence of thofe, whom envy may prompt to afperfe my character.

[2] This paffage fufficiently difcovers the true motive of Plancus's prefent declarations: as they appear evidently to have flowed from fome reafon he had to believe, that the conteft between Antony and the fenate was likely to be adjufted in an amicable manner.

Q 2

In

    In my own particular, I defire no greater re-
ward for my fervices, than the fatisfaction of
having contributed to the fecurity of the repub-
lic. But I think myfelf bound to recommend
thofe brave and worthy men to your efpecial
favour, who partly in compliance with my per-
fuafions, but much more in confidence of your
good faith, would not fuffer themfelves to be
prevailed upon by all the applications that have
been made both to their hopes and their fears,
to depart from their duty to the common-
wealth.

LETTER XVIII.

To PLANCUS.

ALtho' I had received a very full account
from our friend Furnius, of your difpofi-
tion with regard to the republic, and of the mea-
fures you were meditating in its defence; yet the
perufal of your letter [3] afforded me a ftill clearer
view into the whole plan of your patriot purpofes.
Notwithftanding then that you fhould not have an
opportunity of executing your projected fervices,
as the fate of the commonwealth, which depends

---

[3] The foregoing letter to the fenate.

upon a fingle battle, will probably be decided ere
this reaches your hands; yet you have acquired,
neverthelefs, great and univerfal applaufe from
what the world has been informed of your
general good intentions. Accordingly, had either
of the confuls been in Rome [*] when your dif-
patches arrived, the fenate would have declared,
and in terms, I am perfuaded, extremely to your
advantage, the fenfe it entertains of your zea-
lous and acceptable preparations in their caufe.
The proper feafon however for your being re-
warded with honours of this kind, is, in my opi-
nion at leaft, fo far from being elapfed, that on
the contrary it feems to be fcarce fully arrived:
as thofe diftinctions alone appear to me to de-
ferve the name of honours that are conferred by
our country, not in expectation of fervices to
come, but in juft retribution to thofe that have
effectually been performed.   Believe me, if any
form of government fhould fubfift amongft us
where merit can hope to be diftinguifhed, you
will fhine out with all the moft illuftrious dig-
nities it can beftow.   But nothing of this kind
(let me repeat it again) can juftly be called an
honour, but what is given, not as the incentive

----

[*] " The two confuls Hirtius and Panfa were both in Gaul,
" and waiting to attempt a decifive battle with Antony, in
" order to deliver Decimus Brutus from the danger he was
" in at Modena." Mr. *Rofs.*

 of an occafional fervice, but as the recompence of a conftant and uniform courfe of patriotifm. Be it then your earneft endeavour, my dear Plancus, to acquire thefe well-merited rewards, by advancing to the relief of your collegue [5]; by improving that wonderful unanimity which appears in every province for the fupport of the common caufe; and by giving all poffible fuccour to your country in general. Be perfuaded that I fhall always be ready to affift your fchemes with my beft advice, and to promote your honours with my utmoft intereft: in a word, that I fhall act upon every occafion wherein you are concerned, as one who is moft fincerely and moft warmly your friend. I am fo indeed, not only from that intercourfe of affectionate good offices by which we have been long mutually united, but from the love I bear likewife to my country; in tendernefs to which I am more anxious for your life than for my own. Farewel.

March the 30th.

[5] Decimus Brutus,

L E T T E R   XIX.

To Cornificius.

I Agree with you in thinking, that thofe who were concerned in the defign upon Lily-bæum [6], deferved to have been executed upon the fpot.   But you fpared them, it feems, in the apprehenfion that the world would condemn you as too freely indulging a vindictive fpirit: yet as well might you have been apprehenfive, my friend, that the world would condemn you for acting too agreeably to your patriot character.

I very gladly embrace your overtures of renewing that affociation with you for the defence of the republic, in which I was formerly engaged with your father : and I am perfuaded it is an affociation, my dear Cornificius, in which we fhall ever be united.   It is with much pleafure likewife that I find you efteem it unneceffary to fend me any ceremonious acknowledgments of my fervices : formalities indeed would ill agree with that intimacy which fubfifts between us.

A.U.710.

[6] A city in Sicily, oppofite to the coaft of Lybia in Africa. The particulars of the affair alluded to, as well as the perfons concerned in it, are unknown.

A.U. 710.   If the senate were ever holden in the abfence of the confuls, unlefs upon fome very fudden and extraordinary occafion, it would have been more frequently fummoned in order to concert proper meafures for the fupport of your authority. But as neither Hirtius nor Panfa are in Rome, no decree can at prefent be procured in relation to the feveral fums of two millions [7], and of feventy millions [8] of fefterces which you mention. I think, however, that you are fufficiently authorifed to raife this money by way of loan, in virtue of that general decree of the fenate by which you were confirmed in your government.

I imagine you are informed of the ftate of our affairs, by thofe to whom it properly belongs to fend you the intelligence. As for myfelf, I conceive great hopes that things will take a favourable turn. I am not wanting at leaft in my utmoft vigilance and efforts for that purpofe : and I am refolutely waging war againft every foe to the republic. The recovery of our liberties does not feem, indeed, even *now*, to be a matter of great difficulty : I am fure it would have been perfectly eafy, if fome perfons had acted in the manner they ought. Farewel.

[7] About 16000 l. of our money.
[8] About 560000 l.

L E T T E R XX.

To Plancus.

IT is principally for the fake of my country that A.U. 710.
I ought to rejoice in the very powerful fuc-
cours with which you have ftrengthened the re-
public, at a juncture when it is well-nigh reduced
to the laft extremity.   I proteft however by all
my hopes of congratulating you on the victori-
ous deliverance of the commonwealth, that a
confiderable part of the joy which I feel upon
this occafion, arifes from the fhare I take in your
glory.   Great indeed is the reputation you have
already acquired; and great, I am perfuaded, will
be the honours that will hereafter be conferred
upon you: for affure yourfelf nothing could
make a ftronger impreffion upon the fenate than
your late letter [8] to that affembly.   It did fo,
both with refpect to thofe very important fer-
vices which it brought us an account that you
had performed, and with regard to that ftrength
of fentiment and expreffion with which it was
drawn up.   It contained nothing however that
was in the leaft unexpected to myfelf: as I was
not only perfectly well acquainted with your

[8] The letter here mentioned feems to have been a fubfe-
quent one to that which ftands the 17th in the prefent book.

heart,

A.U. 710. heart, and had not forgotten the promifes you had given me in your letters, but as I had received from Furnius a full information of all your defigns. Thefe indeed appeared to the fenate much beyond what they had allowed themfelves to hope: not that they ever entertained the leaft doubt of your difpofition, but becaufe they were by no means fufficiently apprifed either of what you were in a condition to effect, or whither you purpofed to march. It was with infinite pleafure therefore that I read the letter which Marcus Varifidius delivered to me on your part. I received it on the 7th of this month in the morning, amidft a large circle of very worthy citizens who were attending in order to conduct me from my houfe: and I immediately gave them a fhare in my joy. Whilft we were mutually congratulating each other upon this happy occurrence, Munatius came to pay me his ufual morning-vifit: to whom I likewife communicated your letter. It was the firft notice he had received of an exprefs being arrived from you: as Varifidius, in purfuance of your directions, did not deliver any of his difpatches till he had firft waited upon me. A fhort time however after Munatius had left me, he returned with your letter to himfelf, together alfo with that which you wrote to the fenate. We thought proper to carry the latter

imme-

immediately to Cornutus : who as prætor of the A.U.710.
city, fupplies the office of the confuls in their
abfence, agreeably, you know, to an antient
and eftablifhed cuftom. The fenate was in-
ftantly fummoned : and the expectation that
was raifed by the general report of an exprefs
being arrived from you, brought together a very
full affembly.   As foon as your letter was read,
it was objected that Cornutus had not taken the
aufpices in a proper manner : and this fcruple
was confirmed by the general fentiments of our
college [9].   In confequence of this, the fenate
was adjourned to the following day : when I
had a very warm conteft with Servilius, who
ftrenuoufly oppofed the paffing of any decree to
your honour.   For this purpofe he had the inte-
reft to procure his own motion to be firft pro-
pofed to the fenate [1] : which being rejected how-
ever by a great majority, mine was next taken
into confideration.   But when the fenate had
unanimoufly agreed to it, Publius Titius [2], at
the inftigation of Servilius, interpofed his nega-

[9] See rem. 3. p. 279. vol. I.

[1] The fenate could not enter into any debate, unlefs the
fubject of it was propofed to them in form by fome of the
magiftrates ; who had the fole privilege of referring any
queftion to a vote, or of dividing the houfe upon it. *Midlet.
on the Rom. S. p.* 155.

[2] One of the tribunes.   It has already been obferved that
thofe magiftrates had a power of putting a ftop to the pro-
ceedings of the fenate, by their fingle negative.

tive,

A.U. 710. tive. The farther deliberation upon this affair was poftponed therefore to the next day: when Servilius came prepared to fupport an oppofition, which in fome fort might be confidered as injurious to the honour even of Jupiter himfelf; as it was in the Capitol [3] that the fenate, upon this occafion, was affembled. I leave it to your other friends to inform you in what manner I mortified Servilius, and with how much warmth I expofed the contemptible interpofition of Titius. But this I will myfelf affure you, that the fenate

[3] The Capitol was a temple dedicated to Jupiter, and the moft confiderable ftructure of the facred kind in all Rome. The ruins of this celebrated edifice are ftill to be feen. None of the commentators have taken notice of the indirect compliment which Cicero here pays to Plancus: which feems however to deferve a particular explanation. The Capitol was held in fingular veneration, as being built upon the fpot which Jupiter was fuppofed to have chofen for the vifible manifeftation of his perfon. In confequence of this popular fuperftition, both Horace and Virgil often fpeak of the profperity and duration of the Capitol, as a circumftance upon which the fortune of the whole empire depended:

> ——————————————— Stet Capitolium
> Fulgens, triumphatifque poffit
> Roma ferox dare jura Medis.   HoR. Od. iii. 3. 42.

> Dum domus Ænei Capitoli immobile faxum
> Accolet, imperiumque Pater Romanus habebit.   Æn. ix. 448.

Cicero therefore, by a very artful piece of flattery infinuates, that the oppofition Servilius made to the honours which the fenate intended to have paid to Plancus, was in effect an affront to that fupreme and guardian divinity in whofe temple the tranfaction paffed, as being contrary to the intereft of a republic which was diftinguifhed by Jupiter himfelf with his immediate prefence. Vid. Æn. viii. 346.

                                                    could

could not poffibly act with greater dignity and A.U. 710.
fpirit, or fhew a ftronger difpofition to advance
your honours, than it difcovered upon this occa-
fion.   Nor are you lefs in favour with the whole
city in general : as indeed all orders and degrees
of men amongft us, remarkably concur in the fame
common zeal for the deliverance of the republic.
Perfevere then, my friend, in the glorious courfe
upon which you have entered : and let nothing
lefs than immortal fame be the object of your
well-directed ambition.   Defpife the falfe fplendor
of all thofe empty honours that are fhort-lived,
tranfitory and perifhable.   True glory is found-
ed upon virtue alone : which is never fo illuftri-
oufly diftinguifhed as when it difplays itfelf by
important fervices to our country.   You have
at this time a moft favourable opportunity for that
purpofe : which as you have already embraced,
let it not flip out of your hands till you fhall have
employed it to full advantage ; left it be faid, that
you are more obliged to the republic than the re-
public is obliged to you.   As for my own part ;
you will always find me ready to contribute to
the advancement as well as to the fupport of your
dignities : indeed it is what I owe not only to
our friendfhip, but to the commonwealth ; which
is far dearer to me than life itfelf.

Whilft

A.U. 710.

Whilst I was employing my best services for the promotion of your honours, I received great pleasure in observing the prudence and fidelity which Titus Munatius exerted for the same purpose. I had experienced those qualities in him upon other occasions: but the incredible diligence and affection with which he acted for your interest in this affair, shewed them to me in a still stronger and more conspicuous point of view. Farewel.

April the 11th.

LETTER XXI.

To CORNIFICIUS.

MY friendship with Lucius Lamia is well known, I am persuaded, not only to yourself, who are acquainted with all the circumstances of my life, but to every Roman in general. It most conspicuously appeared, indeed, to the whole world, when he was banished by the consul Gabinius [4] for having, with so remarkable a spirit of freedom and fortitude, risen up in my defence [5]. Our friendship however did not commence from that period: it was from an affection

---

[4] See rem. 21. p. 174. vol. i.

[5] When Cicero was persecuted by Clodius.

of

of a much earlier date that he was induced thus A.U. 710.
generoufly to expofe himfelf to every danger in my
caufe. To thefe his meritorious fervices I muft add,
that there is no man whofe company affords me
a more true and exquifite entertainment.   After
what I have thus faid, you will think it needlefs,
furely, that I fhould ufe much rhetoric in recom-
mending him to your favour.   You fee the juft
reafon I have for giving him fo large a fhare of
my affection : whatever terms therefore the
ftrongeft friendfhip can require upon an occa-
fion of this nature, let your imagination fup-
ply for me in the prefent.   I will only affure
you, that your good offices to the agents, the
fervants, and the family of Lamia, in every ar-
ticle wherein his affairs in your province fhall re-
quire them, will be a more acceptable inftance
of your generofity than any you could confer in
my own perfonal concerns.   I am perfuaded in-
deed from your great penetration into the cha-
racters of men, that without my recommenda-
tion you would be perfectly well-difpofed to give
him your beft affiftance.   I muft confefs at the
fame time, I have heard that you fufpect him of
having figned fome decree of the fenate injurious
to your honour.   But I muft affure you, in the
firft place, that he never figned any during the
admi-

A.U. 710. adminiftration of thofe confuls [6] ; and in the next, that almoft all the decrees which were pretended to be paffed at that time, were abfolutely forged. The truth is, you might juft as reafonably fuppofe I was concerned in that decree to which my name was fubfcribed, relating to Sempronius; tho' in fact I was then abfent from Rome, and complained, I remember, of the injury that had been done me, in a letter which I wrote to you upon the occafion. But not to enter farther into this fubject; I moft earneftly intreat you, my dear Cornificius, to confider the intereft of Lamia, in all refpects, as mine, and to let him fee that my recommendation has proved of fingular advantage to his affairs; affuring yourfelf, that you cannot in any inftance more effectually oblige me. Farewel.

[6] It is altogether uncertain to what confuls Cicero alludes : Manutius fuppofes, to Antony and Dolabella.

LETTER XXII.

To the Same.

COrnificius delivered your letter to me on the A.U. 710. 17th of March, about three weeks, as he told me, after he had received it from your hands. 'The senate did not assemble either on that day, or the next; however on the 9th they met: when I defended your cause in a very full house, and with no unpropitious regards from Minerva [1]. I may with peculiar propriety say so, as the statue of that guardian goddess of Rome, which I formerly erected in the Capitol [2], and which had lately been thrown down by an high wind, was at the same time decreed to be replaced. Your letter which Panfa read to the senate was much approved, and afforded great satisfaction to the whole assembly. It fired them at the same time with general indignation against the impudent

[1] It was a sort of proverbial expression among the Romans, when they spoke of any succesful undertaking, to say that it was carried on " not without the approbation of Minerva."

[2] " Cicero a little before his retreat into banishment, took " a small statue of Minerva, which had long been reverenced " in his family as a kind of tutelar deity, and carrying it to " the Capitol, placed it in the temple of Jupiter, under the " title of *Minerva the guardian of the city*." Life of Cic. i. 350.

Vol. III.   R   attempts

 attempts of the horrid *Minotaur* : for fo I may well call thofe combined adverfaries of yours, Calvifius and Taurus[3]. It was propofed therefore that the cenfure of the fenate fhould pafs upon them : but that motion was over-ruled by the more merciful Panfa. However, a decree was voted upon this occafion extremely to your honour.

As for my own good offices in your favour ; be affured, my dear Cornificius, they have not been wanting from the firft moment I conceived a hope of recovering our liberties. Accordingly when I laid a foundation for that purpofe on the 20th of December laft [4], while the reft of thofe who ought to have been equally forward in that work, ftood timidly hefitating in what manner to act, I had a particular view to the preferving you in your prefent poft : and to this end I prevailed with the fenate to agree to my motion concerning the continuance of the proconfuls in their refpective provinces. But my zeal in your caufe

[3] The Minotaur was a fabulous monfter, which the poets defcribe as half man half bull. Cicero therefore in allufion to the name of Taurus who had joined with Calvifius in fome combination againft Cornificius, jocofely gives them the appellation of the Minotaur.

[4] When he fpoke his third and fourth Philippic orations : wherein Cicero endeavoured, amongft other articles, to animate the fenate and the people to vigorous meafures againft Antony.

did

did not terminate here : and I still continued my
attacks upon that person, who in contempt of
the senate, as well as most injuriously to you, had,
even whilst he himself was absent from Rome,
procured your government to be allotted to him.
My frequent, or to speak more properly, my in-
cessant remonstrances against his proceedings,
forced him, much against his inclinations, to en-
ter Rome : where he found himself obliged to re-
linquish the hopes of an honour, which he thought
himself no less sure of than if it had been in his
actual possession. It gives me great pleasure that
these my just and honest invectives against your
adversary, in conjunction with your own exalted
merit, have secured you in your government : as
I rejoice extremely likewise in the distinguished
honours you have there received.

I very reddily admit of your excuse in regard
to Sempronius ; well knowing that your conduct
upon that occasion may justly be imputed to
those errors to which we were all equally liable,
whilst we trod the dark and dubious paths of
bondage. I myself indeed, the grave inspirer of
your counsels and the firm defender of your dig-
nities, even I, my friend, was injudiciously hur-
ried away by my indignation at the times, when
too hastily despairing of liberty, I attempted

 to retire into Greece [6]. But the Etesian winds, like so many patriot-citizens, refused to waft me from the commonwealth: whilst Auster conspiring in their designs, collected his whole force and drove me back again to Regium. From thence I returned to Rome with all the expedition that sails and oars could speed me: and the very next day after my arrival, I shewed the world that I was the only man, amidst a race of the most abject slaves, that dared to assert his freedom and independency [7]. I inveighed indeed against the measures of Antony with so much spirit and indignation, that he lost all manner of patience; and pointing the whole rage of his bacchanalian fury at my devoted head, he at first endeavoured to gain a pretence of assassinating me in the senate: but that project not succeeding, his next resource was to lay wait for my life in private. But I extricated myself from his insidious snares, and drove him, all reeking with the fumes of his nauseous intemperance, into the toils of Octavius [8]. That excellent youth drew

[6] An account of this intended voyage has already been given in a former note. See rem. 3. p. 134. of this vol.

[7] This seems to allude to his having refused to pay obedience to a summons from Antony, to attend a meeting of the senate which was held on that day. See rem. 1. p. 142. of this vol.

[8] Octavius as soon as he returned into Italy after the death of Cæsar, endeavoured to secure Cicero in his interest: as Ci-

together a body of troops, in the firſt place, A.U.710.
for his own and my particular defence; and in
the next for that of the republic in general : which

cero appeared no leſs forward to embrace the friendſhip of
Octavius. They both of them indeed had one of the ſtrongeſt
of all motives, perhaps, for a mutual coalition : as there is
nothing in which men ſeem to unite more amicably, than in
hunting down the ſame common foe.   The league however
into which Cicero entered with Octavius, extended no far-
ther at firſt than to a matter of mere civil controverſy : and
he only engaged to ſupport Octavius in his claim of part of
Cæſar's eſtate, which Antony, it was alledged, injuriouſly
with-held from him.   But even this was going a greater
length, than a true patriot could prudently have ventured.
For tho' the conteſt between Antony and Octavius with re-
ſpect to the money in queſtion was altogether perſonal ; yet
"   by natural conſequence (as the accurate obſerver upon the
"   epiſtles between Cicero and Brutus juſtly remarks) it be-
"   came a matter of more extenſive concern.   In the firſt
"   place, it was joined with the ſucceſſion to the name of Cæ-
"   ſar : which was looked upon by the chiefs of the Cæſarean
"   party as an earneſt of the continuance of the public ſettle-
"   ment made by Cæſar in the perſon of Octavius ; and on
"   the ſame account it was always ſuſpected by the more dif-
"   cerning republicans.   In the next place, it gave Octavius
"   the plauſible occaſion of being the diſtinguiſhed aſſertor of
"   Cæſar's acts, and of the full execution of all his bequeſts :
"   by which means he drew upon himſelf the eyes of all the
"   veterans, the military force of the empire, and intereſted
"   the whole populace of Rome in his cauſe ; ſince it was the
"   common cauſe of all who were expecting with impatience
"   the effect of Cæſar's liberality."   However, had Cicero's
engagements with Octavius ended here ; his conduct might
have been excuſed at leaſt, tho' it certainly could not have
been juſtified.   But when he afterwards armed Octavius with
the power and the dignities of the ſtate ; when he truſted (as
the excellent-author of the obſervations on his life ingeni-
ouſly expreſſes it) *the laſt ſtake of liberty in the hands of a man
who had ſo great temptations to betray it* ; he ſeems clearly to
have acted in contradiction to the ſentiments of his heart,
and to have ſacrificed the cauſe of the republic to the hatred
he bore to Antony. Plutarch expreſly aſſigns this as Cicero's

R 3

if

A.U. 710. if he had not happily raifed, Antony, in his re-
turn from Brundifium, would have fpread defo-
lation, like a wafting peftilence, around the land.
What followed I need not add ; as I imagine you
are well apprifed of all that has happened fubfe-
quent to that period. To return then to what
gave occafion to this digreffion ; let me again af-
fure you, that I am perfectly well fatisfied with
your excufe concerning Sempronius. The truth
is, it was impoffible to act with any deter-
mined fteddinefs and uniformity in times of
fuch total anarchy and confufion. " But other
" days (to ufe an expreffion of Terence) are now
" arrived, and other meafures are now required."
Come then, my friend, let us fail forth together,
and even take our place at the helm. All the
advocates of liberty are embarked in one com-
mon bottom : and it is my utmoft endeavour
to fteer them right. May profperous gales then
attend our voyage ! But whatever winds may arife,

motive for declaring in favour of Octavius : which indeed is
abundantly confirmed by his letters to Atticus. It appears
from thefe that there was fo little difference with refpect to
the republican intereft, whether Antony or Octavius was at
the head of affairs, that neither Atticus, nor Cicero could
determine in that view which to prefer : *valde tibi affentior*,
fays our author to his friend, *fi multum poffit Octavianus,
multò firmius acta tyranni comprobatum iri, quam in telluris :
atque id contra Brutum fieri. Sin autem vincitur, vides into-
lerabilem Antonium ; ut quem velis nefcias.* Ad At. xvi. 14.
Plut. in Brut. Tunftal's obferv. on the epift. between Brut.
and Cic. p. 132. Obferv. on the life of Cic. p. 50.

my

my beſt ſkill, moſt aſſuredly, ſhall not be want-
ing : and is it in the power of patriotiſm to be
anſwerable for more ? In the mean time, let it be
your care to cheriſh in your breaſt every gene-
rous and exalted ſentiment ; remembering always
that your true glory muſt ever be inſeparably
connected with the republic.   Farewel.

A.U. 710.

LETTERS

OF

Marcus Tullius Cicero

TO

Several of his FRIENDS.

BOOK XIV.

LETTER I.

GALBA [1] to CICERO.

ON the 15th of this month, the day on which Panſa intended to join the army of Hirtius, Antony drew out of his lines the ſecond and thirty-fifth legions, toge-

A.U.713.

---

[1] He had been one of Cæſar's lieutenants in Gaul; but not being favoured by him in his purſuit of the conſulſhip, he joined in the conſpiracy with Brutus and Caſſius. He was great-grand-father to the emperor Galba. *Quartier.*

ther

A.U.710. ther with his own prætorian cohort, and that of Silanus [2]; both which were compofed of the Evocati [3]. I happened at this time to be in Panfa's army; having been fent an hundred miles exprefs, in order to haften his march. Antony advanced towards us with thefe troops, in the fuppofition that our forces confifted only of four new-raifed legions: whereas Hirtius, the better to fecure our junction, had taken advantage of the preceding night to reinforce us with the *martial* legion, which I generally commanded, as alfo with two prætorian cohorts. Thefe regiments upon the very firft appearance of Antony's cavalry, could by no means be reftrained from engaging: fo that we were under an abfolute neceffity of following them to the charge. Antony in order to deceive us into a belief that none of his legions were with him, had pofted them at Forum-gallorum [4], and only appeared with his horfe and light-armed troops in view. Panfa when he faw that contrary to his inclination the *martial* legion had rufhed on to the attack, gave directions that two of his new-raifed

[2] He was military tribune in the army of Lepidus; and by the fecret connivance, if not by the exprefs orders, of that general, had conducted a body of troops to the affiftance of Antony in the fiege of Modena. *Dio.* xlvi. p. 336.

[3] See rem. 1. p. 340. vol. i.

[4] Now called Caftel-Franco: a fmall village on the Æmilian way, between Modena and Bologna.

legions

legions which were behind, fhould immediately
come up.   As foon as we had paffed the woods
and a morafs, we formed in order of battle with
twelve cohorts⁵; the other two legions I juft
now mentioned not being yet arrived.   Antony
obferving this, drew all his forces out of the vil-
lage, and inftantly began the engagement.   Both
fides maintained the firft onfet with the moft ob-
ftinate bravery: tho' indeed our right wing, in
which I commanded eight cohorts of the *martial*
legion, at the very beginning of the action re-
pulfed Antony's thirty-fifth legion, and purfued
them above ****⁶ paces out of the field.   But I
no fooner obferved the enemy's cavalry attempt-
ing to furround the wing from which I had ad-
vanced, than I endeavoured to rejoin it; order-
ing at the fame time my light-armed troops to
engage Antony's Moorifh horfe, left they fhould
fall upon us in our rear.   But whilft I was at-
tempting to regain my poft, I found myfelf in
the midft of the enemy's troops, and perceived
Antony himfelf at a fmall diftance behind me.
Upon this, throwing my fhield crofs my fhoul-
ders, I galloped full fpeed towards one of our
new-raifed legions, which I faw advancing from

----

⁵ A cohort confifted of about four or five hundred men.

⁶ " The common editions add here *quingentos:* but it is
" not found either in Dr. Mead's MS. or any other autho-
" rity."   Mr. *Rofs.*

the

the camp; the enemy at the same time pursuing me on the one side, and our own men aiming their pikes at me on the other: but as the latter soon discovered who I was, I had the very extraordinary good fortune to escape. Cæsar's prætorian cohort[6], which was posted on the Æmilian road, made a very long and vigorous resistance. But our left wing, in which were two cohorts of the Martial legion, together with the prætorian cohort, and which formed indeed the weakest division of our army, began to give ground; being hemmed in by Antony's cavalry, in which he is extremely strong. As soon as all our troops had made good their retreat, I began to think of mine; and was the last that entered our camp. Antony considering himself as master of the field, imagined he could likewise take possession of our camp: but after an unsuccessful attempt, he retired with great loss.

As soon as Hirtius was informed of what had passed, he put himself at the head of twenty veteran cohorts, and meeting Antony in his return from the attack of our camp, engaged him upon the very spot where our action had just before happened; and entirely defeated his army. About ten o'clock that night, Antony with his cavalry regained his camp near Mutina; as Hirtius re-

[6] Octavius.

tired

tired to that which Panfa had quitted in the A.U.710. morning, and in which he had left the two legions that repulfed Antony.

The enemy have loft the greateft part of their veteran troops. But this advantage was not to be obtained without a lofs likewife on our fide; the prætorian cohorts, together with the Martial legion, having fomewhat fuffered in this action. We have taken two legionary ftandards [7], together with fixty others: and upon the whole have gained a very confiderable victory. Farewel.

From the camp, April the 20th.

L E T T E R   II.

Plancus to Cicero [8].

IT affords me great pleafure to reflect, that I have amply juftified your favourable reprefentations of me, by having ftrictly fulfilled the promifes I made you. I give you a proof likewife of my particular affection, by acquainting you before any other of my friends, with the

[7] Each legion had a chief ftandard carried before it, upon which was fixed the figure of an eagle: there was a particular one likewife to every company.

[8] When Plancus wrote this letter, he had not received advice of the action between the troops of Antony and thofe of the republic: of which an account has been given in the preceding epiftle.

meafures

A.U.710. meafures I have taken.   I hope you are well per-
fuaded, that the republic will daily receive ftill
ftronger inftances of my attachment : let me af-
fure you at leaft, that you fhall be more and
more convinced of it by the cleareft and moft
unqueftionable evidence.   As to what concerns
my own perfonal intereft; I proteft to you, my
dear Cicero, by all my hopes of refcuing the re-
public from thofe imminent dangers to which it
is expofed, that notwithftanding I efteem thofe il-
luftrious recompences which are conferred by the
fenate as no lefs defirable than immortal fame,
yet, believe me, I fhall not in the leaft remit of my
earneft endeavours to affift the commonwealth,
altho' I fhould never participate of its glorious
rewards.   If the ardor and efficacy of my zeal,
fhould not diftinguifh me, amidft thofe many
excellent citizens who ftand forth in the defence
of our country ; let not your fuffrage contribute
to the increafe of my honours.   I have no ambi-
tion inconfiftent with that general equality for
which I have taken up arms : and am perfectly
well contented to leave it to your own determina-
tion both when and in what manner my fervices
fhall be recompenfed.   Nothing indeed can be
deemed too late or too inconfiderable, which is
given to a man as a public teftimony of his coun-
try's approbation.

9

Having

Having reached the Rhone by long marches, A.U. 710.
I paſſed that river with my whole army on the
27th of April: and immediately ordered a detach-
ment of a thouſand horſe to advance before
me from Vienna [9], by a ſhorter road.   If I meet
with no obſtructions on the part of Lepidus, I
doubt not of giving the republic reaſon to be ſa-
tisfied with my diligence and expedition: but if
he ſhould attempt to intercept my paſſage, I muſt
take my meaſures as circumſtances ſhall require.
Of this however I will now aſſure you, that the
army I am conducting is highly reſpectable,
whether conſidered with regard to the na-
ture, the number, or the fidelity of my troops.
I will only add, that I deſire your friendſhip upon
no other terms than as you are ſure I ſhall al-
ways give you the warmeſt returns of mine.
Farewel.

9 'Tis now called Vienne: a city in the province of Dau-
phiny, ſituated upon the Rhone.

LETTER III.

DECIMUS BRUTUS TO CICERO.

A.U. 710. YOU are senfible how great a lofs the republic has fuftained, by the death of Panfa[1]. It behoves you therefore to exert all your credit and addrefs to prevent our enemies from entertaining any reafonable hope of recovering their ftrength, now that they have thus deprived us of both our confuls[2]. I am preparing to purfue Antony immediately: and I truft fhall be able to render it impoffible either for Antony to continue in Italy, or for Ventidius[3] to efcape out of it.

[1] Panfa died at Bologna a few days after the battle of Mutina, of the wounds he received in that action. *Appian* iii. p. 572.

[2] Hirtius and Octavius after the battle mentioned in the preceding note, "were determined at all hazards to relieve "Modena: and after two or three days fpent in finding the "moft likely place of breaking thro' the intrenchments, they "made their attack with fuch vigor, that Antony rather "than fuffer the town to be fnatched at laft out of his hands, "chofe to draw out his legions and come to a general battle. "The fight was bloody and obftinate: and Antony's men, "tho' obliged to give ground, bravely difputed every inch "of it: till Decimus Brutus, taking the opportunity at the "fame time to fally out of the town at the head of his garrifon, helped greatly to determine and complete the victory. "Hirtius pufhed his advantage with great fpirit, and forced "his way into Antony's camp: but when he had gained "the middle of it, was unfortunately killed near the gene"ral's tent." *Life of Cic.* iii. 204.

[3] Ventidius was a foldier of fortune, who from the meaneft

As I suppose you see very clearly the measures A.U.710.
which Pollio will pursue, I need say nothing to
you upon that article.   But I make it my first
and principal request that you would send to
Lepidus, in order, if possible, to prevent that
light and inconstant man from renewing the war,
by joining with Antony: as both Lepidus and
Pollio are at the head of very numerous and
powerful armies.   I do not mention this as ima-
gining that you are not equally attentive to these
important points; but from the firm persuasion

original became one of the most distinguished captains of
the age.   The father of Pompey having taken the city of
Ascalum in the Italic or social war, reserved part of the in-
habitants to grace his triumphal entry into Rome; among
which was the mother of Ventidius, who walked before the
victor's car with her infant son at her breast.   When he
grew up, he gained his livelihood by serving as a groom;
in which employment having gotten together a little money,
he furnished himself with some mules and carriages, which
he let out to the government for the use of the proconsuls
in their way to the provinces.   In this capacity he became
known to Cæsar, who observing in him a genius much supe-
rior to his station, took him into Gaul, where he advanced
him in his army; and after the civil wars were ended, gave
him a place in the senate, and created him prætor.   After
the death of Cæsar, he attached himself to the interest of
Antony: to whose assistance he was at this time marching
at the head of a considerable body of troops, which he had
raised out of Cæsar's veteran legions that were dispersed in
different parts of Italy.   Towards the end of the present
year, the triumvirate appointed him consul. Having shortly
afterwards obtained a signal victory over the Parthians, his
conduct and bravery were rewarded with a triumph: and
to crown the series of his glory, he was honoured at his
death with a public funeral. *Aul. Gel.* xv. 4. *Dio.* xliii.
p. 239. *Vel. Paterc.* ii. 65.

A.U.710. that Lepidus, however dubious it may perhaps appear to the senate, will never of himself act in the manner he ought. Let me intreat you likewise to confirm Plancus in his present resolutions : who, I should hope, when he sees Antony driven out of Italy, will not be wanting in his assistance to the republic. If the latter should have crossed the Alps, I purpose to post a proper number of forces to guard the passes of those mountains [4]: and you may depend upon my giving you regular notice of all my motions. Farewel.

From my camp at Regium [5].
April the 29th.

LETTER IV.

TO PLANCUS.

HOW pleasing was the letter I received from you two days before our victory at Mutina! wherein you gave me an account of the state of your troops, of your zeal to the republic, and of the expedition with which you were ad-

[4] The intent of this guard seems to have been what Mr. Rols conjectures, in order to intercept the march of Ventidius, and prevent him from following Antony over the Alps.

[5] A town upon the Æmilian way, between Modena and Parma. It is now called Reggio.

vancing

vancing to the relief of Brutus. But notwith-
standing that the enemy was defeated before you
could join our army: the hopes neverthelefs of
the commonwealth are ftill fixed entirely upon
you: as the principal leaders of thefe infamous
rebels have efcaped, it is faid, from the field of
battle. You will remember therefore, that to
exterminate the remains of this party, will be a
fervice no lefs acceptable to the fenate, than if
you had given them the firft repulfe.

I am waiting, as well as many others, with
great impatience for the return of your couriers.
I hope that our late fuccefs will now induce even
Lepidus himfelf to act in concert with you, for
the defence of the common caufe. I intreat you,
my dear Plancus, to employ your utmoft endea-
vours for this important purpofe; that every
fpark of this horrid war may be utterly and for
ever extinguifhed. If you fhould be able to effect
this, you will render a moft godlike fervice to
your country, and at the fame time procure im-
mortal honour to yourfelf. Farewel.

May the 5th.

LETTER V.

To the Same.

A.U. 710.

I Seifed the very firft opportunity of contributing to the augmentation of your dignities : and I omitted no diftinction that could be confidered either as the applaufe or reward of merit. This you will perceive by the decree which has been voted to your honour with the utmoft zeal and unanimity in a very full houfe : and it is expreffed in the very words I dictated from a paper which I had drawn up for that purpofe. I was fenfible at the fame time from your letter, that it was more your ambition to approve your actions to every honeft mind, than to be diftinguifhed with thefe infigns of glory : but I thought it incumbent upon the republic to confider, not what you defire, but what you deferve. Let me only intreat you to finifh the work which others have fo happily begun ; remembering that whoever fhall deftroy Antony, will have the whole honour of concluding this war. It is thus that Homer gives the glory, not to Ajax, nor Achilles, but to Ulyffes alone, of having exterminated Troy [6]. Farewel.

---

[6] In the original it is, *Homerus non Ajacem, nec Achillem, fed Ulyffem appellavit* πλοιπορθιον ; which is not ftrictly

LET-

L E T T E R VI.

Decimus Brutus to Cicero.

I Look upon the obligations I have received A.U.710. from you, as nothing inferior even to thofe which I have conferred upon the republic: but I am not capable, you are well affured, of making you fo ill a return as I have experienced from fome of my ungrateful countrymen. It might perhaps in the prefent conjuncture, be thought to have fomewhat the air of flattery were I to fay, that your fingle applaufe outweighs, in my efteem, their whole united approbation. It is certain however, that you view my actions by the faithful light of difpaffionate truth, and reafon: whereas they, on the contrary, look upon them through the clouds of envy and malevolence. But I am little concerned how much foever they may oppofe my honours; provided they do not obftruct me in my fervices to the republic: the very dangerous fituation of which, let me now point out to you in as few words as poffible.

true: for Homer frequently gives that epithet to Achilles. Plancus however could not miftake the hint, that any ftratagem would be fair and honourable which fhould for ever remove Antony out of their way.

S 3

In

A.U.710.   In the first place then, you are sensible what great disturbances the death of the consuls [7] may create in Rome: as it may give occasion to all the dangerous practices that ambition will suggest to those, who are desirous of succeeding to their office [8]. This is all that prudence will allow me to say in a letter: and all indeed that is necessary to be said to a man of your penetration. As to Antony, notwithstanding he made his escape from the field of battle with but a very few troops, and those too entirely disarmed; yet by setting open the prisons, and by pressing all sorts of men that fell in his way, he has collected no contemptible number of forces. These have likewise been considerably augmented by the accession of the veteran and other troops of Ventidius: who after a very difficult march over the Apennine mountains, has found means to join Antony in the fens of Sabata [9]. The only possible scheme which the latter can pursue, is, either to have recourse to Lepidus, if that general should be disposed to receive him; or to post himself on the Alps and Apennines, in order to make depreda-

[7] Hirtius and Panfa.

[8] This seems plainly to point at Octavius; who in fact soon after procured himself to be elected consul, in conjunction with Quintus Pedius.

[9] Between the Alps and the Apennines, on the coast of Genoa.

tions

tions with his cavalry (in which he is exceedingly A.U. 710.
ſtrong) on the neighbouring country ; or to
march into Etruria [1], where we have no army to
oppoſe him. Had Cæſar however paſſed the
Apennine mountains agreeably to my advice [2], I
ſhould have driven Antony into ſuch difficulties,
that perhaps without ſtriking a ſingle blow, I
ſhould have been able to have waſted his whole
army by famine. But the misfortune is, that
Cæſar will neither be governed by me, nor will
his army be governed by him: both which are
very unhappy circumſtances for our cauſe. This
then being the ſad ſtate of public affairs, can I
be follicitous, as I ſaid above, what oppoſition
I may meet with in reſpect to my own perſonal
honours? The particulars I have here mentioned
are of ſo very delicate a nature, that I know not
how you will be able to touch upon them in the
ſenate : or if you ſhould, I fear it will be to no

[1] Tuſcany.

[2] " Octavius from the beginning had no thoughts of
" purſuing Antony. He had already gained what he
" aimed at ; had reduced Antony's power ſo low, and
" raiſed his own ſo high, as to be in a condition of making
" his own terms with him in the partition of the empire :
" whereas if Antony had been wholly deſtroyed, the repub-
" lican party would have probably been too ſtrong for him
" and Lepidus. When Octavius was preſſed therefore to
" purſue Antony, he contrived ſtill to delay it until it was
" too late ; taking himſelf to be more uſefully employed in
" ſecuring to his intereſt the troops of the conſuls." *Life
of Cic.* iii. 214.

S 4   purpoſe.

A.U. 710. purpofe. In the mean time I am in no condition to fubfift my troops any longer. When I firft took up arms for the deliverance of the commonwealth, I had above four hundred thoufand feftertia [3] in ready money: but at prefent I have not only mortgaged every part of my eftate, but have borrowed all I could poffibly raife on the credit of my friends. I leave you to judge therefore with what difficulty I now maintain feven legions at my own expence. The truth is, I fhould not be equal to fo great a charge, were I poffeffed of all Varro's [4] immenfe treafures.

As foon as I fhall receive any certain information of Antony's motions, I will give you notice. In the mean time, I will only add, that I defire the continuance of your friendfhip upon no other terms than as you fhall find an equal return of mine. Farewel.

From my camp at Tertona [5], May the 5th.

---

[3] About 320,000l. fterling.

[4] Who this man of immenfe wealth was, is not known. There is no reafon to believe, that he was the celebrated Terentius Varro, to whom feveral letters in the preceding part of this collection are addreffed.

[5] *Tortona*, about thirty miles north from Genoa.

LET-

L E T T E R VII.

Plancus to Cicero.

I Give you a thousand and a thousand thanks A.U.710. for your late favours: which as long as I live I shall always most gratefully acknowledge. More than this I dare not venture to promise. For I fear it will never be in my power to acquit such uncommon obligations : unless you should think (what your letter endeavours indeed with much serious eloquence to persuade me) that to remember them is to return them. You could not have acted with a more affectionate zeal, if the dignities of your own son had been in question : and I am perfectly sensible of the high honours that were decreed to me in consequence of your first motion for that purpose. I am sensible too, that all your subsequent votes in my behalf, were entirely conformable to the circumstances of the times and the opinion of my friends: as I am informed likewise of the advantageous colours in which you are perpetually representing me, as well as of the frequent contests you sustain with my injurious detractors. It is incumbent upon me therefore, in the first place, to endeavour to convince the republic that I am worthy of the praises you bestow upon

me ;

A.U.710. me; and in the next place, to render you fen-
fible, that I gratefully bear your friendfhip in re-
membrance. I will only add under this article,
that I defire you to protect me in the honours I
have thus procured by your influence: but I
defire it no otherwife than as my actions fhall
prove that I am the man you wifh to find me.

As foon as I had paffed the Rhone, I detached
a body of three thoufand horfe under the com-
mand of my brother, with orders to advance
towards Mutina: to which place I intended to
follow them with the reft of my army. But on
my march thither I received advice, that an action
had happened and that the fiege was raifed. An-
tony, I find, has no other refource left but to
retire into thefe parts with the remains of his
broken forces. IIis only hopes indeed are, that
he may be able to gain either Lepidus, or his
army: in which there are fome troops no lefs
difaffected to the republic than thofe which
ferved under Antony himfelf. I thought proper
therefore to recall my cavalry, and to halt in the
country of the Allobroges[7]; that I may be ready

---

[6] In the fecond letter of this book, Plancus fays this de-
tachment confifted only of a thoufand horfe: in one or other
therefore of thefe paffages the tranfcribers muft have com-
mitted fome miftake.

[7] It comprehended the territories of Geneva with part of
Savoy and Dauphine: and formed a diftrict of the province
under the command of Lepidus.

to

to act as circumftances fhall require.   If Antony A.U.710.
fhould retire into this country, deftitute of men;
I make no doubt, notwithftanding that he fhould
be received by the army of Lepidus, to be able
to give a good account of him with my prefent
forces.   Should he even appear at the head of
fome troops, and fhould the tenth veteran legion
revolt, which, together with the reft of thofe
regiments, was by my means prevailed upon to
engage in the fervice of the republic; yet I fhall
endeavour, by acting on the defenfive, to prevent
him from gaining any advantage over us : which
I hope to effect, till a reinforcement from Italy
fhall enable me to exterminate this defperate
crew.   I will venture at leaft to affure you, my
dear Cicero, that neither zeal nor vigilance fhall
be wanting on my part for that purpofe.   It is
my fincere wifh indeed, that the fenate may have
no farther fears : but if any fhould ftill remain,
no man will enter into their caufe with greater
warmth and fpirit, nor be willing to fuffer more
in the fupport of it, than myfelf.

I am endeavouring to engage Lepidus to join
with me in the fame views : and I have promifed
him, if he will act with a regard to the intereft
of the republic, that I fhall upon all occafions
yield him an entire deference.   I have employed
my brother, together with Furnius and Late-
renfis,

 renfis[9], to negotiate this affociation between us: and no private injury done to myfelf fhall ever prevent me from concurring with my greateft enemy, whenever it may be neceffary for the defence of the commonwealth. But fhould thefe overtures prove unfuccefsful, I fhall ftill perfevere with the fame zeal (and perhaps with more glory) in my endeavours to give fatiffaction to the fenate. Take care of your health, and allow me an equal return of your friendfhip. Farewel.

LETTER VIII.

DECIMUS BRUTUS, Conful elect, to CICERO.

I Have received a duplicate of the letter you fent me by my couriers: to which I can only fay in return, that my obligations to you rife much higher than I can eafily difcharge.

I gave you an account in my laft, of the pofture of our affairs: fince which I have received intelligence, that Antony is on his march towards Lepidus. Among fome papers of Antony which are fallen into my hands, I found a lift of the feveral perfons whom he intended to em-

---

[9] Furnius, it has already been obferved, was lieutenant to Plancus: as Laterenfis acted in the fame capacity under Lepidus.

ploy

ploy as mediators in his behalf with Pollio, Le- A.U. 710.
pidus and Plancus: so that he has not yet, it
seems, given up all hopes of gaining the latter.
Nevertheless, I did not hesitate to send an imme-
diate express to Plancus with advice of Antony's
march.   I expect within a few days to receive
ambassadors from the Allobroges and all the other
districts of this province: and I doubt not of
dismissing them strongly confirmed in their alle-
giance to the republic. You will be attentive on
your part, I dare say, to promote all such neces-
sary measures at Rome as shall be agreeable to
your sentiments, and to the interest of the com-
monwealth.   I am equally persuaded that you
will prevent, if it be possible to prevent, the
malevolent schemes of my enemies.   But if you
should not succeed in these generous endeavours,
you will at least have the satisfaction to find
that no indignities they can throw upon me,
are capable of deterring me from my purposes.
Farewel.

From my camp on the frontiers of the Statiel-
lenses [1].   May the 5th.

---

[1] A territory in Liguria, the principal town of which
was *Aquæ Statiellorum*, now called Aqui, in the district of
Montferat.

LETTER IX.

PLANCUS to CICERO.

A.U. 710. SOME occurrences have arisen since I closed my former letter, of which I think it may import the republic that you should be apprised: as both the commonwealth and myself, I hope, have reaped advantage from my assiduity in the affair I am going to mention. I sollicited Lepidus by repeated expresses to lay aside all animosities between us, and amicably unite with me in concerting measures for the succour of the republic; conjuring him to prefer the interest of his family and his country to that of a contemptible and desperate rebel; and assuring him if he did so, that he might entirely command me upon all occasions. Accordingly by the intervention of Laterensis, I have succeeded in my negociation: and Lepidus has given me his honour, that if he cannot prevent Antony from entering his province [2], he will most certainly lead his army against him. He requests likewise that I would join him with my forces; and the rather, as Antony is extremely strong in cavalry, whereas that

---

[2] Narbonensian Gaul: which together with part of Spain composed the province of Lepidus.

of

of Lepidus is very inconfiderable: and out of thefe few, ten of his beft men have lately deferted to my camp. As foon as I received this ex- prefs, I loft no time to forward and affift the good intentions of Lepidus. I clearly faw indeed the advantage that would arife from my joining him: as my horfe would be of fervice in purfu- ing and deftroying Antony's cavalry, and as the prefence of my troops in general would be a re- ftraint upon the difaffected part of thofe under his command. To this end, having fpent a day in throwing a bridge acrofs the Ifara [1], a very confi- derable river, that bounds the territories of the Allobroges, I paffed it with my whole army on the 12th of May. But having received advice that Lucius Antonius [2] was advancing towards us with fome regiments of horfe and foot, and that he was actually arrived at Forum Julii [4]; I ordered on the 14th a detachment of four thoufand horfe to meet him under the command of my brother: whom I purpofe to follow by long marches with four light-armed legions and the remainder of my ca- valry. And fhould that Fortune which prefides over the republic, prove in any degree favourable

[1] It is now called the *Ifere*, a river in Dauphiné which falls into the Rhone.

[2] A brother of Mark Antony.

[4] Now called Frejus, a city in Provence.

A.U. 710. to my arms, I shall soon put an end at once both to our own fears, and to the hopes of these insolent rebels. But if the infamous Antony, apprised of our approach, should retire towards Italy; it will be the business of Brutus to intercept his march: and Brutus, I am persuaded, will not be wanting either in courage or conduct for that purpose. Nevertheless I shall in that case send my brother with a detachment of horse to harrass Antony in his retreat, and to protect Italy from his depredations. Farewel.

LETTER X.

Cassius, Proconsul, to Cicero.

YOUR letter [s] affords me a new proof of your extraordinary friendship. I find by it, that you are not only a well-wisher to my interest, (as you have at all times been indeed, for the sake of the republic as well as for my own) but enter into it with the warmest and most anxious follicitude. I was persuaded therefore, that as you could not suppose me capable of being inactive at a season when my country laboured under a general oppression, you would be

---

[s] This seems to be an answer to the 15th letter of the preceding Book, p. 219.

im-

impatient to hear both of my perfonal welfare and A.U. 711.
of the fuccefs of my military preparations. For
this reafon, as foon as Aulus Allienus had refigned
thofe legions into my hands which he brought
from Egypt [6], I wrote to you by different cou-
riers whom I difpatched to Rome. I fent a letter
at the fame time to the fenate: and if my people
obeyed their inftructions, it was not delivered till
it was firft read to you. But if thefe expreffes
fhould not be arrived, I am perfuaded they have
been intercepted by Dolabella: who after having
moft villainoufly murdered Trebonius [7], has
made himfelf mafter of his province.

[6] See rem. 3. p. 206. of this vol.

[7] It has already been obferved in rem. 4. p. 194. of
this vol. that Dolabella left Rome before the expiration of
his confulfhip, in order to poffefs himfelf of the govern-
ment of Syria. In his way thither he arrived at Smyrna;
where Trebonius, proconful of Afia Minor, refided. Tre-
bonius refufed him admittance into the city; but treated
him however with great civility, and many compliments
mutually paffed between them. With thefe Dolabella ap-
peared fatisfied, and pretending to purfue his march, pro-
ceeded towards Ephefus: but he returned in the night, and
making himfelf mafter of the city by furprife, feifed Trebo-
nius in his bed. Cicero in one of his Philippics, expatiates
upon the cruelties which Dolabella exercifed on this his un-
fortunate but illuftrious prifoner. He kept him two days un-
der torture to extort a difcovery of the public money in his
cuftody, infulting him at the fame time with the moft op-
probrious language: he then ordered his head to be cut off
and exhibited to the populace on the point of a fpear, his
body to be dragged through the principal ftreets of Smyrna,
and afterwards to be thrown into the fea. See rem. 8. p. 99.
of this vol. *Appian. B. C.* iii. p. 542. *Phil.* xi. 2, 3.

 All the troops which I found in Syria, have submitted to my authority. However I have been a little retarded in my preparations, in order to diftribute fome donatives which I had promifed to the foldiers : but I have now difcharged my engagements.

If you are fenfible that I have refufed no labours nor dangers for the fervice of my country; if it was by your advice and perfuafion that I took up arms againft thofe infamous invaders of our liberties ; if I have not only raifed an army for the defence of the commonwealth, but have even fnatched it from moft cruel and oppreffive hands ; let thefe confiderations recommend my interefts to your care and protection. Had Dolabella indeed poffeffed himfelf of thefe forces, the expectation of fuch an additional body of troops, even before they had actually joined Antony, would greatly have confirmed and ftrengthened his party. If upon this account therefore you think thefe foldiers deferve highly of the republic, let them experience the benefit of your patronage; nor fuffer them to have reafon to regret, that they preferred their duty to the commonwealth to all the powerful temptations of plunder and rapine. I muft alfo recommend it to your care, that due honours be paid to the generals Marcus and Crif-
pus.

pus [8].   As to Baſſus, he obſtinately refuſed to
deliver up the legion under his command : and
had they not without his conſent deputed ſome
of their officers to treat with me, he would
have ſhut the gates of Apamea, and forced me
to have entered the town by aſſault.   I make
theſe requeſts then, as well in the name of our
friendſhip, which I truſt will have much weight
with you; as in that of the republic, which has
ever, I know, been the object of your warmeſt
affection.   Believe me, the army under my com-
mand is zealouſly attached not only to the ſenate,
and to every friend of our country, but particularly
to yourſelf.   The frequent accounts indeed they
hear of your patriot-diſpoſition, have extremely
endeared you to them : and ſhould they find their
intereſts to be a part of your concern, they will
conſider you in all reſpects as their firſt and
greateſt benefactor.

Since I wrote the above, I have received intel-
ligence that Dolabella is marched into Cilicia :
whither I purpoſe immediately to follow him. I
will give you early notice of the event of this ex-
pedition : and may I ſo prove ſuccefsful as I
ſhall endeavour to deſerve well of the republic.

[8] Some account of theſe perſons, as well as of Baſſus men-
tioned in the next ſentence, has been given in the preceding
remarks.

T 2

Take

 Take care of your health and continue your friendſhip to me.   Farewel.

From my camp, May the 7th.

LETTER XI.

To Decimus Brutus, Conſul elect.

THE meſſage you commiſſioned Galba and Volumnius to deliver to the ſenate, ſufficiently intimates the nature of thoſe fears and ſuſpicions which you imagine we have reaſon to entertain.   But I muſt confeſs that the apprehenſions you would thus infuſe into us, ſeem by no means worthy of that glorious victory you have obtained over the enemies of the commonwealth.   Believe me, my dear Brutus, both the ſenate and the generals that ſupport its cauſe, are animated with an undaunted reſolution: we were ſorry therefore that you, whom we eſteem the braveſt captain that ever the republic employed, ſhould think us capable of any timidity.   Is it poſſible indeed, after having confidently repoſed our hopes on your courage and conduct when you were inveſted by Antony in all the fulneſs of his ſtrength and power, that any of us ſhould harbour the leaſt fear now that the ſiege is raiſed, and the enemy's army entirely

tirely overthrown ? Nor have we any thing, A.U. 710.
furely, to apprehend from Lepidus. For who
can imagine him fo utterly void of all rational
conduct, as to have profeſſed himſelf an advocate
for peace when we were engaged in a moſt ne-
ceſſary and important war, and yet to take up
arms againſt the republic the moment that moſt
defirable peace is reſtored ? You are far too
fagacious, I doubt not, to entertain ſuch a
thought [9]. Neverthelefs the fears you have re-
newed amongſt us at a time when every temple
throughout Rome is refounding with our thankf-
givings for your deliverance, have caſt a very
confiderable damp upon our joy. May the fact
prove then, (what indeed I am inclined to believe
as well as hope) that Antony is completely van-
quiſhed.   But ſhould he happen to recover fome
degree of ſtrength, he will moſt aſſuredly find
that neither the ſenate is deſtitute of wiſdom, nor
the people of courage : I will add too, nor the
republic of a general, fo long as you ſhall be alive
to lead forth her armies.   Farewel.

May the 19th.

[9] It will appear in the progreſs of thefe letters, that if
Cicero was really in earneſt in what he here ſays concern-
ing Lepidus, it was he himſelf, and not Brutus, who want-
ed fagacity.

LETTER XII.

PLANCUS to CICERO.

A.U.710. ANtony arrived at Forum-Julii with the van of his army, on the 15th of May: and Ventidius is only two days march behind him. Lepidus writes me word, that he propofes to wait for me at Forum-Voconii [1], where he is at prefent encamped: a place about four-and-twenty miles diftant from Forum-Julii. If he and Fortune do not deceive my expectations, the fenate may depend upon my fpeedily terminating this bufinefs to their full fatisfaction.

I mentioned to you in a former letter, that the great fatigues which my brother had undergone by his continual marches, had extremely impaired his conftitution. However, as foon as he was fufficiently recovered to get abroad, he confidered his health as an acquifition which he had gained as much for the fervice of the republic, as for himfelf: and was the firft therefore to engage in every hazardous expedition. But I have recommended it to him, and indeed infifted, that he fhould return to Rome: as he would be much more likely to wear himfelf away by

___
[1] Now called *Le Luc*, in Provence.

con-

continuing in the camp, than be able to give me A.U.710.
any affiftance. Befides, I imagined now that
the republic was moft unhappily deprived of
both the confuls, that the prefence of fo worthy
a magiftrate would be abfolutely neceffary at
Rome. But if any of you fhould think other-
wife; let *me* be cenfured for my imprudent ad-
vice; but let not my brother be condemned as
failing in his duty.

Lepidus, agreeably to my requeft, has deli-
vered Apella into my hands, as an hoftage for
the faithful execution of his engagements to co-
operate with me in the defence of the common-
wealth. Lucius Gellius has given me proofs of
his zeal: as he has acted alfo in the affair of the
three brothers, to the fatisfaction of Sextus Ga-
vianus. I have lately employed the latter in
fome negotiations between Lepidus and myfelf:
and I have found him firmly attached to the in-
tereft of the republic. It is with great pleafure I
give this teftimony in his favour: a tribute which
I fhall always be ready to pay where-ever it is de-
ferved.

Take care of your health, and allow me the
fame fhare of your heart which you moft affured-
ly poffefs of mine. I recommend my dignities
likewife to your protection: and I hope, if I can

T 4

plead

A.U.710. plead any merit, you will continue your good offices to me with the fame fingular affection you have hitherto difcovered.   Farewel.

LETTER XIII.

To CORNIFICIUS.

YOU recommend a friend of my own, when you defire my good offices to Lucceius: be affured I fhall faithfully fupport his intereft by every mean in my power.

We have loft our collegues [2] Hirtius and Panfa: and the death of thefe excellent confuls, who difcharged their office with great advantage to the republic, has happened at a very unfeafonable conjuncture.   For tho' we are at prefent deliver-ed from the oppreffions of Antony; we are not wholly free from all apprehenfions of danger. But if I may be permitted, I fhall continue my ufual endeavours to preferve the commonwealth from ruin: tho' I muft confefs, I am full weary of the work.   No laffitude, however, ought to obftruct the duties we owe to our country.—But I forbear to enter farther into this fubject; as I had rather you fhould hear of my actions from others, than from myfelf. The account I receive of yours is entirely agreeable to my wifhes: but

[2] In the college of augurs.

it is far otherwife with refpect to the reports con-A.U. 710.
cerning Minucius.   They are indeed very unfa-
vourable to his character; notwithftanding all
the fine things you faid of him in one of your
letters.   I fhould be glad to know the truth of
the cafe: and to be informed of every thing elfe
which is tranfacting in your province.   Fare-
wel.

LETTER XIV.

To Decimus Brutus, Conful elect.

IT is with infinite fatisfaction, my dear Brutus,
that I find you approve of my conduct in the
fenate with refpect both to the decemvirs [9],
and to the honours decreed to our young [1] man.
Yet after all, what have my labours availed? Be-
lieve me, my friend, (and you know I am not
apt to boaft) the fenate was the grand engine of
my power: but all thofe fprings which I ufed
fo fuccefsfully to manage, have utterly loft

[9] Thefe decemvirs were probably the ten perfons whom
the fenate in the firft tranfports of their fuppofed compleat
victory before the walls of Modena, had appointed to inquire
into the conduct of Antony during his adminiftration of the
confular office. *Vid. Appian. B. C.* iii. 578.

[1] Octavius.   The honours here mentioned were perhaps,
the ovation, (a kind of inferior and lefs fplendid triumph)
which by the influence of Cicero was decreed to young Cæfar
for his fervices at the fiege of Modena.   See *Life of Cic.* iii.
P. 211.

their

A.U.710. their force, and I can no longer direct its motions. The truth of it is, the news of your glorious fally from the garrifon of Mutina ; of Antony's flight ; and of his army being entirely cut to pieces ; had infpired fuch confident hopes of a complete victory, that the difappointment has caft a general damp upon the fpirit I had raifed againft our enemies : and all my ardent invectives feem at laft to have proved juft as infignificant as if I had been combating with my own fhadow.— But to the purpofe of your letter.—Thofe who are acquainted with the difpofitions of the fourth and the *martial* legions, affure me, they will never be prevailed on to ferve under you. As to the fupply of money which you defire ; fome meafures may, and moft affuredly fhall, be taken in order to raife it.—I am wholly in your fentiments with regard to the calling Brutus [2] out of Greece, and retaining Cæfar here for the protection of Italy. I agree with you likewife, my dear Brutus, that you have enemies : and tho' I find it no very difficult matter to fuftain their attacks, yet ftill however, they fomewhat embarrafs my fchemes in your favour.

The legions from Africa [3] are daily expected. In the mean time the world is greatly aftonifhed

[2] Marcus Brutus.

[3] Thefe were fome of the veteran legions that had ferved under Julius Cæfar. See rem. 4. on let. 18. of this book.

to find that the war is broke out again in your A.U. 710.
province.   Nothing, in truth, ever happened so
unexpectedly: as we had promised ourselves,
from the account of the victory which was
brought to us on your birth-day, that the peace
of the republic was established for many genera-
tions.   But now all our fears are revived with as
much strength as ever.

You mentioned in your letter dated the 15th
of May, that you were just informed by an ex-
press from Plancus, that Lepidus had refused to
receive Antony.   Should this prove to be fact,
our business will be so much the easier; if not,
we shall have a very difficult struggle to main-
tain: and it depends upon you to ease me of my
great apprehensions for the event.   As for my
own part, I have exhausted all my powers; and
I am utterly incapable of doing more than I have
already performed.   It is far otherwise however,
with my friend: and I not only wish, but expect,
to see you the greatest and most distinguished
of Romans.   Farewel.

LETTER XV.

TO PLANCUS.

 NOthing, my dear Plancus, could be more glorious to yourself, nor more acceptable to the senate, than the letter you lately addressed to that assembly: I will add too, nothing could be more opportune than the particular juncture in which it was delivered. Cornutus received it in the presence of a very full house, just as he had communicated to us a cold and irresolute letter from Lepidus. Yours was read immediately afterwards: and it was heard with the loudest exclamations of applause. It was highly pleasing indeed to the senate, not only from the importance of its contents and those zealous services to the republic of which it gave us an account, but from that strength and elegance of expression with which it was animated. The senate was extremely urgent that it might immediately be taken into consideration: but Cornutus thought proper to decline their request. However, the whole assembly expressing great indignation at his refusal, the question was put by five of the tribunes of the people. When Servilius was called upon for his opinion, he

8

moved

moved that the debate might be adjourned. A.U. 710.
What my fentiments were (and I was fupported
in them by the unanimous concurrence of the
whole houfe) you will fee by the decree that paffed
upon this occafion.

I am fenfible that your own fuperior judgment
is abundantly fufficient to direct you in all emer-
gencies; yet I cannot forbear advifing you not
to wait for the fanction of the fenate in fo critical
a conjuncture as the prefent, and which undoubt-
edly muft often demand immediate action. Be
a fenate, my friend, to yourfelf: and without
any other authority fcruple not to purfue fuch
meafures as the intereft of the republic fhall re-
quire. In one word, let your actions anticipate
our expectations, and give us the pleafure of
hearing that you have executed fome glorious
exploits, ere we are fo much as apprifed that you
even had it in your intention. I will venture to
affure you, that the fenate will moft certainly
approve both your zeal and your judgment in
whatever you fhall thus undertake. Farewel.

LETTER XVI.

To DECIMUS BRUTUS, Conful elect.

A.U. 710.

I Am indebted to you for your fhort letter by Flaccus Volumnius, as well as for two others more full ; one of which was brought by the courier of Titus Vibius, the other was forwarded to me by Lupus : and all of them came to my hands on the fame day. I find by your own account as well as by that which Græceius has given me, that the war, far from being extinguifhed, feems to be breaking out again with greater violence. You are fenfible if Antony fhould gain any ftrength, that all your illuftrious fervices to the republic will be utterly fruftrated. The firft accounts we received here, and which indeed were univerfally credited, reprefented him as having run away in great confternation, attended only with a few frightened and difarmed foldiers. But if the truth, after all, fhould be (what Græceius affures me) that Antony is in fact fo ftrong as to render it unfafe to give him battle; he does not feem fo much to have fled from Mutina, as to have changed the feat of war. This unexpected

9

news has given all Rome another countenance, A.U. 710. and a general air of difappointment appears in every face. There are even fome amongſt us who complain of your not having immediately purſued Antony: for they imagine if no time had been loſt, that he muſt inevitably have been deſtroyed. But it is uſual with the people in all governments, and eſpecially in ours, to be particularly diſpoſed to abuſe their liberty, by licentious reflections on thoſe to whom they are indebted for the enjoyment of it. However, one ſhould be careful not to give them any juſt cauſe for their cenſures.

To ſay all in one word; whoever deſtroys Antony, will have the glory of terminating the war: a hint which I had rather leave to your own reflections, than enter myſelf into a more open explanation [3]. Farewel.

LETTER XVII.

DECIMUS BRUTUS to CICERO.

I Will no longer attempt to make any formal acknowledgments of the repeated inſtances I receive of your friendſhip: mere words are a very

---

[3] See rem. 6. p. 260. of this vol.

in-

 inadequate return to thofe obligations which my beft fervices can but ill repay. If you will look back upon my former letters, you cannot be at a lofs to difcover the reafons that prevented me from purfuing Antony immediately after the battle of Mutina. The truth, my dear Cicero, is, that I was not only unprovided both with cavalry and baggage-horfes, but not having at that time had an interview with Cæfar, I could not depend on his affiftance: and I was wholly ignorant likewife, that Hirtius was killed. This will account for my not having purfued Antony on the day of the engagement. The day following I received an exprefs from Panfa to attend him at Bononia: but in my way thither, being informed of his death, I immediately returned back to join my little corps. I may juftly call them fo indeed, as my forces are extremely diminifhed, and in a very bad condition from the great hardfhips they fuffered during the fiege. It was by thefe means that Antony got two days advance of me: and as he marched in diforder, he could retire much fafter than it was in my power to purfue. He increafed his forces likewife by prefling the inhabitants and throwing open the prifons in every town thro' which he paffed: and in this manner he continued his march till he arrived in the fens of Sabata. This is a place with which I muft

bring

bring you acquainted. It is situated between the A.U.710.
Alps and the Apennines, and the roads that lie
about it are scarce practicable. When I had
reached within thirty miles of Antony, I was in-
formed that he had been joined by Ventidius, and
had made a speech at the head of their combined
troops, to persuade them to follow him over the
Alps ; assuring them that Lepidus had agreed to
support him. Nevertheless, not only his own
soldiers (which indeed are a very inconsiderable
number) but those likewise of Ventidius repeat-
edly and unanimously declared that they were de-
termined either to conquer, or perish in Italy : and
at the same time desired that they might be con-
ducted to Pollentia *. Antony found it in vain to
oppose them : however, he deferred his march till
the ensuing day. As soon as I received this in-
telligence, I detached five cohorts to Pollentia :
and am now following them with the remainder
of my troops. This detachment threw themselves
into that city an hour before Trebellius arrived
with his cavalry : a circumstance which gives me
great satisfaction, as it is a point, I think, upon
which our whole success depends. When the
enemy found that their designs were thus frus-
trated, they conceived hopes of crossing the Alps
into Gaul : as they supposed the four legions com-

---

* Some remains of this city still subsist, under the name of
Polenzo. It is situated at the confluence of the Stura and the
Tanaro in Piemont.

 manded by Plancus would not be able to withstand their united forces; and that an army from Italy could not overtake them foon enough to prevent their paffage. However the Allobroges together with my detachment have hitherto been fufficient to prevent their defign: which I truft they will find ftill more difficult to effect, when I fhall come up with the reft of my forces. But fhould they happen in the mean time to pafs the Ifara, I fhall exert my utmoft endeavours that this circumftance may not be attended with any ill confequences to the commonwealth.

Let it raife the fpirits and the hopes of the fenate, to obferve that Plancus and myfelf, together with our refpective armies, act in perfect concert with each other, and are ready to hazard every danger in fupport of the common caufe. However, whilft you thus confidently rely on our zeal and diligence, you will remit nothing, I hope, of your own; but employ your utmoft care to fend us a reinforcement as well as every other neceffary fupply, that may render us in a condition to defend your liberties againft thofe who have infamoufly confpired their ruin. One cannot indeed but look upon thefe our enemies with fo much the greater indignation, as they have acted with the vileft hypocrify; and fuddenly turned thofe troops againft their country, which they long pretended to have raifed for its defence. Farewel.

L E T T E R   XVIII.

Decimus Brutus to Cicero.

I Wish you would peruse the letter I have ad-
dressed to the senate, and make what altera-
tions you shall judge proper.   You will find by
it, that I am under an absolute necessity of thus
applying to them.   Whilst I imagined that I
should be joined by the fourth and martial le-
gions [4], agreeably to the decree of the senate
which passed for that purpose on the motion of
Paulus and Drusus, I was less sollicitous about the
rest: but now that I have only some new-raised
regiments, and those too extremely ill accoutred,
I cannot but be apprehensive upon your accounts,
as well as upon my own.

The citizens of Vicentia [5] have always dif-
tinguished Marcus Brutus and myself by their
particular regard.   I intreat you therefore to en-
deavour that justice be done them by the senate, in
the affair concerning the slaves. They are indeed

----

[4] These were veteran legions which had served under C
far.   But notwithstanding that they entered into th
the late consuls Hirtius and Pansa, they could b; no
be prevailed with to join Decimus Brutus : in resent
probable, of the part he bore in the conspiracy agai
favourite general. *Vid. Ep. Famil.* xi. 14.

[5] *Vicenza:* a maritime city in the territories of the V
tians.

                 en-

A.U.710. entitled to your favour both by the equity of their
cauſe, and the fidelity with which they have upon
all occaſions perſevered in their allegiance to the
republic: whereas their adverſaries, on the con-
trary, are a moſt ſeditious and faithleſs people.
Farewel.

Vercellæ [6], May the 21ſt.

LETTER XIX.

MARCUS LEPIDUS [b] to CICERO.

HAving received advice that Antony was ad-
vancing with his troops towards my pro-
vince, and had ſent before him a detachment of
his cavalry under the command of his brother
Lucius; I moved with my army from the con-
fluence of the Rhone and the Arar [7], in order to
oppoſe their paſſage. I continued my march
without halting, till I arrived at Forum Voconii:
and am now encamped ſomewhat beyond that
town, on the river Argenteus [8], oppoſite to An-
tony. Ventidius has joined him with his three
legions; and has formed his camp a little above
mine. Antony before this conjunction had the

---

[6] Vercelli: in the dutchy of Milan.

[b] See rem. [a] p. 217. of this vol.

[7] The *Saone:* which falls into the Rhone at Lyons.

[8] The Argens, in Provence: it empties itſelf into the Me-
diterranean a few miles below Frejus.

ſecond

second legion entire, together with a confiderable A.U. 710.
number of men, tho' indeed wholly unarmed,
who efcaped from the general flaughter of his
other legions.   He is extremely ftrong in caval-
ry : for as none of thofe troops fuffered in the
late action, he has no lefs than *** [9] horfe. Great
numbers of his foldiers, both horfe and foot, are
continually deferting to my camp ; fo that his
troops diminifh every day.   Both Silanus [1] and
Culeo [2] have left his army, and are returned to
mine. But notwithftanding I was greatly offended
by their going to Antony, contrary to my incli-
nation; yet in regard to the connections that
fubfift between us, and in compliance with my
ufual clemency, I have thought proper to par-
don them. However, I do not upon any occafion
employ their fervices ; nor indeed fuffer them to
remain in the camp.

As to what concerns my conduct in this war;
you may depend upon it I fhall not be wanting in
my duty either to the fenate or the republic : and
whatever farther meafures I fhall take to this end,
I fhall not fail to communicate them to you.

[9] The number is omitted in all the antient MSS.

[1] See rem. 2. p. 250. of this vol.

[2] He had been fent by Lepidus with a body of men, under
the pretence of guarding the paffes of the Alps : but moft pro-
bably with fecret inftructions to favour the march of Antony
over thofe mountains in his way to the camp of Lepidus : for
he fuffered Antony to pafs them without the leaft obftruction.
Appian, B. C. iii. p. 579.

U 3

The

The friendſhip between us, has upon all occaſions been inviolably preſerved on both ſides; and we have mutually vied in our beſt good offices to each other. But I doubt not that ſince this great and ſudden commotion has been raiſed in the commonwealth, ſome falſe and injurious reports have been ſpread of me by my enemies, which, in the zeal of your heart for the intereſt of the republic, have given you much uneaſineſs. I have the ſatisfaction however to be informed by my agents at Rome, that you are by no means diſpoſed eaſily to credit theſe idle rumours: for which I think myſelf, as I juſtly ought, extremely obliged to you. I am ſo, likewiſe, for the former inſtances of your friendſhip in promoting my public honours: the grateful remembrance of which, be aſſured, is indelibly impreſſed upon my heart.

Let me conjure you, my dear Cicero, if you are ſenſible that my public conduct has upon all occaſions been worthy of the name I bear, to be perſuaded that I ſhall continue to act with equal, or, if poſſible, even with ſuperior zeal [a]. Let me hope too, that the greater the favours are which

---

[a] There was ſo little of truth in theſe profeſſions, that Lepidus within a very few days from the date of this letter openly joined with Antony againſt the ſenate. See let. 28. of this book.

you

you have conferred upon me, the more you will A.U.710.
think yourfelf engaged to fupport my credit and
character.   Farewel.

From my camp, at Pons Argenteus,
     May the 22d.

LETTER XX.

PLANCUS to CICERO.

YOU have been apprifed, no doubt, by Læ-
vus and Nerva, as well as by the letter they
delivered to you on my part, of the defign I was
meditating when they left me : as indeed they
have conftantly borne a fhare in all my councils
and meafures of every kind.   It has happened,
however, to me, what happens not unfrequently,
I fuppofe, to every man who is tender of his re-
putation, and defirous of approving his conduct
to the friends of his country : I have given up a
fafer fcheme, as being liable, perhaps, to fome ill-
natured exceptions, in exchange for a more dan-
gerous one that may better evince my zeal.   I
am to inform you then, that after the departure
of my lieutenants *, I received two letters from
Lepidus, intreating me to join him.   Thefe were
feconded by the much ftronger follicitations of

* Lævus and Nerva ; the perfons mentioned above.

A.U.710. Laterensis: who earneftly reprefented to me
—(what indeed I am alfo apprehenfive of myfelf)
that there is great reafon to fear a mutiny among
the difaffected troops under the conduct of Lepi-
dus. I determined immediately therefore to
march to his affiftance, and take an equal fhare
in the dangers with which he was threatened. I
was fenfible at the fame time, that to wait on the
banks of the Ifara till Brutus fhould pafs that
river with his army, and to meet the enemy in
conjunction with my collegue, whofe forces, as
well as their general, would act in perfect har-
mony with me and my troops, would be much
the moft cautious meafure with refpect to my
own perfonal fecurity. But I reflected, that if
any miffortune fhould attend Lepidus, it would
be wholly imputed to me: and I fhould be con-
demned either as obftinately fuffering my refent-
ment to prevent me from giving fuccour to my
enemy in the caufe of the republic, or of timidly
avoiding to take part in the danger of a moft juft
and neceffary war. As my prefence therefore
might be a mean of protecting Lepidus, and of
bringing his army into a better difpofition, I re-
folved to expofe myfelf to all hazards, rather than
appear to act with too much circumfpection. But
never was any man more anxious in an affair for
which he was in no fort anfwerable, than I am

in

in the prefent : for tho' I fhould have no manner A.U. 710.
of doubt if the army of Lepidus were not con-
cerned; yet under that circumftance, I am full
of apprehenfions for the event.   Had it been my
fortune to have met Antony before my junction
with Lepidus, I am fure he would not have been
able to have kept the field againft me even a
fingle hour: fuch is the confidence I have in my
own troops, and fo heartily do I defpife his bro-
ken forces, as well as thofe of that paltry mule-
teer, the contemptible Ventidius '.   But as the
cafe is now circumftanced, I dread to think what
may be the confequence fhould any ill humours lie
concealed in the army of Lepidus : as they may
poffibly break out in all their malignity, before
they can be remedied, or even difcovered.   It
is certain however, that Lepidus, together
with the well-affected part of his army, would be
expofed to great danger, if we fhould not act in
conjunction : befides, that our infamous enemies
would gain a very confiderable advantage, fhould
they draw off any of his forces.   If my prefence
therefore fhould prove a mean of preventing thefe
evils, I fhall think myfelf much indebted to my
courage and good fortune for engaging me to
make the experiment.   With this defign I moved
with my army from the banks of the Ifara on the

' See rem. 3. p. 256. of this vol.

 21ſt of May; having firſt erected a fort at each end of the bridge which I had thrown over that river, and placed a ſtrong party to defend it: that when Brutus ſhall arrive he may have nothing to retard his paſſage. I have only to add, that I hope to join Lepidus within eight days from the date of this letter. Farewel.

LETTER XXI.

From the Same to CICERO.

I Should be aſhamed that this letter is ſo little conſiſtent with my former, if it aroſe from any inſtability of my own. But it is much otherwiſe: and I have ſteadily purſued every meaſure in my power to engage Lepidus to act in concert with me for the defence of the republic; imagining it would render you leſs apprehenſive of my ſucceſs againſt our wretched enemies. To this end, I not only complied with all the conditions he propoſed, but even engaged for more than he demanded: and I had ſo much confidence in the ſincerity of his intentions, that I ventured to aſſure you no longer than two days ago, that he would zealouſly co-operate with me in carrying on the war upon one common plan. I depended indeed upon the promiſes he had given me under his own hand, to-

gether

gether with the affurances I had likewife received A.U. 710.
from Laterenfis, who was at that time in my
camp, and who earneftly conjured me to forget
all refentments againft Lepidus, and to rely upon
his good faith.   But Lepidus has now put it out
of my power to entertain thefe favourable hopes
of him any longer: however, I have taken, and
fhall continue to take, all neceffary precautions,
that the republic may not be prejudiced by my
too eafy credulity.   I am to inform you then, that
after I had ufed the utmoft expedition (agree-
ably to his own earneft requeft) to tranfport my
army over the Ifara, and for that purpofe had,
in the fpace of a fingle day, thrown a bridge
acrofs that river; I received a counter-exprefs
from him, requiring me to advance no farther;
as he fhould not have occafion, he faid, for my
affiftance.   Neverthelefs, I will own to you, I
was fo imprudent as to proceed in my march;
believing that the true reafon of his thus changing
his mind, arofe from an unwillingnefs to have
a partner with him in his glory.   I imagined
that without depriving him of any fhare of that
honour, which he feemed fo defirous to monopo-
lize, I might poft myfelf at fome convenient di-
ftance, in order to be ready to fupport him with
my troops in cafe he fhould be preffed by the
enemy: an event which, in the fimplicity of

my

 my heart, I thought not improbable. In the mean time I received a letter from the excellent Laterenſis, which was conceived in terms full of deſpair. He complained that he had been greatly deceived, and aſſured me that neither Lepidus, nor his army, were to be truſted. He expreſly cautioned me at the ſame time to be upon my guard againſt their artifices; adding that he had faithfully diſcharged the engagements he had entered into on his part, and hoped I would act with the ſame fidelity to the republic on mine. I have ſent a copy of this letter to Titius: and purpoſe to tranſmit the originals of all the reſt relating to this affair, by the hands of Lævus Ciſpius, who was privy to the whole tranſaction. I ſhall inſert in this packet the letters of Lepidus to which I did not give any credit, as well as thoſe to which I did.

I muſt not forget to add, that when Lepidus harangued his ſoldiers, theſe mighty honeſt fellows were exceedingly clamorous for peace. They proteſted that after the loſs of both the conſuls; after the deſtruction of ſo many brave men who had periſhed in defence of their country; and after Antony and his adherents had been declared enemies of the commonwealth and their eſtates confiſcated; they were determined not to draw their ſwords any more either on the one ſide or the other. They were prompted to be-
haave

A.U. 710.

have thus mutinously, not only by the infolent fuggeſtions of their own hearts, but by the encouragement alſo of their officers, particularly Canidius, Rufrenus, and others whoſe names the ſenate ſhall be acquainted with at a proper ſeaſon. Lepidus was ſo far from puniſhing this ſedition, that he did not take even a ſingle ſtep to reſtrain it. I thought therefore that it would be the higheſt temerity to expoſe my own faithful troops, together with my auxiliaries, which are commanded by ſome of the moſt conſiderable chiefs of Gaul, and in effect too my whole province, to their combined armies. I conſidered, if I ſhould thus loſe my life, and involve the republic in my own deſtruction, I ſhould fall, not only without honour, but without pity. In conſequence of theſe reflections, I have determined to march my forces back again, that our wretched enemies may not have ſo great an advantage as my advancing any farther might poſſibly give them. I ſhall endeavour to poſt my army ſo advantageouſly as to cover the province under my command from being inſulted, even ſuppoſing the troops of Lepidus ſhould actually revolt. In ſhort, it ſhall be my care to preſerve every thing in its preſent ſituation till the ſenate ſhall ſend an army hither, and vindicate the liberties of the republic with the ſame ſucceſs in this part of the world, as

attended

 attended their arms before the walls of Mutina. In the mean time be assured, that no man will act with more fervent zeal than myself in all the various occurrences of the war: and I shall most readily either encounter the enemy in the field, or sustain the hardships of a siege, or even lay down my life itself, as any of these circumstances shall prove necessary for the service of the senate. Let me exhort you then, my dear Cicero, to exert your utmost efforts to send a speedy reinforcement to me, ere Antony shall have encreased the number of his forces, or our own shall be entirely dispirited. For if dispatch be given to this affair, these infamous banditti will undoubtedly be extirpated, and the republic remain in full possession of her late victory. Take care of your health, and continue your friendship to me.

P. S. I know not whether it may be necessary to make any excuse for the absence of my brother, who was prevented from attending me in this expedition by a slow fever, occasioned by the great fatigues he has lately undergone. As no man has shewn more zeal or courage in the cause of the republic, he will undoubtedly return to the duties of his post the very first moment his health shall permit.

I recommend my honours to your protection: tho' I must confess at the same time that all my

desires

desires ought to be satisfied, since I enjoy the pri- A.U. 710.
vilege of your friendship, and the satisfaction of
seeing you invested with the high credit and au-
thority I have ever wished you. I will leave it
therefore entirely to yourself, both when and in
what manner I shall experience the effect of your
good offices: and will only request you to suffer
me to succeed Hirtius in your affection, as I cer-
tainly do in the respect and esteem he bore you.
Farewel.

L E T T E R   XXII.

To F U R N I U S [7].

IF the interest of the republic requires the conti-
nuance of your services, and it be necessary (as all
the world indeed is of opinion it is) that you should
bear a part in those important operations which
must extinguish the remaining flames of the war;
you cannot, surely, be engaged in a more wor-
thy, a more laudable, or a more illustrious pur-
suit. I think therefore, you should by no means
interrupt your applauded efforts in the cause of
liberty, for the sake of obtaining the prætorship
somewhat earlier than you are regularly entitled

---

[7] He had been tribune in the year of Rome 703, and was
as this time in the army of Plancus as one of his lieutenants.

 to enjoy it.   I fay your *applanded* efforts: for let not my friend be ignorant of the fame which his conduct has acquired.   Believe me, it is inferior only to that of Plancus himfelf, both by his own confeffion, and in the judgment too of all the world.   If there is any farther fervice then remaining for you to perform to your country, you ought to purfue it with an unbroken application, as an employment of all others the moft truly honourable: and what, my friend, fhall ftand in competition with true honour? But fhould you imagine, that you have amply fatisfied the duties you owe to the commonwealth; I do not diffuade you from haftening hither when the time of the elections fhall approach: provided this ambitious impatience fhall nothing diminifh from the luftre of that reputation you have fo juftly obtained.   I could name however many inftances of perfons of great diftinction, who during their engagements in the fervice of the republic abroad, have renounced their legal pretenfions of foliciting employments at home: a facrifice which in your own cafe will be fo much the lefs, as you are not at prefent ftrictly qualified to offer yourfelf as a candidate. Had you already indeed paffed through the office of ædile, and two years [8] had intervened fince

----

[8] By the laws of Rome a man could not be chofen prætor

                                               your

your exercifing that function; the felf-denial would have been greater: whereas now you will forego nothing of the ufual and ftated time of petitioning for the poft in queftion. I am very fenfible that your intereft is much too ftrong to require the affiftance of Plancus: neverthelefs, fhould his arms be attended with the fuccefs we wifh, your applications would certainly appear with greater advantage were they deferred till the time of his confulate.

Thus much (as I was willing you fhould know my fentiments) I thought proper to fay: but more, I am perfuaded, your own good fenfe and judgment would render unneceffary. The fum of all then, is fhortly this: that I would have you regulate your conduct upon all occurrences, not by the common ftandard of popular ambi-tion, but by that of true and folid glory; and look upon a lafting reputation as of more value than the tranfient honour of enjoying the prætorian office fomewhat earlier than ufual. I had a confultation the other day at my houfe upon this fubject, with your very good friends Cæcina, Calvifius, and my brother, at which your freed-man Dardanus was likewife prefent: and they every one of them joined with me in the opinion

till two years after he had ferved the office of ædile; and the fame diftance of time was likewife required between the prætorfhip and the confulate.

 I have here given you.   But after all, you your-
self are the beft and moft competent judge.
Farewel.

LETTER XXIII.

Decimus Brutus to Cicero.

FRiendfhip and gratitude make me feel upon
your account, what I never felt upon my
own; and I will confefs, that I am not without
fear in regard to a ftory which has been propa-
gated concerning you. I thought it by no means
a matter to be defpifed when I had only heard of
it, as I frequently did, from common report:
but it has lately been mentioned to me likewife
by Segulius.   This man tells me (tho' what he
fays indeed is generally of a piece with the reft of
his character) that paying a vifit at Cæfar's, where
you were much the fubject of the converfation,
Cæfar complained (and it was the only charge, it
feems, which he brought againft you) of an am-
biguous expreffion * which you had made ufe of

---

* The expreffion itfelf is inferted in the original; but as it
turns upon an ambiguity that will not hold in our language,
it was impoffible to preferve it in the tranflation. *Laudan-
dum adolefcentem*, Cicero is charged with having faid, *or-
nandum, tollendum:* the laft of which words is capable of a
double meaning, and may imply either that Octavius fhould
be advanced to the dignities of the ftate, or that his life

concerning

concerning him.   I fufpect the whole to be a A.U. 710.
mere fiction of Segulius; or at leaft that it was
he himfelf who reported thefe words to Cæfar.
Segulius endeavoured at the fame time to per-
fuade me, that you are in great danger of falling
a victim to the refentment of the veteran legions,
who fpeak of you, he pretends, with much in-
dignation.   The principal caufe, it feems, of
their difpleafure is, that both Cæfar and myfelf
are left out of the commiffion for dividing the
lands [5] among the foldiers, and that every thing
is difpofed of juft as you and your friends at
Rome think proper.

Notwithftanding that I was on my march [6]
when I received this account, yet I thought it
would not be advifable to pafs the Alps till I

fhould be taken away.   The polite and learned panegyrift
of Cicero's conduct, has endeavoured to vindicate his ad-
mired hero from a charge fo little favourable both to his
prudence and his honour: and it is to be wifhed that his
arguments were as convincing as they are plaufible.   In a
point however, that does not admit of any pofitive proof,
candour will incline on the favourable fide : tho' I cannot
but agree with an excellent author, that if the accufation
was true, " it very much takes off from the ingratitude of
" Octavius in confenting to the death of his benefactor :
" fince fuch double-dealing could hardly deferve the name
" of an obligation, let the effects of it be ever fo ad-
" vantageous." *Life of Cic.* iii. p. 240. *Obferv. on the
Life of Cic.* iii. p. 54.

[5] Thefe were lands which the fenate feem to have pro-
mifed as an encouragement to their troops, upon the break-
ing out of the war againft Antony. *Vid. Philip.* xiv. 13.

[6] In order to join Plancus.

X 2

had

A.U. 710. had informed myself how affairs stand. I am
well perfuaded, neverthelefs, that with refpect
to yourfelf, thefe reports and menaces of the
veterans aim at nothing farther than by alarming
your fears and incenfing the young Cæfar againft
you, to obtain for themfelves a more confider-
able proportion of the rewards decreed by the
fenate. But I do not intend by faying this, to
diffuade you from ftanding upon your guard:
as nothing, be affured, is more valuable to me
than your life. Let me only caution you not to
fuffer your fears to run you into greater dangers,
than thofe you would avoid. However, I would
advife you to obviate the clamours of thefe ve-
terans, as far as you reafonably may; and to
comply with their defires both in regard to the
decemvirs [7], and to the diftribution of their re-
wards. As to thofe forfeited eftates which be-
longed to the veterans who ferved under Antony;
I fhould be glad, if you think proper, that
Cæfar and myfelf may be nominated to affign
them to the troops. But in reference to the
pecuniary donative which they have been alfo
promifed; it will be proper to act with more de-
liberation, and as the circumftances of the public
finances fhall require: to which end it may be

[7] The perfons appointed to execute the commiffion for
the diftribution of the lands above mentioned.

fignified

signified to them, that the senate will take these their claims into consideration. As to those other four legions to whom the senate has also decreed an allotment of lands; I imagine that the estates in Campania together with those which were formerly seised by Sylla, will be sufficient for the purpose. I should think too that the best method of division would be, either to parcel out those lands in equal shares to the several legions, or to determine their respective proportions by lot. But when I thus give you my opinion, it is by no means as pretending to superior judgment, but merely from the affection of my heart towards you, and from my sincere desire that the public tranquillity may be preserved: which I am very sensible, if any accident should happen to you, cannot possibly be maintained.

I do not purpose to march out of Italy, unless I should find it greatly expedient. Mean while I am employed in disciplining my troops and furnishing them with arms: and I hope to appear with no contemptible body of forces, upon any emergency that shall again call me into the field. But Cæsar however has not sent back the legion to me, which served in Pansa's army.

I request your immediate answer to this letter: and if you should have any thing of importance to communicate to me, which requires particular

X 3

secrecy,

 fecrecy, I defire you would convey it by one of your own domeftics.   Farewel.

Eporedia ˢ, May the 24th.

LETTER XXIV.

From the Same to CICERO.

ALL things here go on well ⁹ : and it fhall be my endeavour to render them ftill better. Lepidus feems to be favourably difpofed towards me : and indeed we have reafon to diveft ourfelves of all our fears, and to act with undaunted freedom in defence of the commonwealth. But had our affairs a far lefs promifing afpect; yet it might juftly animate and augment that courage which I know always refides in your breaft, to reflect that we have three powerful armies ' devoted to the fervice of the republic, and that Fortune has already declared in our favour.

The report which I mentioned in my former letter is evidently calculated to intimidate you. But believe me if you exert a proper fpirit, the

---

ˢ A town not far from Vercellæ ; from whence the laft letter from Brutus was dated. See p. 292. of this vol.

⁹ " Brutus having received moft probably fome frefh in-
" telligence concerning Lepidus, wrote this letter to Cicero
" the day after he had written the former." Mr. Rofs.

' That of Octavius, Plancus, and his own.

whole

whole united party will be unable to withſtand A.U. 710.
your eloquence.

I purpoſe, agreeably to what I told you in my
laſt, to remain in Italy till I ſhall hear from you.
Farewel.

Eporedia, May the 25th.

L E T T E R XXV.

To Plancus.

THE news from your part of the world is ſo
extremely variable and cortradictory, that
I am utterly at a loſs what to write. Sometimes
the accounts we receive of Lepidus are agreeable
to our wiſhes, and at others entirely the reverſe.
All reports however concur in aſſuring us, that
you are ſuperior to every danger either from
fraud or force. If you are in ſome degree in-
debted for the latter to Fortune; it is certain
that the former at leaſt is owing to your prudence
alone.

I am informed by a letter from your colleguc [a],
dated the 15th of May, that you mentioned in
one of your expreſſes to him, that Lepidus
had refuſed to receive Antony. We ſhould have
been more diſpoſed to credit this intelligence, if
you had taken notice of it in any of your diſ-
patches to Rome. But perhaps you would not

[a] Decimus Brutus.

X 4   venture

 venture to communicate to us this piece of good
news, as having been a little premature in an ac-
count of the fame kind in your laft.   Every man
indeed is liable to be deceived by his wifhes;
but all the world knows that you can never be
impofed upon by any other means.   In the pre-
fent inftance however, all poffibility of farther
error is removed : for *to ftumble twice againft the
fame ftone*, is a difgrace, you know, even to a
proverb.   Should the truth prove agreeable then
to what you mentioned in your letter to your col-
legue, all our fears are at an end : neverthelefs
we fhall not difmifs them, till we recei.e a confir-
mation of this account from your own hand.

I have often affured you of my firm perfua-
fion, that the whole credit of delivering the
commonwealth from this civil war, will devolve
entirely upon that general who fhall extinguifh
thefe its laft furviving flames : an honour which I
hope, and believe, is referved folely for yourfelf.

It is with great pleafure, tho' without the leaft
furprife, that I find you entertain fuch grateful
fentiments of my zeal in your fervice.   Higher,
indeed, it cannot poffibly rife : but you may de-
pend upon my exerting it to more important pur-
pofes, if affairs in your part of the world fhould
fucceed as we wifh.   Farewel.

May the 29th.

LET-

LETTER XXVI.

LENTULUS [2] to CICERO.

AS I found when I applied to Brutus in Ma- A. U. 710.
cedonia, that he would not soon be pre-
pared to march to the assistance of this province [3],
I determined to return hither in order to collect
what remained of the public money, and to remit
it with all possible expedition to Rome.   In the
interval I received intelligence, that Dolabella's
fleet appeared upon the coast of Lycia [4], and that
he had procured above an hundred transport-
vessels ; intending, if he should not succeed in
his designs upon Syria [5], to sail directly with
his forces to Italy, and join the Antonys and
the rest of those infamous rebels.   I was so
much alarmed at this account, that I thought
proper to postpone all other affairs, and imme-
diately proceed in quest of this fleet.   And not-
withstanding my ships were unequal both in

[2] He was the son of Publius Lentulus to whom several
letters in the first and second books are addressed.   He at-
tended Trebonius into Asia Minor as his quæstor in that
province : from whence the present letter was written.

[3] In order to quell the commotions which Dolabella had
raised.   See rem. 7. p. 273. of this vol.

[4] It formed part of the province of Asia Minor : it is now
called Aldinelli.

[5] See rem. 4. p. 194. of this vol.

5   number

A.U. 710. number and fize to thofe of the enemy; I fhould probably have deftroyed their whole fleet, if I had not been obftructed by the Rhodians: however I have difabled the greateft part of it, and difperfed the reft. I have taken likewife every one of their tranfports: the foldiers and officers on board having quitted them upon the firft notice of my approach. In a word, I have fucceeded in the main of my defign; having defeated a fcheme which I greatly dreaded, and prevented Dolabella from ftrengthening our enemies by tranfporting his forces into Italy.

I refer you to the letter which I have written to the fenate [6], for an account of the ill treatment I received from the Rhodians: tho' indeed I have by no means reprefented it in its ftrongeft colours. Thefe people, in confequence of their imagining that the affairs of the commonwealth were utterly defperate, behaved towards me with the moft infufferable infolence. But their affronts to my own perfon, is in no fort the foundation of my complaints: I have ever difregarded injuries of this kind that centered entirely in myfelf. It is their difaffection to the republic; their attachment to the oppofite party; their conftant ill-offices to all thofe who diftinguifh themfelves in the fupport of our liberties, that I

[6] The following letter.

thought

thought demanded my refentment.   Let me not A.U. 710.
be underftood, however, as pafling an indifcri-
minate cenfure upon the whole ifland in general:
far am I indeed from thinking them all equally
infected with the fame principles.   But I know
not by what fatality it happens, that thofe very
magiftrates who refufed to give protection to my
father, to Lucius Lentulus, to Pompey, and to
the reft of thofe illuftrious chiefs who fled into
this ifland after the battle of Pharfalia; are all of
them at this juncture either actually in the ad-
miniftration themfelves, or poffefs an unlimited
influence over thofe who are.   Accordingly they
have conducted themfelves in this affair with
their ufual malevolence : and it is not only expe-
dient, but indeed abfolutely neceffary that the
republic fhould interpofe her authority, left the
infolence of this people fhould rife to ftill greater
heights, by pafling any longer unchaftifed.

Let me hope you will continue, as ufual, to
take my interefts under your protection : and
that you will upon all occafions, both in the fe-
nate and in every other inftance, promote my ho-
nours with your fuffrage.   As the province of Afia
is decreed to the confuls [7], with a power of ap-

---

[7] Hirtius and Panfa : the news of whofe death, together
with that of the battles in which they fell, had not yet
reached the knowledge of Lentulus.

pointing

A.U.710. pointing whomfoever they fhall think proper to adminifter the government till their arrival; I intreat you to employ your intereft with them to confer this dignity upon me. The fituation of affairs in this province does by no means require their prefence before the expiration of their confular office, or in any fort render it neceffary that they fhould fend hither an army. For Dolabella is now in Syria: and, agreeably to what you declared with your ufual prophetic difcernment, he will certainly be defeated by Caffius ere the confuls can poffibly arrive. Accordingly he has been obliged to abandon the fiege of Antiochia, and has retreated to Laodicea, a fea-port town in Syria, as the only city in which he could confide. I hope he will foon meet with the fate he fo well deferves; or rather indeed, I am perfuaded it has already attended him: for he has no other place to which he can retreat, and it is impoffible he fhould make any long or effectual refiftance againft fo powerful an army as that which Caffius has led againft him [8]. I imagine therefore that Panfa and Hirtius will be in no hafte to come

---

[8] This fhortly afterwards proved to be the fact. For Caffius having forced the city of Laodicea to furrender; Dolabella, in order to avoid falling into the hands of his enemy, put an end to his own life by the affiftance of one of his flaves, whom he commanded to be his executioner. *Vel. Paterc.* ii. 69.

into

into thefe provinces, but rather choofe to finifh A.U.713.
their confular year at Rome. For this reafon I
am inclined to hope that you may prevail with
them to appoint me their fubftitute.

I have received affurances from both of them,
as well in perfon as by letter, that no fucceffor
fhould be elected to my office during their con-
fulate : and Panfa has lately repeated the fame
promife to my friend Verrius. Believe me,
it is not from any ambitious views that I de-
fire to be continued fome time longer in this
province. But as I have met with many dif-
ficulties and difadvantages in the difcharge of
my functions, I fhould extremely regret the be-
ing obliged to refign my poft before I fhall have
fully reaped the fruit of my labours. If it were in
my power to remit to Rome the whole of thofe
affeffinents I had actually levied, I fhould be fo
far from wifhing to remain here, that I fhould
defire to be recalled. But I am very follicitous
to receive the money I advanced to Caffius; to
replace what I loft by the death of Trebonius,
and the oppreffions of Dolabella; as well as to re-
cover the feveral fums which are due to me from
thofe who have perfidioufly broken the good faith
they owed both to myfelf and to the republic.
Now thefe are points which I can by no means
effect, unlefs the time of my continuance in this
province

 province be prolonged : a privilege which I hope to obtain by the interpofition of your ufual good offices.

I perfuade myfelf that my fervices to the commonwealth give me juft reafon to expect, not the honour only of adminiftering this province, but as high dignities as Caffius and the two Bruti : as I not only fhared with them in forming the defign and undergoing the hazard of that ever-memorable enterprife againft Cæfar [9], but have exerted myfelf with equal zeal and fpirit in all our prefent commotions. I was the firft, let me boaft, that bid defiance to the oppreffive laws of Antony. I was the firft that brought over the cavalry of Dolabella to the intereft of the republic, and delivered them into the hands of Caffius. I was the firft who levied troops in defence of our common liberties againft the infamous attempts of thofe who have confpired our deftruction : and it is owing entirely to me that Syria, together with the army in that province, joined themfelves under Caffius in the fupport of the republic. The truth is, if I had not very expeditiously con-

[9] Plutarch (as Manutius in his remark upon this paffage obferves) taking notice that feveral affected to be thought affociates in the confpiracy againft Cæfar, who in truth were no way concerned in that affair ; particularly mentions Lentulus as one in that number. But he paid dear for his boaft ; as it coft him his life when Octavius got into power. *Plut. in vit. Cæfar.*

tributed

tributed thofe large fubfidies both of men and A.U. 710.
money with which I fupplied Caffius, he would
not have ventured to march into Syria: and the
name of Dolabella would now have been no lefs
formidable to the republic than that of Antony
himfelf.   Yet at the fame time that I acted thus
warmly for the intereft of the republic, I had
every private bias that could draw me to the
oppofite party.   Dolabella was my friend and
companion; as the Antonys were my neareft
relations : and it was by the united good offices
of the latter that I obtained the quæftorfhip of
this province.   But the love of my country was
fuperior to every other attachment: and I ftood
forth the firft to declare war againft the ftrongeft
and moft endearing connections both of blood
and friendfhip.   Inconfiderable, it muft be ac-
knowledged, is the fruit which I have hitherto
reaped from thefe inftances of my patriotifm.
However, I do not defpair: and I fhall unwea-
riedly perfevere, not only in difplaying my zeal
for our liberties, but in expofing myfelf to every
difficulty and every danger for their fupport.
Neverthelefs I cannot but add, if I were to be
encouraged by fome of thofe honours I have
merited from the fenate and from every friend to
our country, they would give me an authority

10   which

 which would enable me to act with greater advantage to the common cauſe.

I did not ſee your ſon when I was with Brutus, as he was juſt gone into winter-quarters with the cavalry [1]. But I had the ſatisfaction of finding that he was in general eſteem: which gave me great pleaſure, not only on his account and yours, but likewiſe upon my own. For I cannot but conſider a ſon of yours that thus copies out his father's virtues, as ſtanding in the relation to me of a brother. Farewel.

Perga [a], May the 29th.

[1] "Brutus, when he firſt left Italy, ſailed directly for
"Athens, where he ſpent ſome time in concerting meaſures
"how to make himſelf maſter of Greece and Macedonia:
"which was the great deſign that he had in view. Here he
"gathered about him all the young nobility and gentry of
"Rome, who for the opportunity of their education, had
"been ſent to this celebrated ſeat of learning: but of them
"all, he took the moſt notice of young Cicero. He made
"him therefore one of his lieutenants, tho' he was but
"twenty years old: gave him the command of his horſe;
"and employed him in ſeveral commiſſions of great truſt
"and importance; in all which the young man diſtinguiſhed
"both his courage and conduct." *Life of Cic.* iii. 142.

[a] A city of Pamphylia, in Aſia Minor: now called *Pirgi*.

L E T T E R XXVII.

Lentulus, Proquæstor and Proprætor, to the
Consuls, the Prætors, the Tribunes of the
People, the Senate and the Commons of Rome.

AS soon as Dolabella had possessed himself of
Asia [2] by the most infamous and cruel act
of treachery [3], I applied immediately to the army
in Macedonia under the command of the illustri-
ous Marcus Brutus ; as the nearest assistance to
which I could have recourse, in order to recover
this province as soon as possible to the dominion
of the commonwealth.   But Dolabella being ap-
prehensive of my design, advanced with so much
rapidity, that he had got out of these territories
before it was possible that the forces I had solli-
cited could arrive.   In his march however, he
laid the whole country waste ; seised upon the
public money ; and not only plundered the Ro-
man citizens of their effects, but most inhu-
manly sold them as slaves.   I did not think
it necessary therefore to defer my departure
out of Macedonia, till the troops of Brutus
should be ready.   It appeared to be most for

A.U. 710.

---

[2] Asia Minor.   See rem. 8. p. 309. vol. ii.
[3] See rem. 7. p. 273. of this vol.

the advantage of the republic, that I fhould re-
turn with all expedition to the duties of my poft,
in order to levy the remainder of the public
taxes, to collect the money I had depofited, to
inquire what part of it had been feifed, and by
whofe neglect: in a word, to tranfmit to you
a full and faithful account of the ftate in which
I fhould find the affairs of this province. With
thefe views, I embarked: but as I was failing
among the Greek iflands, I received intelligence,
that Dolabella's fleet lay off the coaft of Lycia,
and that the Rhodians had a confiderable num-
ber of fhips of war ready to fail. I refolved
therefore to put back to Rhodes with the fhips
that attended me, and which were now joined by
thofe under the command of Patifcus the pro-
quæftor: a perfon whom I muft mention as moft
intimately united with me, not only by the ties
of friendfhip, but by the fame common fentiments
towards the republic. I affured myfelf that the
Rhodians would give me affiftance, in the firft place,
from their regard to the authority of your decree,
by which Dolabella is declared an enemy to
his country: and, in the next, as they ftood en-
gaged by a folemn treaty renewed with us in
the confulate of Marcus Marcellus and Servius
Sulpicius, to confider the enemies of the republic

in

in all refpects as their own.   But I was greatly A.U.710.
deceived in my expectation : they were fo far
from being inclined to ftrengthen my fleet with
any of their own fhips, that they would not fuf-
fer it to enter their harbour.   They even refufed
to furnifh our foldiers with provifions and wa-
ter : and it was with difficulty I obtained permif-
fion myfelf to fail into their port with two fmall
veffels.   However, I did not think proper to re-
fent this infult upon the rights and the majefty of
the Roman people : deeming it of more im-
portance in the prefent conjuncture to fruftrate
the defigns of Dolabella.   For I had difcovered
by fome intercepted letters, that it was his pur-
pofe, if he failed in his attempt upon Syria and
Egypt, (as fail I was fure he muft) to proceed
directly with his band of robbers and their plun-
der to Italy.   Accordingly in view to this his
fcheme, he had preffed, out of the ports of Ly-
cia, a confiderable number of tranfports, none of
them lefs than fifty-fix tons burthen [3] : and thefe
were ftrongly guarded by his fleet. Being great-
ly alarmed therefore, confcript [4] fathers, at this

[3] Thefe veffels were much inferior to thofe employed for
the fame purpofes in our fervice : the largeft of which are
of 300 tons, and the fmalleft of 100.

[4] This appellation was at firft given as a mark of diftinc-
tion to thofe particular fenators who were added by Tar-

A.U.710. dangerous defign; I refolved to bear with the in-
jurious treatment of the Rhodians, and to fubmit
to every milder expedient of gaining them over
to our intereft.. For this purpofe, I fuffered my-
felf to be introduced into their fenate in the man-
ner they thought proper: where I reprefented,
in the ftrongeft terms I was capable, the danger
to which the republic would be expofed, if that
infamous rebel fhould tranfport his forces in-
to Italy. But I found them moft perverfely dif-
pofed to imagine, that the friends of the republic
were the weaker party; that the general affocia-.
tion in favour of our liberties was by no means.
voluntary; that the fenate would ftill patiently
fuffer the infolence of Dolabella; and that no man
would venture to vote him a public enemy. To
be fhort, they were more inclined to believe the
falfe reports that had been propagated by the dif-
affected, than to credit my reprefentations, tho'
entirely agreeable to truth. 'In conformity with
this difpofition, they had fent, before my arrival
in the ifland, two feveral embaffies to Dolabella,
notwithftanding his late affaffination of Trebo-

quinius Prifcus, or by the people at the fettling of the com-
monwealth, to the hundred which originally compofed the
fenate as it was inftituted by Romulus. But in after-times
it became a common title which was promifcuoufly made ufe
of in all addreffes to that great council of the republic. *Vid.*
Manut. de fenat.

nius,

nius, and the many other flagitious acts which he A.U.710.
committed in this province.   And this they did
by an unexampled violation of their laws, and
contrary to the exprefs prohibitions of the magi-
ftrates who were then in office.   But whether this
conduct was owing to their fears for the territo-
ries they poffefs on the continent, as they them-
felves alledge; or whether it is to be imputed to
the factious influence of a few of their principal
magiftrates, who formerly treated fome of our
illuftrious countrymen with equal indignity, I
know not.   This however is certain, that I
could not prevail with them to take any mea-
fures to obviate an evil, which it was very
eafy for them to prevent: and all the arguments
I could ufe either with refpect to my own perfonal
danger, or in regard to that which threatened the
republic if this traytor with his banditti, after
being driven from Syria, fhould tranfport them-
felves into Italy, proved utterly ineffectual.   It
was even fufpected that the magiftrates them-
felves amufed us with various pretences of delay,
till they could fend intelligence to Dolabella's
fleet of our approach.   And indeed there were
fome circumftances that greatly increafed this
fufpicion; particularly, that Sextius Marius, and
Caius Titius, the lieutenants of Dolabella, fud-
denly quitted the fleet, and abandoned their

Y 3   tranfports

A.U. 710. tranfports which had coft them fo much time and pains to colleƈt. Be that as it will, I purfued my voyage from Rhodes towards Lycia, and falling in with the enemy, I took all their tranfports, and have reftored them to their owners. By thefe means I have obftruƈted what I fo much feared, and have removed all apprehenfions of Dolabella's paffing into Italy with his rafcal crew. I chafed the enemy as far as Sida, which is the utmoft limit of my province; where I learnt that part of them were feparated, and that the reft had fteered in company together towards Syra and the ifland of Cyprus. Having thus difperfed this fquadron, and knowing That brave commander and excellent patriot, the illuftrious Caius Caffius, had a confiderable fleet in thofe feas, I returned to the duties of my employment: and it fhall be my endeavour, confcript fathers, to give both you and the republic full proofs of my indefatigable zeal. To this end, I fhall exert my utmoft affiduity in colleƈting the public revenues, which I fhall tranfmit to you, together with all my accounts, as expeditioufly as poffible. If I fhould have time, likewife, to make a progrefs thro' the province in order to inquire into the conduƈt of thofe with whom I entrufted the care of the finances, I fhall not fail to fend a lift of fuch who fhall appear to have been faithful to

their

their truft, as well as of thofe who by voluntarily
betraying it, have rendered themfelves partners
in the guilt of Dolabella.   Let me add, that if
you fhall think proper to chaftife thefe laft ac-
cording to their demerits, the execution of your
juftice will greatly ftrengthen my authority, and
enable me with more facility to raife and preferve
the remainder of the public taxes.   In the mean
while, the better to fecure the public revenue,
and to protect this province from future infults,
I have formed (what indeed was extremely want-
ing) a body of troops compofed entirely of vo-
lunteers.

Since I wrote the above, about thirty Afiatic
foldiers who deferted from Dolabella in Syria,
are arrived in Pamphylia.   They relate that Do-
labella appeared before the walls of Antiochia in
Syria, and finding that the inhabitants had fhut
the city-gates againft him, he made feveral at-
tempts to enter by force; but was always
repulfed with great difadvantage.   At length
having loft about an hundred men, he retired
in the night and fled towards Laodicea;
leaving all his fick and wounded behind him.
They add, that the fame night almoft the whole
of his Afiatic troops deferted; eight hundred
of which returned to Antiochia, and furren-
dered themfelves to the officers of the garrifon

Y 4   which

A.U.710. which Caffius had left in that town ; the reft, (of
which number thefe foldiers are) came down into
Cilicia by mount Amanus : in fine, that Caffius
with his whole army was reported to have been
but four days march from Laodicea when Dola-
bella retired towards that city. I am perfuaded
therefore that this moft infamous villain will meet
with the punifhment he deferves much fooner
than we expected.

LETTER XXVIII.

LEPIDUS, Imperator and fovereign Pontif[2], to
the Senate and People of Rome[3].

HEaven and earth will bear me witnefs, con-
fcript fathers, that there is nothing I have
at all times more fincerely defired, than the pre-
fervation of our common liberties : and I fhould

---

[2] The function of the Roman pontifs was to give judg-
ment in all caufes relating to religion, and to regulate the
feftivals, facrifices, and all other facred inftitutions. The
fovereign pontif, or fuperintendant of thefe *pontifices*, was
one of the moft honourable offices in the commonwealth.

[3] This letter was written by Lepidus to the fenate, in or-
der to excufe the junction of his forces with thofe of Antony;
which was effected the day before its date. But tho' he re-
prefents himfelf as merely paffive in that tranfaction, and to
have been forced into it by a general revolt of his troops; yet
it moft evidently appears to have been in confequence of a
fecret treaty which had been in agitation during fome months
before, between him and Antony.

foon have convinced you of this truth, if Fortune A.U. 710.
had not forced me to renounce thofe meafures I
purpofed to purfue.   My whole army indeed ex-
preffed their ufual tendernefs towards their fellow
countrymen, by a mutinous oppofition to my
defigns : and to own the truth, they abfolutely
compelled me not to refufe my protection to fuch
a multitude of Roman citizens.   I conjure you
then, confcript fathers, to judge of this affair,
not by the fuggeftions of private refentment, but
by the intereft of the commonwealth : nor let
it be imputed as a crime to me and my army,
that amidft our civil diffentions we yielded to the
dictates of compaffion and humanity.   Be affur-
ed, that by acting with an equal regard to the
fafety and honour of all parties, you will beft
confult both your own and your country's advan-
tage.   Farewel.

> From my camp, at Pons Argenteus,
>   May the 30th.

LETTERS

OF

Marcus Tullius Cicero

TO

Several of his FRIENDS.

BOOK XV.

LETTER I.

To Plancus.

THO' I am too well affured of the dif- A.U.710.
pofition of your heart, to require any
formal declarations of your gratitude;
yet I cannot but confefs, that I received your ac-
knowledgments with great pleafure, as they af-
forded me the moſt evident proof of the affection

you

 you bear me.   I was always indeed perfectly fen-
fible of your friendfhip : but it never appeared to
me in a ftronger or more advantageous light.

, Your letter to the fenate was extremely well
received, not only from the important account it
brought us of your wife and heroic meafures, but
as it was greatly admired likewife for the ftrength
and elegance of its compofition.   Let it be your
earneft labour, my dear Plancus, to extinguifh
the remains of this war: which if you fhould
happily effect, you will acquire the moft con-
fummate credit and reputation.   I wifh all pof-
fible profperity to the republic: yet, believe me,
fpent as I am with my utmoft efforts to preferve
it from deftruction, I am fcarce more follicitous
for the liberties of my country, than for the
glory of my friend.   I hope that the immortal
gods have placed within your power a moft fa-
vourable opportunity of increafing your fame:
and let me entreat you to embrace it, my dear
Plancus, in the full perfuafion that whoever fhall
deftroy Antony, will have the honour of ter-
minating this moft execrable and alarming war.
Farewel.

LETTER II.

Asinius Pollio[1], to Cicero.

IT is owing to Lepidus, who detained my cou- A.U.710.
riers above a week, that I did not receive
earlier advice of the feveral actions near Mutina :
tho' indeed I fhould be glad to have been the laft
that was informed of this unhappy news, if it
were utterly out of my power to be of any affift-
ance in redreffing its confequences. I wifh the
fenate had ordered me into Italy, when they
fent for Plancus and Lepidus : for if I had been
prefent, the republic would not have received this
cruel wound. And tho' fome perhaps may re-
joice in this event, from the great number of
principal officers and veteran foldiers of the Cæfa-
rian party, who have perifhed ; yet they will un-
doubtedly find reafon to lament it, when they
fhall be fenfible of the terrible defolation it has
brought upon their country. For if what is re-
lated concerning the number of the flain, be in
any degree true ; the flower and ftrength of our
armies are entirely cut off.

I was well aware of the great advantage it
would have proved to the republic, if I could

<hr>

[1] See rem. 6. p. 207. and rem. 1. p. 209. of this vol.

have

 have joined Lepidus: as I fhould have been able, and efpecially with the affiftance of Plancus, to have diffipated thofe doubts which occafioned his delay in declaring for the fenate. But the letters which I received from him being written (as you will perceive by the copies I herewith tranfmit) in the fame fpirit with thofe fpeeches, which it is faid, he made to his army at [2] Narbo; I found it neceffary to act with fome fort of artifice towards him, if I hoped to obtain leave to march my troops tho' his province. I was apprehenfive likewife, if an engagement fhould happen before I could execute my defigns, that the known friendfhip I had with Antony (tho' not fuperior indeed to that which Plancus entertained for him) would give my enemies an occafion of mifreprefenting my intentions. For thefe reafons I difpatched two couriers from Gades [3] in the month of April by two different fhips, with letters, not only to you, and to Octavius, but to the confuls alfo, requefting to be informed in what manner my fervices might moft avail the republic. But, if I am right in my calculation, thefe fhips did not fail till the very day on which the battle was fought between Panfa and Antony: as that was the fooneft, I

[2] Narbonne in Provence.
[3] Cadiz.

think,

think, since the winter, that these seas were na-
vigable.   To these reasons for not marching, I
must add, that I had so little apprehension of this
civil war, that I settled the winter-quarters of my
troops in the very remotest parts of Lusitania [4].
Both armies, it should seem, were as eager to
come to an action, as if their greatest fears on
each side were, lest some less destructive expedi-
ent might be found of composing our disturb-
ances.   However, if circumstances required so
much precipitation, I must do Hirtius the justice
to acknowledge, that he conducted himself with
all the skill and courage of a consummate ge-
neral.

I am informed by my letters from that part of
Gaul which is under the command of Lepidus,
that Pansa's whole army is cut to pieces, and that
he himself is since dead of his wounds.   They
add, that the *martial* legion is entirely destroyed,
and that Lucius Fabatus, Caius Peducæus, and
Decimus Carfulenus are among the number of
the slain.   My intelligence farther assures me,
that in the subsequent attack by Hirtius, both he
and Antony lost all their legions ; that the fourth
legion, after having taken Antony's camp, was
engaged and defeated by the fifth, with terrible
slaughter ; that Hirtius, together with Pontius

***

4 Portugal.

Aquila,

 Aquila, and, as it is reported, Octavius likewise, were killed in the action. If this should prove true, (which the gods forbid) I shall be very greatly concerned. My advices farther import, that Antony has with great disgrace abandoned the siege of Mutina; however, that he has [a] *** complete regiments of horse still remaining, together with one which belongs to Publius Bagiennus, as also a considerable number of disarmed soldiers; that Ventidius has joined him with the seventh, the eighth, and the ninth legions; and that Antony is determined, if there should be no hopes of gaining Lepidus, to have recourse to the last expedient, and arm not only the provincials, but even the slaves: in fine, that Lucius Antonius, after having plundered the city of Parma, has posted himself upon the Alps. If these several particulars are true, there is no time to be lost: and every man who wishes that the republic, or even the name of the Roman people may subsist, should immediately, without waiting for the express orders of the senate, contribute his utmost assistance to extinguish these dreadful flames. I hear that Decimus Brutus is at the head of only seventeen cohorts, together with two incomplete legions of new-raised troops, which had been levied by Antony. I doubt not however, that the remains of the forces

[a] The number is omitted in the MSS.

forces commanded by Hirtius will join him. A.U.710. I hope fo at leaft: as there is little, I think, to be expected from any new recruits that may be raifed; efpecially fince nothing can be more dangerous than to give Antony time to recover ftrength.

My next letters from Italy will determine the plan of my operations: and as the corn is now cut down, and partly carried in, I fhall be more at liberty to execute them without obftruction from the feafon of the year. In the mean time let me affure you, that I will neither defert, nor furvive[s], the republic. It is a misfortune however that my diftance from the fcene of action is fo great, and the roads fo infefted, that it is often fix weeks, and fometimes more, ere I can be informed of any event that has happened. Farewel.

[s] Notwithftanding Pollio's pious refolutions of expiring with the republic, he was contented to live on long after its total deftruction, and died in a good old age in the court and favour of Auguftus. It was not many months indeed from the date of this letter, that he united with the enemies of his country, by joining his troops with thofe of Antony and Lepidus. *Auct. Dial. de Cauf. Corrupt. Eloquent.*

LETTER III.
Decimus Brutus to Cicero.

A.U. 710. IT affords me some consolation in the midst of my great concern [6], that the world is at length convinced that my fears were not without just foundation [a]. I have sent by this express a full account of the whole affair to the senate. And now let them deliberate, if they please, whether they shall call home their troops from Africa and Sardinia; whether they shall send for Marcus Brutus; and whether they shall order the payment of my forces. But of this you may be well assured, that unless they act with regard to these several articles in the manner I have pointed out in my letter, we shall all of us be exposed to the utmost danger.

I intreat you to be extremely cautious whom the senate shall employ to conduct the troops that are to reinforce me : as it is a trust which requires great fidelity and expedition. Farewel.

From my camp, June 3d.

[6] Occasioned by the treachery of Lepidus in having deserted the cause of the republic, and joined himself to Antony. This letter appears to have been written a few days after that event; being dated the 3d of June, and the junction between the two armies of Lepidus and Antony having been effected on the 29th of May.

[a] See the 11th letter of the preceding book, p. 276. to which this seems particularly to allude.

LET-

L E T T E R IV.

To Decimus Brutus[7].

MAY every god confound that most infa- A.U. 710.
mous of all human beings, the execrable
Segulius! For do you imagine, my friend, that
he has told this idle tale to none but Cæsar, or
to you? Be assured he has related it to every
mortal that would give him the hearing. I am
much obliged to you however, for informing me
of this contemptible report: as it is a very strong
instance, my dear Brutus, of the share you allow
me in your friendship.

As to what he mentioned concerning the com-
plaints of the veterans, that you and Cæsar are
left out of the commission for dividing the lands;
I sincerely wish I had likewise been excluded from
so troublesome an office. But it is by no means to
be imputed to me, that you were not both nominat-
ed : on the contrary, I moved that all our generals
should be included. But the clamours of those who
always endeavour to obstruct your honours, car-
ried it against me : and you were both excepted,

" This letter is an answer to the 23d of the foregoing
book : and was written before any of the letters which give
an account of Antony's being received by Lepidus had come
to Cicero's hands.

 in oppofition to my warmeft efforts. Unheeded then by me, let Segulius propagate his impotent calumnies! For all that the man means, is nothing more than to repair his broken fortunes. Not that he can be charged with having diffipated his patrimony: for patrimony he never had. He has only fquandered in luxury what he acquired by infamy.

. You may be perfectly at eafe, my dear and excellent Brutus, with regard to thofe fears which you fo generoufly entertain upon my account, at the fame time that you feel none, you tell me, upon your own. Be affured I fhall expofe myfelf to no dangers which prudence can prevent: and as to thofe againft which no precaution can avail, I am little follicitous. High indeed would my prefumption be, were I to defire to be privileged beyond the common lot of human nature.

The advice you give me not to fuffer my fears to lead me into greater dangers than thofe they would avoid; fupplies me at once with a proof both of your judgment and your friendfhip: but the caution is altogether unneceffary. The truth of it is, diftinguifhed as you are by a fortitude of mind which renders you incapable of fear upon any occafion; yet there is no man who approaches nearer to you in that quality than myfelf. Neverthelefs, I fhall always be upon my

guard,

guard, though I fhall never be afraid.   Indeed
if I fhould have any reafon ; will it not be
wholly owing, my dear Brutus, to yourfelf?
For were I of a difpofition apt to take alarm,
yet I fhould be perfectly compofed, in the con-
fidence of that protection I fhall receive from
your approaching confulate: efpecially as the
world is no lefs fenfible than I am, of the fin-
gular fhare I enjoy of your affection.

I agree entirely with your opinion concerning
the four legions : as alfo that both you and Cæfar
fhould have the diftribution of thofe eftates you
mention. This is an office on which fome of
my collegues had caft a very wifhful eye : how-
ever I have difappointed their longing, by re-
ferving it wholly for you and Cæfar. In the
mean time, if any occurrence fhould arife that
requires particular fecrecy, I fhall obferve your
directions and communicate it to you by one of
my own domeftics.   Farewel.

June the 4th.

LETTER V.

Plancus to Cicero.

A.U. 710.
I Shall never regret to undergo the greatest dangers in the cause of my country, provided, my dear Cicero, that whatever happens to myself, I may not justly be accused of temerity. But I should not scruple to confess, that I had been guilty of an imprudence, if I had ever acted in reliance upon the sincerity of Lepidus. Too easy a disposition to give credit to fair pretences, cannot so properly be called a fault as an error : but an error into which the nobleft minds are generally moft liable to fall. It was not however, from a miftake of this nature that I had lately well-nigh been deceived : for the character of Lepidus I perfectly well knew. It was entirely owing to a certain fenfibility of what my detractors might fay : a quality, I will freely acknowledge, particularly prejudicial in the affair of war. I was apprehenfive if I remained in my camp, that thofe who are inclined to mifconftrue my actions, might reprefent me as the occafion of the war being protracted, by obftinately indulging my refentment againft Lepidus : and therefore I advanced almoft within fight of him and Antony. I encamped indeed at no greater

diftance

distance from them than forty miles, that I might A.U. 710.
be able, as circumstances should require, either
speedily to join the army of Lepidus, or safely to
retreat with my own.   In marking out my camp,
I chose a spot of ground that gave me the advan-
tage of having a large river in my front, which
would take up some time in passing, and that lay
contiguous likewise to the country of the Vocon-
tii[8]: who I was sure would favour my retreat.
When Lepidus found himself disappointed of
what he so much wished, and that there was no
hopes of my approaching nearer, he immediately
threw off the mask; and on the 29th of May he
joined Antony.   The combined armies moved
the same day in order to invest my camp: and
they had actually advanced within 20 miles, be-
fore I received advice of their junction. However
I struck my tents with so much expedition, that
by the favour of the gods, I had the happiness
to escape them.   My retreat was conducted with
so much good order, that no part of my baggage,
nor even a single man, was either left behind or in-
tercepted by these incensed villains.   On the 4th
of this month I repassed the Isara with my whole
army: after which I broke down the bridge I had
thrown across that river.   I took this precau-
tion, that my troops might have time to refresh

* A people of Narbonensian Gaul.

Z 4   them

A.U. 710. themfelves, as well as to give my collegue [9] an opportunity of coming up to me: which I imagine he will be able to effect in three days from the date of this letter.

I muft always acknowledge the zeal and fidelity which Laterenfis has fhewn to the republic, in his negotiations between Lepidus and myfelf: but it is certain that his great partiality towards Lepidus, prevented him from difcerning the dangers into which I have been led. However, as foon as he difcovered how grofsly he had been impofed upon, he attempted to turn that fword againft his own breaft, which with much more juftice had been plunged in the heart of Lepidus. But he was prevented from completing his purpofe: and it is faid (tho' I by no means mention it as a certainty) that the wound he has given himfelf is not mortal [1].

My efcape from thefe traitors has proved an extreme mortification to them: as they marched to attack me with the fame unrelenting fury which inftigates them againft their country. Some late circumftances particularly contributed to inflame their refentment. I had frequently and warmly urged Lepidus to extinguifh this civil war: I had difapproved of the conferences that were holden,

[9] Decimus Brutus.

[1] It proved otherwife: and the fenate in honour of his patriotifm, not only decreed him a public funeral; but ordered a ftatue to be erected to his memory. *Dio.* p. 324.

with

with the enemy : I had refufed to fee the lieute- A.U.710.
nants whom Antony deputed to me under the
paffports of Lepidus : and had intercepted Catius
Veftinus, whom the former had fent exprefs to
the latter.   But it is with pleafure I reflect, that
the more earneftly they wifhed to get me into
their hands, the more they fuffer in the difap-
pointment.

· Continue, my dear Cicero, to employ the fame
vigorous efforts you have hitherto exerted, that
we who are in arms for the defence of the repub-
lic, may have fuitable honours paid to our fer-
vices.   In the mean time I wifh that Cæfar would
join us with thofe brave troops he commands;
or, if his affairs will not permit him, that at leaft
they might be fent under the conduct of fome
other general : for moft certainly his own perfo-
nal intereft is at ftake [2].   The whole force of the
difaffected party is united againft our country :
and fhall we not put forth our utmoft ftrength in
its defence ? As for what concerns myfelf, I will
venture to affure you, that if you at Rome are
not wanting on your parts, I will abundantly per-
form every thing that can be expected on mine.

The obligations I am continually receiving from
your hands, endear you to me every day more and

---

[2] Octavius was at this time fecretly carrying on a treaty
with Lepidus and Antony, which fhortly after ended in an
alliance, which every reader is acquainted with under the
name of the *Triumvirate*.

A.U.710. more; at the same time that they animate me to act in such a manner as not to forfeit in any degree your esteem and affection.

I will only add my wishes, that I were able in person to give you such proofs of my gratitude, as might afford you greater reason to rejoice in the good offices you have conferred upon me. Farewel.

Cularo, on the frontiers of the Allobroges [3], June the 6th.

LETTER VI.

TO DECIMUS BRUTUS.

TO tell you the truth [4], I was once inclined to be somewhat angry at the shortness of your letters : but I am now so well reconciled to your concise manner, that I condemn my own as downright loquacity, and shall make your epistles the models of mine. How short, yet how expressive are you when you tell me, that "all "things go well with you, and that you shall "endeavour to render them still better; that Le- "pidus seems favourably disposed; and that we

[3] A people of the Narbonensian Gaul, in which Cularo, now called Grenoble, was situated.

[4] When Cicero wrote this letter, which is an answer to the 24th of the preceding book, p. 310. of this vol. he had not yet received the news of Antony's junction with Lepidus.

"have

" have every thing to expect from our three ar-   A.U. 710.
mies [1]!" Were I ever so full of fears, these sig-
nificant sentences would banish them all.   But I
exert the spirit you recommend: and indeed if
at the time when you were closely blocked up in
Mutina, my hopes nevertheless were fixed en-
tirely upon you; how much higher, think you,
must they be raised now?

I should be glad, my dear Brutus, to resign to
you my post of *observation*, if I might do so with-
out incurring the censure of deserting it.   As to
what you mentioned of continuing in Italy till
you should hear from me; I do not disapprove
of it, if the motions of the enemy should not call
you elsewhere: as there are many points upon
the carpet at Rome, which may render it pru-
dent for you not to remove to a farther distance.
But at all events, if your presence here may
prove a means of terminating the war; it is un-
doubtedly the first and principal scheme you
should have in view.

The senate has decreed the first money that
could be raised, for the payment of your troops.
—Servius is extremely your friend: and you
may always depend upon me.   Farewel.

June the 8th.

[1] Those of Decimus Brutus, Plancus, and Octavius.

I. F. T.

LETTER VII.

ASINIUS POLLIO to CICERO.

A.U.710. BALBUS[6], my quæstor, has withdrawn from Gades with very confiderable effects in his hands which he had received of the public taxes [7], confifting of a large quantity of uncoined gold, a much larger of filver [8], together with a great fum of ready money: and what adds to his iniquity, is, that he has not difcharged even the pay of the troops [9]. In his flight he was detained three days by contrary winds at Calpe[1]; from whence however he failed on the 1ſt of this month: and has tranfported himfelf together with his treafure into the dominions of Bogud, king of Mauritania[2]. But whether the prefent

[6] He was nephew to Lucius Cornelius Balbus, the great friend and favourite of Cæfar, and of whom frequent mention has been made in the preceding letters.

[7] The quæftor was receiver-general of the provincial taxes.

[8] The province of Spain abounded in valuable mines of every fort, particularly in thofe of filver and gold: the proprietors of which paid a certain proportion to the government, of the pure ore which thefe mines produced. *Strab. iii. Burman. de vectigal. P. R. differt. p.* 107.

[9] The payment of the forces was a part of the bufinefs belonging to the provincial quæftors.

[1] Gibraltar.

[2] One of the moft confiderable kingdoms in antient Africa; comprehending thofe of Fez and Morocco, together with part

pre-

prevailing reports [3] will bring him back to Ga- A.U. 710.
des, or carry him to Rome, I know not: for I
hear that his refolutions vary with every different
exprefs that arrives.   But befides the robberies
and the extortions he has committed in this pro-
vince, and the cruelties he has exercifed towards
our allies, he affected in feveral inftances to imitate
(as he himfelf ufed to boaft) the actions of Cæfar.
Accordingly on the laft day of the games which he
exhibited at Gades, he prefented Herennius Gal-
lus, a comedian, with the golden ring; and con-
ducted him to one of the 14 benches of the the-
atre, which he had appropriated to thofe of the
equeftrian order. He likewife continued himfelf
in the fupreme magiftracy of Gades, by his own
fingle authority: and at two immediately fuccef-
five affemblies of the people, he nominated for
the two next following years fuch of his creatures
whom he thought proper to fucceed him in the
government of that city. He alfo recalled from
exile, not indeed thofe unfortunate men who were
banifhed on account of the prefent commotions,
but thofe infamous rebels who were concerned

of Algiers and Billedulgerid. Bogud, the prince of this
country, had in the late civil wars favoured and affifted Cæ-
far, by whom he had been greatly diftinguifhed: as he af-
terwards fupported Antony in the war between him and
Octavius. It is probable therefore that Balbus withdrew
with thefe treafures, not in order to convert them to his pri-
vate ufe, but to employ them in the caufe of Antony. *Hirt.
de Bel. Alex.* 59. *de Bel. Afric.* 25.
    [3] Concerning the junction of Lepidus with Antony.

in

 in the sedition which was raised in Gades, during the proconsulate of Sextus Varrus [4]; and in which all the members of their council were either assassinated, or expelled. Thus far he had Cæsar for his model: but in the instances I am going to mention, he exceeded even Cæsar himself. He caused a play to be acted at the public games, upon the subject of his embassy to Lucius Lentulus [5], the proconsul: and the good man was so affected with the remembrance of those transactions which the scenes of this drama recalled to his mind, that he melted into tears. At the gladiatorial games, he gave a specimen of his cruelty with regard to one Fadius, who had served in Pompey's army. This man had twice, it seems, voluntarily entered the lists in combats of this kind; but upon the present occasion he

---

[4] It does not appear who this person was, nor at what time he presided as governor of Spain.

[5] He was consul in the year 704, when the civil war broke out: in which he took part with Pompey. He accompanied that general in his retreat to Brundisium, and from thence passed over with him into Greece. But before Lentulus left Italy, Balbus was employed by Cæsar (as Manutius observes) to prevail with him to return to Rome. Balbus afterwards (as appears by a passage which the same commentator cites from Paterculus) executed a much more difficult commission of this kind, at the siege of Dyrrachium: where he undertook to carry some farther overtures from Cæsar to Lentulus who was in that garrison, and which he executed with equal address and intrepidity. It was this adventure, it is probable, that formed the subject of the play which Pollio here mentions. *Ad At.* viii. 11. *Vel. Paterc.* ii. 51.

refused

refufed to fight, tho' peremptorily required by A.U.710.
Balbus: and accordingly threw himfelf upon the
protection of the populace. But the mob having
pelted Balbus with ftones when he attempted to
recover him out of their hands, he let loofe upon
them a party of his Gallic horfe. Balbus having
by thefe means got the unfortunate Fadius into
his poffeffion, ordered him to be fixed in a pit
which was dug for that purpofe in the place
where the games were exhibited, and caufed him
in this manner to be burnt alive. This was per-
formed foon after Balbus had dined [6], who was
prefent during the whole execution, walking
about bare-footed, with his hands behind him,
and his tunic loofe, in the moft unconcerned and
indecent manner : and while the unhappy fuf-
ferer cried out that he was a Roman citizen ;
" Why do you not run now (faid the infulting

[6] There feems to have been fome peculiar indecorum in
this circumftance, tho' it is not very eafy to determine where-
in it precifely confifted. It may be, that public executions
at this time of the day, were thought indecent : it is certain
at leaft that it was deemed improper to hold courts of judica-
ture for the trial of criminal matters in an afternoon. For
Plutarch takes notice that the younger Cato was accufed of
this practice during his prætorfhip : and thinks it neceffary
for the credit of that illuftrious Roman, to deny the truth of
the charge. Or perhaps Pollio might point out this circum-
ftance as a mark of uncommon cruelty of difpofition in Bal-
bus, who could rife from table with a temper of mind fo dif-
ferent from that which pleafures of this fort are naturally apt
to infpire; and turn from a chearful meal to a fcene of the
utmoft horror and barbarity. *Plut. in vit. Caton. Uticen.*

" and

 " and relentlefs Balbus) to implore the protec-
" tion of the people?" But this was not the
fingle cruelty he exercifed. He expofed like-
wife feveral Roman citizens to wild beafts; par-
ticularly a certain noted auctioneer in the city of
Hifpalis [7]: and this for no other reafon but be-
caufe the poor man was exceffively deformed.
Such is the monfter with whom I had the mif-
fortune to be connected! But more of him when
we meet. In the mean time (to turn to a point
of much greater importance) I fhould be glad
the fenate would determine in what manner they
would have me act. I am at the head of three
brave legions: one of which Antony took great
pains to draw over to his intereft at the com-
mencement of the war. For this purpofe he
caufed it to be fignified to them, that the very
firft day they fhould enter into his camp, every
foldier fhould receive five hundred [8] denarii;
befides which he alfo affured them that if he ob-
tained the victory, they fhould receive an equal
fhare of the fpoils with his own troops: a reward
which all the world knows would have been
without end or meafure. Thefe promifes made
a deep impreffion upon them: and it was with
great difficulty I kept them from deferting. I

[7] The city of Seville in Spain.
[8] About 14 l. fterling.

fhould

ſhould not indeed have been able to have effected this, if I had not cantoned them in diſtant quarters: as ſome of the cohorts, notwithſtanding they were thus ſeparated, had the inſolence to mutiny. Antony endeavoured likewiſe to gain the reſt of the legions by immenſe offers. Nor was Lepidus leſs importunate with me to ſend him the thirtieth legion: which he ſollicited both by his own letters, and by thoſe which he cauſed Antony to write. The ſenate will do me the juſtice therefore to believe; as no advantages could tempt me to ſell my troops, nor any dangers which I had reaſon to apprehend if Antony and Lepidus ſhould prove conquerors, could prevail with me to diminiſh their number, that I was thus tenacious of my army for no other purpoſe but to employ it in the ſervice of the republic [q]. And let the readineſs with which I have obeyed all the orders I received from the ſenate, be a proof that I would have complied in the ſame manner with every other they ſhould have thought proper to have ſent me. I have preſerved the tranquillity of this province; I have maintained my authority over the army; and have never once moved beyond the limits of my own juriſdiction. I muſt add likewiſe, that I have never employed any ſoldier either of my

[q] See rem. 5. p. 337. of this vol.

 own troops, or thoſe of my auxiliaries in carry-
ing any diſpatches whatſoever: and I have con-
ſtantly puniſhed ſuch of my cavalry whom I have
found at any time attempting to deſert. I ſhall
think theſe cares ſufficiently rewarded, in ſeeing
the peace and ſecurity of the republic reſtored.
But if the majority of the ſenate and the com-
monwealth indeed in general, had known me
for what I am, I ſhould have been able to have
rendered them much more important ſervices.

I have ſent you a copy of the letter which I
wrote to Balbus juſt before he left this province:
and if you have any curioſity to read his play
which I mentioned above; it is in the hands of
my friend Gallus Cornelius, to whom you may
apply for it. Farewel.

Corduba, June the 8th.

LETTER VIII.

To Plancus.

ALL our hopes are entirely fixed (and fixed
too with the approbation of the gods them-
ſelves) upon you and your collegue [1]. The
perfect unanimity therefore that appears by your
reſpective letters to the ſenate to ſubſiſt between
you, affords great ſatisfaction, not only to that

[1] Decimus Brutus.

aſſembly

affembly in particular, but to the whole city in general.

As to what you wrote to me concerning the commiffion for dividing the lands; if that affair had been brought before the fenate, I fhould have been the firft to have propofed the moft honourable decree in your favour. But the flownefs of their deliberations in the bufinefs which was then under their confideration, together with other obftructions which attended their debates, having prevented them from coming to any refolution ; both your brother and myfelf were of opinion, that it was moft advifable to proceed upon the former decree : and I take it for granted that he has acquainted you, to whom it is owing that it was not drawn up in the manner we propofed. But if in this inftance, or in any other, your inclinations fhould not be intirely gratified ; be well perfuaded however, that you are in fuch high efteem with all the friends of the republic, that there is no fort of honours they are not difpofed to confer upon you.——I wait with great impatience for an exprefs from you, as I expect it will bring us the news I moft wifh. Farewel.

LETTER IX.

TO CORNIFICIUS [*].

A.U.710. IS it really so, my friend: and have I never written to you but when I had occasion to recommend the cause of some litigious suitor? I confefs I have frequently troubled you with letters of this kind: but muft you not thank your own obliging partiality towards me, if the world is perfuaded that no recommendation has so much weight with you as mine? Tell me, however, when did I omit writing, if your family gave me notice of an opportunity? In fact, nothing affords me greater fatisfaction, now that I cannot converfe with you in perfon, than this intercourfe of letters. I only lament that my public occupations prevent me from correfponding with you as frequently as I wifh. If I had more leifure indeed, I fhould not only provoke you to enter with me into a commerce of this epiftolary kind, but I fhould challenge you with whole volumes of my works: a challenge, which I ought to have received from you, as your engagements, I imagine, are not altogether

[*] See rem. 6. p. 61. of this vol.

so

fo numerous as mine. But if I am miſtaken A.U.710.
in this ſuppoſition; how ſhall I acquit you of
being a little unreaſonable in expecting frequent
letters on my part, when you have ſo ſeldom
leiſure to ſend me any on yours? If I have
hitherto been engaged in the moſt important
occupations, as holding myſelf bound to exert
all my cares in the defence of the republic; I
may ſtill more ſtrongly urge that plea at pre-
ſent.   For as a relapſe is always more dangerous
than a firſt attack; ſo the re-kindling of this
war after it was almoſt totally extinguiſhed,
demands a double portion of my labour and
vigilance. But not to enter farther into this ſub-
ject, believe me, my dear Cornificius, I ſhould
think myſelf moſt inexcuſably indolent, not to
ſay ill-mannered, were I capable of ſuffering you
to gain the ſuperiority over me in any inſtance
of friendſhip. That I enjoy yours, is a point
of which I never once had the leaſt doubt : but
the converſation I have lately had with Cherip-
pus, has rendered it ſtill more evident.   As
agreeable as he always was to my taſte, I could
not but look upon him in his laſt viſit with
more than ordinary pleaſure : as he not only
acquainted me with the ſentiments of your heart
in the meſſage he delivered to me, but as he
repreſented at the ſame time a lively image of
A a 3   your

 your very air and countenance.   You had no
reafon then to be apprehenfive that I fhould be
difpleafed at your having fent me the fame com-
mon letter which you addreffed to all your friends
in general.   If I defired a more particular me-
morial, it was merely from the affection of my
heart, and by no means as a point upon which I
infifted.

The lofs of both our confuls [4], together with
the incredible fcarcity of money in the treafury,
puts it out of my power to eafe you of your great
and continual expence in your military prepara-
tions.   We are trying all expedients in order to
raife fupplies for difcharging thofe donatives we
promifed to the troops that behaved well :   and
I imagined that we fhall at laft be obliged to have
recourfe to a tax [5].

I am perfuaded there is no truth in the report
concerning Attius Dionyfius : as Stratorius has
not mentioned a word to me upon that fubject.
With regard to Publius Lucceius ; be well per-
fuaded that his intereft is no lefs my concern

---

[4] Hirtius and Panfa.

[5] " This was a fort of capitation tax, proportioned to each
" man's fubftance ; but had wholly been difufed in Rome
" from the conqueft of Macedonia by Paulus Æmilius,
" which furnifhed money and rents fufficient to eafe the
" city ever after of that burthen, till the neceffity of the
" prefent times obliged them to renew it. *Val. Max.* iv.
" 3." *Life of Cic.* iii. p. 249.

than it is yours: for indeed he is extremely my
friend.   I could not however prevail with the
managers of the auction to adjourn the sale:
their engagements and their oath obliging them,
they assure me, to the contrary.   I would by all
means therefore advise him to hasten into Italy:
and if the summons I sent him some time since
had any weight, he will be at Rome when you
read this letter.   As to the affairs you mention,
and particularly the money; I find you were not
apprised of Pansa's death when you wrote your
letter, by the hopes that you express that thro' my
interest he would comply with your request.   And
most undoubtedly he would, had he been living:
for he held you in great esteem.   But as he is
dead, I do not see that any thing can now be
done in this matter.

I approve, in general, of your measures with
respect to Venullius, Latinus, and Horatius;
and particularly, that you have deprived them
of their lictors.   But I am not altogether so
well pleased, that in order to render this circum-
stance the less uneasy to them, you have taken
away these attendants likewise from your own
lieutenants.   Those who deserve the highest ho-
nours ought not to have been thus levelled with
a set of men, who certainly merit the utmost
disgrace: and if they will not depart from your

 province in obedience to the decree of the senate, I think you should use compulsory methods for that purpose.

I have nothing farther to add in answer to your last letter (of which I received a duplicate) but that I hope you will be persuaded, your credit and reputation are no less sacred to me than my own [6].   Farewel.

LETTER X.

TO DECIMUS BRUTUS.

THO' I always receive your letters with the highest satisfaction, yet I am much better pleased that you employed your collegue Plancus to make an excuse to me, than if you had interrupted your very important occupations by writing yourself.   He has executed your commission very fully: and nothing can render your character more truly amiable to me, than the account he gives of your zeal and diligence.

[6] This letter closes the correspondence between Cicero and Cornificius.   The latter not long afterwards lost his life in bravely defending his province against the troops of Sextius : who claimed it in the name of Octavius, by virtue of the general division of the Roman dominions that had been agreed upon between the triumvirs. *Appian. de B. C.* p. 620.

The

The junction of your forces with thofe of A.U.710.
Plancus, and the harmony with which you act
together, as appears by your common letter to
the fenate, was extremely agreeable both to that
affembly and to the people in general. What
remains then, my dear Brutus, but to conjure
you to perfevere in the fame unanimity, and to
endeavour, I will not fay to excel others, but
(what is far worthier of your ambition) to rife
above yourfelf.   I need add no more : efpecially
as I am writing to one whofe epiftolary concife-
nefs I purpofe to imitate.

I wait with impatience for your next difpatches:
as I imagine they will bring us fuch accounts as
are agreeable to our wifhes.   Farewel.

L E T T E R   XI.

To Furnius [7].

WHEN your letter affured me, that it
was abfolutely neceffary either to flight
Narbonenfian Gaul [8], or to attack the enemy
with great difadvantage ; I was glad to find that
the former had been chofen : as I much more
dreaded the confequences of coming to an en-

---

[7] See rem. 7. p. 303. of this vol.

[8] In which province were the combined armies of Antony
and Lepidus.

gagement

 gagement upon unequal terms. What you men-
tioned likewife concerning the harmony between
Plancus and Brutus, afforded me great pleafure:
for it is a circumftance upon which I found my
principal hopes of our fuccefs.

Notwithftanding you modeftly refer it to time
to inform me to whom we owe that general zeal
which appears in your province [9]; be affured it
is a point of which I am already perfectly well
apprifed.   I could not therefore but read the lat-
ter part of your letter, which in all other refpects
was extremely agreeable to me, with fome con-
cern.   You there tell me, that if the election for
ædiles is fixed for the month of Auguft, you will
foon be at Rome; but if it is already over, you
will be there much fooner: " for wherefore,"
you afk, " fhould you weakly continue to hazard
" your life, without the profpect of any recom-
" penfe?" O! my friend, is it poffible that
you who judge fo well concerning the interefts
of others, fhould be thus a ftranger to your own?
But as I am fenfible of the ftrong impulfe of
your heart towards true glory, I cannot believe
that thefe are its genuine fentiments: at leaft if
they be, I muft condemn my own judgment as
well as yours, for being fo greatly deceived in

* Tranfalpine Gaul: in which province Furnius was lieu-
tenant to Plancus.

your

your character.   Shall the ambition of antici-
pating a flight and common honour, (for fo I
muft call the office you have in view, if obtained
in the manner by which fo many others have
rifen to it before you) induce you to withdraw
from a theatre where you are acting with fuch
univerfal and well-merited applaufe? Shall it be
a queftion with you, whether to offer yourfelf
as a candidate now, or at the next election for
prætors: and is it none, how you fhall deferve
every illuftrious diftinction which the common-
wealth can beftow? Are you a ftranger to the
exalted reputation you have acquired? Or do
you confider it as of no value, thus to rife in
the efteem of your country? If you are igno-
rant indeed of the high credit in which you ftand
with the public; it is an ignorance for which
we who are your friends are undoubtedly to be
blamed.   But if you already know it; tell me,
my Furnius, can any prætorfhip afford you a
fatisfaction fuperior to what you feel in difcharg-
ing the duty you owe to your country, and in
reaping immortal glory? an acquifition, which
tho' few indeed endeavour to deferve, yet every
man, moft certainly, wifhes to enjoy.   Calvifius,
who is much your friend, and a man of great
judgment alfo, frequently joins with me in com-
plaining of you upon this article.   However,
                                             fince

A.U. 710. fince you are fo defirous to attain this office ; I
fhall endeavour that the election may be deferred
till the month of January : as this adjournment
will upon many accounts, I think, prove for the
advantage likewife of the republic. Farewel:
and may victory attend you !

LETTER XII.

To Caius Cassius.

I Imagine you are informed by the public jour-
nals, which I know are duly tranfmitted to
you, of the infamous conduct of that moft light
and inconftant man, your relation Lepidus [1].
We are again therefore involved in a war, which
we flattered ourfelves was entirely over: and all
our hopes are now placed upon Decimus [2] and
Plancus; or to fpeak more truly indeed, upon
Brutus [3] and upon you. For it is from you two
that we expect, not only a prefent affiftance, in
cafe any misfortune (which the gods avert!)
fhould attend our arms, but a firm and lafting
re-eftablifhment of our liberties.

The reports in regard to Dolabella [4], are in all

[1] Lepidus and Caffius were married to the two fifters of
Marcus Brutus.

[2] Brutus.

[3] Marcus.

[4] That he was defeated by Caffius.

refpects

respects agreeable to our wishes, excepting only A.U. 710.
that they want confirmation.   In the mean time
be assured, that the opinion and expectations
of the world concerning you, are such as evi-
dently shew that they look upon you as a truly
great man.   Let this animate you to the noblest
atchievements: in the full persuasion that there
is nothing so confiderable which your country
does not hope to obtain by your courage and
conduct.   Farewel.

L E T T E R XIII.

To the Same.

I Take example from the concisenefs of your
letters, to shorten mine: tho' to say truth,
nothing occurs at prefent that can tempt me to
lengthen them. For as to *our* tranfactions, I well
know you are acquainted with them by the public
journals: and we are perfectly ignorant of every
thing that concerns yours.   One would imagine
indeed that all communication were cut off be-
tween us and Afia: for we have received no
intelligence from thence, excepting only fome
uncertain, tho' indeed repeated, rumours in re-
lation to the defeat of Dolabella.

We

We imagined that the flames of this civil war were entirely extinguiſhed : but in the midſt of this pleaſing perſuaſion, we were ſuddenly and greatly alarmed by the conduct of your relation Lepidus. Be aſſured therefore, that the hopes of the republic are wholly fixed upon you and your army. We have, it is true, a very powerful body of troops in this part of the world: neverthelefs, your preſence here is extremely neceſſary to give our affairs all the ſucceſs we wiſh. I will not ſay that we have no hopes of recovering our liberties : but I muſt ſay our hopes are ſmall. Such as they are, however, they are entirely founded upon your future conſulate [5]. Farewel.

LETTER XIV.
CASSIUS [6], Quæſtor, to CICERO.

THE preſervation of the republic by the victory we have lately obtained, gives me inexpreſſible joy : as the honours that have been

[5] Caſſius and Brutus were prætors the laſt year: and the laws entitled a man to ſue for the conſulate two years after he had ſerved the office of prætor.

[6] It is altogether uncertain whether the author of this letter was Lucius Caſſius the brother of Caius Caſſius, or another Caſſius, diſtinguiſhed by the addition of *Parmenſis*, from Parma, the place of his nativity. There is nothing indeed, in the hiſtory of theſe two Caſſii, or in the letter itſelf, that can render it more reaſonable to ſuppoſe it to have been written by the one, rather than the other: for

paid

paid my friend [7], afford me likewise a very senfi-
fible pleafure.   I cannot fufficiently indulge my
admiration when I confider you as thus rifing
above yourfelf in glory; and that the confular [8]
fhould fhine forth even with more luftre than
the conful.   Some uncommon privilege of fate,
moft certainly attends your patriot virtues: as
we have often, I am fure, experienced.   How
elfe fhould your fingle eloquence be of more avail
than the arms of all our generals? You have a
fecond time indeed refcued the well-nigh van-
quifhed republic from the hands of our enemies;
and once more reftored her to us again.   From
this period therefore I date the return of our
liberties: and I fhall now be honoured with the
public applaufe of the moft diftinguifhed of pa-

they were both in the number of the confpirators againft
Cæfar; and both afterwards acted with Brutus and Caflius
in Afia.   This epiftle appears to have been written from
the ifland of Cyprus foon after the news of Antony's defeat
at the battle of Mutina had reached that part of the world.
Cafaubon. ad Suet. Jul. 80.   *Appian. B. C. p.* 671.

[7] This feems to allude to the honours that were paid to
Cicero by the populace, upon the news that Antony had
been forced to abandon the fiege of Mutina.   "The whole
" body of the people (to give the relation of this fact in
the words of Dr. Middleton) " affembled about Cicero's
" houfe, and carried him in a kind of triumph to the Ca-
" pitol: where, on their return, they placed him in the
" roftra, to give them an account of the victory: and then
" conducted him home with infinite acclamations."   *Phil.*
xiv. 5.   *Life of Cic.* iii. 197.

[8] Thofe who had paffed thro' the office of conful, were
ftiled confulars.

 triots.   Yes, my friend, you will now declare
(what you promifed to conceal till the recovery
of our freedom fhould render it to my advantage
to be known) you will now declare to the whole
world thofe inftances you received of my tender
attachment both to you and to the republic;
during the dark and dangerous feafon of our
fervitude.   I am much lefs follicitous, however;
that you fhould publifh my praifes, than that you
fhould be perfuaded I deferve them: and I had
rather ftand approved by your filent judgment,
than without that internal verdict in my favour,
to enjoy by your recommendation the good
opinion of the whole world.   It is my great
ambition indeed, that you fhould efteem my
late conduct to have been, not the effect of a
fudden and irregular impulfe, but the natural
refult of the fame uniform principles of which
you have been a witnefs: in a word, that you
fhould think of me, as of one from whom the
republic has fo much to expect, as may well
juftify every honour to which I fhall be ad-
vanced.   I am fenfible, my dear Cicero, that
your own family, as they are well worthy of the
relation they bear to you, deferve your firft and
moft tender regard.   But thofe furely have a right
to the next place in your affection, who endeavour
to imitate your patriot virtues: and I fhall be
glad

glad to find that their number is confiderable.   I
imagine, however, that it is not fo great as to ex-
clude me from a fhare in your good offices, and
prevent you from procuring any public diftinc-
tions in my favour which fhall be agreeable to
your inclination and your judgment.   That I am
not unworthy of them with refpect to the difpo-
fition of my heart, I have already, perhaps, fuf-
ficiently convinced you : and as to my talents,
whatever they may be, the general oppreffion un-
der which our country fo long laboured, would
not fuffer them to appear in their full advantage.

I drew together out of the ports of this Afiatic
province and of the neighbouring iflands, all the
fhips of war I could poffibly collect : and, con-
fidering the great oppofition I met with from the
feveral cities, I mann'd them with tolerable expe-
dition.   With this fleet I purfued that of Dola-
bella, commanded by Lucilius : who after hav-
ing frequently made a fhew of coming over to
me, but ftill however continuing to retreat, fail-
ed at length into the port of Corycus [9]; where he
blocked himfelf up.   I did not think proper to
follow him thither ; not only as judging it moft
advifable to join our land forces, but as Turuli-
us the Quæftor lay behind me with a fquadron
which Tullius Cimber fitted out the laft year

[9] In Cilicia.

A.U.710. from Bythinia. I put in therefore at Cyprus: from whence I take this firſt opportunity of acquainting you with the intelligence I have here received. I am to inform you then, that the city of Laodicea, (in purſuance of the example of our faithleſs allies the Tarſenſes [1], tho' indeed with a greater degree of folly) have voluntarily called in Dolabella. From thoſe two cities he has compoſed an army (as far as numbers can make an army) of Greek ſoldiers, and is encamped before Laodicea; having thrown down part of the walls, in order to join his camp with the town. On the other hand, Caſſius [2] is encamped about twenty miles diſtant from him at Paltos. His army conſiſts of ten legions, and twenty auxiliary cohorts, together with four thouſand horſe. He imagines, that he ſhall be able to oblige the enemy to ſurrender, without hazarding a battle : as wheat is ſo ſcarce in Dolabella's camp that it is ſold for twelve drachmæ. The enemy muſt neceſſarily, indeed, be deſtroyed by famine, if they are not ſoon ſupplied by the ſhips that belong to Laodicea. This, however, we ſhall with great eaſe prevent: for, beſides the three ſquadrons under Turulius, Patiſcus, and myſelf; Caſſius has a conſiderable fleet in theſe ſeas commanded by Sextilius

---

[1] The citizens of Tarſus.
[2] Caius Caſſius.

Rufus.

Rufus. Let me encourage you then to hope, A.U. 710.
that we fhall foon vindicate our liberties with the
fame fuccefs [3] in this part of the world, as has
attended your army in Italy.   Farewel.

Cromyacris, in Cyprus, June the 13th.

L E T T E R   XV.

To Decimus Brutus.

I Was expecting every day to hear from you,
when our friend Lupus gave me notice that
he was juft fetting out to you, and defired to
know if I had any thing to write. But tho' I
have nothing worth communicating, more than
what you are furnifhed with by the public jour-
nals; and that you are no friend, I am told, to
letters of mere empty form; yet I cannot forbear
following your example, and fending you two or
three fhort words.   Be affured then, that all our
hopes reft upon you and your collegue [4].   As to
Brutus [5], I am not able to give you any certain
account of him: I can only fay, that in purfuance
of your advice, I endeavour to perfuade him in
all my letters to come over into Italy, and to take

[3] See rem. 8. p. 316. of this vol.
[4] Plancus.
[5] Marcus Brutus.

A.U.710. a part in this general war [6]. I much wish he were now here: as his presence would render me less apprehensive of the consequences of these intestine commotions [7] which prevail in Rome; and which are by no means, indeed, inconsiderable. —But I forget that I proposed to imitate your laconic brevity, and am running on in a second page. Farewel then, and may success attend your arms [8]!

June 18th.

[6] The conduct of Marcus Brutus, as far as can be judged of it at this great distance, appears altogether unaccountable. Before the battle of Mutina, he had drawn down all his forces to the coast, in order to embark for Italy, if any accident should make his assistance necessary. But upon the news of Antony's defeat, he retired to the remotest parts of Greece and Macedonia, to oppose the attempts of Dolabella: and from that time (as Dr. Middleton observes) seemed deaf to the call of the senate, and to all Cicero's letters, which urged him so strongly to come to their relief. But had Brutus and Cassius (as the same ingenious historian remarks) marched with their armies towards Italy, at the time when Cicero first pressed it, before the desertion of Plancus and the death of Decimus; it seems reasonable to believe, that the immediate ruin of the republic might have been prevented. *Life of Cic.* iii. 247.

[7] The disturbances to which Cicero alludes, were probably those that were occasioned by the violent measures of Octavius in order to obtain the consulate. See rem. 8. p. 381. of this vol.

[8] Decimus Brutus soon after the date of this letter, was most treacherously deserted by Plancus: who drew off his troops from those of his collegue, and went over with them to the camp of Antony and Lepidus. " Decimus Brutus " being thus abandoned and left to shift for himself, with a " needy mutinous army, eager to desert, and ready to give " him up to his enemies, had no other way to save himself " than by flying to Marcus Brutus in Macedonia. But the

LET-

L E T T E R XVI.

To Caius Cassius.

YOUR relation and my friend the *worthy* Lepidus, together with all his adherents, were by an unanimous decree of the senate which paſſed on the 30th of June laſt, declared public enemies to their country: but at the ſame time a full pardon was offered to ſuch as ſhall return to their allegiance before the firſt of September. The ſenate acts with great ſpirit: but it is the expectation of being ſupported by your army that chiefly animates them in their vigorous meaſures. I fear indeed, that we ſhall have occaſion for all your aſſiſtance: as the war is now become extremely formidable by the villainy of Lepidus.

The accounts which daily arrive concerning Dolabella, are altogether agreeable to our wiſhes: but at preſent they are nothing more than mere rumours. However your letter addreſſed to the

" diſtance was ſo great, and the country ſo guarded, that
" he was often forced to change his road, for fear of being
" taken; 'till having diſmiſſed all his attendants, and wan-
" dered for ſome time alone in diſguiſe and diſtreſs, he con-
" mitted himſelf to the protection of an old acquaintance and
" hoſt, whom he had formerly obliged: where either thro'
" treachery or accident, he was ſurpriſed by Antony's ſol-
" diers, who immediately killed him, and returned with his
" head to their general. *Vel. Paterc.* ii. 64. *App.* iii. 588.
" *Val. Max.* ix. 13." *Life of Cic.* iii. 242.

A.U. 710. fenate, dated from the camp on the 9th of May,
has raifed a general perfuafion in Rome, that he
is actually defeated.   Accordingly it is imagined
that you are now upon your march into Italy,
with a view on the one hand, of fuccouring us
with your troops, if any of thofe accidents fo
common in war fhould have rendered our arms
unfuccefsful : or on the other hand, of affifting
us with your counfels and authority, in cafe we
fhould have proved victorious.   You may be af-
fured, in the mean while, that no endeavours of
mine fhall be wanting to procure the forces un-
der your command all poffible honours.   How-
ever I muft wait a proper feafon for this purpofe,
when it fhall be known how far they have availed,
or are likely to avail, the republic.   At prefent
we have only heard of their endeavours in the caufe
of liberty : and glorious, it muft be acknowledg-
ed, their endeavours have been.   But ftill fome
pofitive fervices are expected : and thefe ex-
pectations, I dare be confident, either already
are, or foon will be, perfectly anfwered. No man,
indeed, poffeffes a more patriot or heroic fpirit
than yourfelf : and it is for this reafon that we
wifh to fee you in Italy as foon as poffible.   The
fact is, if you and Brutus were here, we fhould
look upon the republic as reftored.

                                             If

If Lepidus had not received Antony, weak A.U. 710. and defencelefs as he was, when he fled after the battle of Mutina, we fhould have obtained a complete victory.   This infamous ftep therefore has rendered him far more odious in Rome even than Antony himfelf ever was.   For Antony raifed a war at a time when the republic was in the utmoft ferment: whereas Lepidus has kindled the flames in the midft of peace and victory.   We have the confuls elect [9] to lead our armies againft him: but tho' we greatly depend upon their courage and conduct; ftill however the uncertain event of war, leaves us much to fear.   Be affured therefore, that our principal reliance is upon you and Brutus; whom we hope foon to fee in Italy: and Brutus indeed we expect every day.   Should we have defeated our enemies, as I hope we fhall, before your arrival; the authority, neverthelefs, of two fuch illuftrious citizens will be of infinite fervice in raifing up the republic, and fixing it upon fome tolerable bafis.   All our bufinefs indeed will by no means be over, notwithftanding we fhould be delivered from the infamous defigns of our enemies: as there are many other diforders of a different kind, which it will be ftill neceffary to redrefs.   Farewel.

[9] Decimus Brutus and Plancus.

LETTER XVII.

TO AMPIUS [1].

A.U. 710. YOUR family has informed you, I imagine, of my zealous labours to procure your restoration: as I have the pleasure to be assured that they are abundantly satisfied with my services. Uncommon indeed as the affection is which they every one of them bear towards you; yet I cannot allow that they are more sincerely desirous of your welfare than myself. I am sure at least, their power of assisting you in this conjuncture, is by no means equal to mine. I have employed it, and shall continue to employ it for your benefit: and I have already gained a very considerable point, which will much contribute to facilitate your return. In the mean while, preserve a firm and manly spirit: and be well persuaded that my good offices shall not be wanting to you upon any occasion. Farewel.

[1] In some MSS. the superscription of this letter is to Appius, and in others to Ampius Balbus. The time when this letter was written is no less uncertain than the person to whom it is addressed.

LETTER XVIII.

PLANCUS, Consul elect, to CICERO.

I Cannot forbear to exprefs upon every occafion, A.U. 710. the fentiments I entertain of your repeated favours: tho' at the fame time it is with fome referve that I indulge myfelf in this fatisfaction. The great intimacy indeed which you allow me to enjoy with you, renders all formal acknowledgments of this kind unneceffary: nor would I make fo cheap a return to the many important obligations I owe to you, as that of mere empty profeffions. I had much rather referve the proofs of my gratitude, to fome future opportunity of teftifying it in perfon: and if I live I will convince you by the affiduity of my good offices, and by every inftance of refpect and efteem, that you have not a friend, nor even a relation, who is fo warmly attached to you as myfelf. In the mean time I am at a lofs to determine, whether the daily pleafure I receive, or the lafting honour I fhall derive from your affectionate regard, be greater.

I find the intereft of my troops has been a part of your care. It was not with any intention of

advancing

advancing my own power, that I was defirous they fhould be diftinguifhed by the fenate: as I am confcious of having no views but what regard the welfare of the republic. My reafons were, in the firft place, becaufe I thought they deferved to be rewarded; and in the next place, becaufe I was defirous they might upon all occafions be ftill more attached to the commonwealth. I hoped likewife by thefe means fo ftrongly to fortify them againft all follicitations, that I might be anfwerable for their continuing to act with the fame unfhaken fidelity which they have hitherto preferved.

I have kept entirely upon the defenfive: and tho' I am well apprifed with how much juft impatience the public wifhes for a decifive action, yet I perfuade myfelf that the fenate will approve my conduct. If any misfortune indeed fhould attend our armies in this part of the world, the republic would not very foon be in a condition to oppofe any fudden incurfion of thefe rapacious traitors. As to the ftate of our forces; I imagine you already know that thofe under my command confift of three veteran legions, together with one new-raifed regiment: which laft however is compofed of far the beft difciplined troops I ever faw of this fort. Brutus[2], is at

[2] Decimus.

the

the head of ten legions ; one of which is veteran ; A.U.710.
another has been upon the eftablifhment about
two years ; and all the reft are lately raifed.
Thus you fee, tho' our army is very numerous,
it is not extremely ftrong.   The republic indeed
has but too often had occafion to be convinced,
how little is to be expected from raw and un-
experienced forces.   However, if we had been
joined either by the African legions [1], which
are compofed wholly of veteran troops, or by
Cæfar's [2], we fhould without hefitation have ha-
zarded a general engagement.   As the troops
of the latter were fomewhat nearer than the for-
mer, I frequently preffed Cæfar by letters, to
advance : and he accordingly promifed to join
us with all expedition.   But other views, I per-
ceive, have diverted him from thefe intentions.
Neverthelefs, I have difpatched my lieutenant
Furnius with another letter to him, if happily it
may any thing avail.   You are fenfible, my dear
Cicero, that I take an equal part with you in the

[1] Thefe legions compofed part of that army with which
Julius Cæfar defeated Scipio in Africa : from whence they
had lately been recalled by the fenate.   But foon after their
landing they were corrupted by the other foldiers ; and de-
ferting the fenate, they joined themfelves to Octavius.   *Life
of Cic.* iii. 241.

[2] Octavius.

affection

 affection you bear to Octavius. He has a right to my friendship, not only from that intimacy which I enjoyed with his uncle , but in regard also to his own difposition: which as far as I could ever difcover, is regulated by principles of great moderation and humanity. It would ill indeed become that diftinguifhed amity which fubfifted between Julius Cæfar and myfelf, not to look upon Octavius with all the tendernefs which is due to the fon of my friend; after he has been adopted as fuch by Cæfar's will, and that adoption approved by the fenate. What I am going to fay therefore is more the dictate of concern than refentment: but it muft be acknowledged, that if Antony ftill lives; if he has been joined by Lepidus; if their armies are by no means contemptible: in a word, all their hopes and all their attempts, are fingly owing to Cæfar [6]. Not to look farther back than to his promife of joining me : had he fulfilled the affu-rances he gave me for that purpofe, the war would by this time either have been totally at an end, or driven into Spain; where the enemy could not have carried it on without great difadvan-tage, as that province is utterly averfe to them.

[5] Julius Cæfar.
[6] See rem. 2. p. 263. of this vol.

I am

I am at a lofs to conceive therefore, with what A.U. 710.
view, or by whofe advice, Cæfar was diverted
from a meafure fo greatly to his intereft and his
honour, in order to turn his purfuits towards a
confulfhip of a few months duration [7]: much
to the terror at the fame time of the republic [8],
and with pretenfions too, exceedingly ridicu-
lous [9]. The remonftrances of his friends might
be extremely ferviceable upon this occafion, both
to himfelf and to the commonwealth. But none
of them, I am perfuaded, would have fo much in-
fluence over him as yours [10]; as there is no man

[7] To the end of the current year: of which there re-
mained about five or fix months unexpired when Octavius
was declared conful.

[8] Octavius advanced towards Rome at the head of feveral
legions, in order to demand the confulate: which threw
the city into the utmoft confternation and diforder. *Dio.*
p. 319. *Appian.* p. 585, 6.

[9] Perhaps the abfurdity to which Plancus here alluded,
was, that Octavius, who was but a youth of twenty, and
confequently who wanted above twenty years of the age
prefcribed by the laws for being qualified to fue for the con-
fular office, fhould entertain fo extravagant a thought as to
afpire to the fupreme magiftracy.

[10] Plancus chofe a very improper man to diffuade Octavius
from purfuing his defign upon the confulate, when he fixed
upon Cicero as the molt likely perfon to prevail with him for
that purpofe. It appears indeed that Octavius had artfully
enfnared Cicero to enter into his views, by perfuading him
that he was defirous of having him for his collegue in the
confular office, and promifing to leave the fole adminiftra-
tion of it to Cicero's fuperior wifdom and experience. The
bait was too well adapted to his vanity and ambition, to be
thrown out in vain: and Cicero undertook the management

 who is fo much obliged to you except myfelf:
for I fhall ever acknowledge that the favours I
have received from you are great and innumer-
able. I have given inftructions to Furnius to
follicit Cæfar upon this fubject: and if I fhould
have that authority with him which I am fure I
ought, he will hereafter thank me for my advice.
In the mean time, we have a very difficult part
to fuftain here: as on the one hand, we do not

of this affair upon the terms propofed. Plutarch, Appian,
and Dion Caffius all concur in giving teftimony to the truth
of this fact: but as it is a fact which proves that Cicero
was by no means at this juncture acting the part of a pa-
triot: the polite apologift of his conduct has endeavoured
to difcredit the evidence of thefe hiftorians. To this end
Dr. Middleton produces the following paffage from the let-
ters to Brutus, as an inconteftable proof, " that no man
" was more 'fhocked at Octavius's attempt, or took more
" pains to diffuade it, than Cicero." *Cæfarem———— impro-
biffimis litteris quidam fallacibufque nunciis impulerunt in fpem
certiffimam confulatus. Quod fimulatque fenfi, neque ego illum
abfentem litteris monere deftiti, nec accufare præfentes ejus necef-
farios, qui ejus cupiditati fuffragari videbantur; nec in fenatu
fceleratiffimorum confiliorum fontes aperire dubitavi. Epift. ad
Brut.* 10. Now there feems to be the ftrongeft reafon to
queftion either the authenticity, or the veracity, of this
letter: becaufe it is moft certain from one of Cicero's
Philippics, that he actually did favour the earlieft poffible
promotion of Octavius to the confulate. *Quid eft enim P. C.*
(fays he) *cur eum (Octavium) non* quam primum ampliffi-
mos honores *capere cupiamus? Legibus enim annalibus cum
grandiorem ætatem ad confulatum conftituebant, adolefcentiæ
temeritatem verebantur. C. Cæfar ineunte ætate docuit ab ex-
cellenti eximiaque virtute,* progreffum ætatis expectari non
oportere. *In hoc fpes libertatis pofita eft; ab hoc accepta jam
falus, huic* fummi honores *et exquiruntur et parati funt, Phil.*
v. 17, 18. Could Cicero, after this, without being guilty
of the wildeft and the weakeft inconfiftency, " admonifh

think

think   ourſelves altogether ſtrong enough to AU.710.
hazard an engagement : and on the other, muſt
take care not to expoſe the republic to greater
dangers by declining one.   However, if Cæſar
ſhould comply with the dictates of his intereſt
and his honour : or if the African legions ſhould
ſpeedily join us : you may depend upon having
nothing to fear from this quarter.——Let me in-
treat you to continue your friendſhip to me, and

" Octavius by letter againſt his deſigns upon the conſul-
" ſhip ; reproach thoſe to their face who encouraged him
" in that ambitious view : and lay open the ſource of theſe
" traiterous counſels in the ſenate ;" (all which the epiſtle
in queſtion affirms that he did ;) when he had himſelf in
the ſpeech and in the paſſage above cited, ſaid every thing
that his wit and eloquence could ſuggeſt in favour of Octa-
vius's premature advancement to the conſular office ? Either
the letters then to Brutus are not genuine ; or Cicero to
ſerve a preſent purpoſe, pretended that he had acted a part
which he did not. The former of theſe ſuppoſitions is
maintained by ſome very learned and judicious critics : and
the latter will by no means be thought improbable, if there
is any weight in the ſeveral inſtances of the ſame kind
which have been occaſionally produced in the courſe of
theſe remarks.   But whichever of theſe alternatives be the
fact, it equally concludes in ſupport of that hiſtorical evi-
dence for which I have been contending.   In farther con-
firmation of which it may be obſerved, that Plutarch cites
the authority of Octavius himſelf, for what he affirms con-
cerning the private agreement between Octavius and Cicero
in regard to the conſulate.   And it is probable he took this
piece of ſecret hiſtory from thoſe memoirs which Octavius
wrote of his own life : as it is certain that both Plutarch
and Appian made great uſe of them in compiling their hiſ-
tories. *Plut. in vit. Cic. Appian.* p. 578, 9. 385. *Dio.* p.
519. *Middlet. on the epiſt. to Brut.* p. 134. *rem.* 8. *Tunſtal's
obſerv. on the epiſt. to Brut.* p. 222. *et Suet. in Aug.* 85.

6

to

 to be affured that I am entirely yours. Farewel ".

　　　From my camp, July the 28th.

[11] Plancus foon after the date of this letter, abandoned his collegue Decimus Brutus, and went over with his troops to Antony and Lepidus. See rem. 8. on letter 15. of this Book. About four months likewife from the time when this letter was written, the celebrated coalition was formed between Cæfar, Antony and Lepidus : in confequence of which, Cicero, it is well known, was facrificed to Antony's refentment. In the laft moments of his life he behaved with great compofure : and it is the only circumftance in all his misfortunes, that he bore with a becoming fortitude. He had indeed fo much the lefs reafon to complain of his fate, as it is certain that he fuffered nothing more than he would have inflicted, had Fortune put Antony into his power. *Omnium adverforum,* fays Livy, *nibil ut viro dignum erat, tulit, præter mortem : quæ, vere æftimanti, minus indigne videri potuit, quod a victore inimico nibil crudelius paffurus erat, quàm quod ejufdem fortunæ compos ipfe feciffet. Liv. fragm. apud Senec. Suafor.* 6. This is the judgment which the nobleft and moft impartial of the Roman hiftorians has paffed upon Cicero : and the truth of it is abundantly confirmed by the foregoing letters.

A N

A N
I N D E X,

Referring to the Order in which the Letters of this Volume ſtand in the Edition of Grævius.

THE END.

www.ingramcontent.com/pod-product-compliance
Lightning Source LLC
Chambersburg PA
CBHW021533110726
47902CB00004B/857